Blessed Souls

The Teachings of Sri Karunamayi

Volume Four

Bhagavati Sri Sri Sri Vijayeswari Devi

Sri Matrudevi Viswashanti Ashram Trust, Inc.
(SMVA Trust, Inc.)
New York, U.S.A.

Published under the auspices of:

SRI MATRUDEVI VISWASHANTI ASHRAM TRUST
Penusilakshetram, Nellore Dt., Andhra Pradesh 524342, India.

KARUNAMAYI SHANTI DHAMA
14/5, 6th Cross, Ashok Nagar, Banashankari lst Stage,
Bangalore 560050, India. Ph: 650 9588 Fax: 660 0518

SRI MATRUDEVI VISWASHANTI ASHRAM TRUST, INC.
Millwood, NY 10598, U.S.A.

SRI MATRUDEVI VISWASHANTI ASHRAM TRUST, INC.
London, England, U.K.

1st Edition 1000 copies

Cover design: Jesse Arana

Printed by: McNaughton & Gunn, Inc.
Saline, Michigan, USA

Sri Karunamayi, Bhagavati Sri Sri Sri Vijayeswari Devi is revered as the incarnation of Divine Mother. She was born on Vijaya Dashami in Gudur, Nellore District, Andhra Pradesh, India. Vijaya Dashami is the culmination of the sacred nine day Navaratri celebration honoring the Divine Mother, and commemorates Her victory over the negative forces of the universe. Hence Sri Vijayeswari's name—Goddess of Victory. She is also known as Karunamayi, the Compassionate Mother, or simply and more intimately as Amma, our own beloved mother.

The purpose of Sri Karunamayi's mission is universal peace and the spiritual upliftment of humanity. She offers to lead everyone to higher levels of consciousness through the regular practice of meditation.

ACKNOWLEDGEMENTS

This book would not have been possible but for the dedicated efforts of the crew, who travel all over the States every year with Sri Karunamayi and record every word She lovingly speaks to Her "most beloved children." Many transcribers and editors have worked behind the scenes to bring these divine words of wisdom to seekers all around the globe.

TABLE OF CONTENTS

Introduction vii

Pronunciation Key. x

Divine Discourses

Spirituality is Like a Diamond 1

Sri Lalita Sahasranama — The Thousand Petal Lotus 11

Devi's Self Luminous Feet 26

Mental Renunciation is the Greatest Virtue 47

Practice Mind Control 66

Divine Mother's Address 84

Mother is the Guru of Brahma, Vishnu and Ishwara 94

Mother's Day—"Sri Mata is Your True Mother" 109

Know Divine Mother Through Meditation 127

Lalita Devi is Most Tender 149

You are the Soul, You are Pure! 160

Sri Mata is Always in Front of You 175

Offer the Fragrant Inner Flowers to Amma 195

Meditate - Meditate on Mother Divine 211

Appendices

INTRODUCTION

Sri Karunamayi's teachings are simple and ancient, yet profound and new. They are universal. Amma's beloved children are always captivated by Her melodious voice, sweet smile, all-embracing love and boundless compassion. She soothes their minds and hearts with soft, enlightening words. *Blessed Souls, Volume 4*, is a compilation of Amma's discourses which form a continuation of talks given in the summer of 1997 during Her third U.S. tour. This book should not be thought of as a mere collection of discourses, for it is a veritable treasure chest of priceless gems to be distributed to one and all.

Amma's teachings have greatly enriched the lives of those who have come into contact with Her. For many of us there has been a new beginning, a new meaning and purpose to life for which we are extremely grateful. Throughout Her travels in the US, Amma has been very pleased that almost all the people who sought Her blessings asked for spiritual growth and salvation. And in this *Kali yuga*, Amma reminds us, it is very easy to attain *moksha* just by praying to Mother with a pure heart.

Amma gently leads us into the depths of *Sri Lalita Sahasranama* and explains that these thousand names of Divine Mother contain the essence of all four *Vedas* and the secrets of all *yogas*. Just one name of Divine Mother, when chanted with deep devotion is enough to burn away all impurities from billions of births. *Sri Lalita Sahasranama* is the elixir of all *yogas*, and is a sure way to have a permanent connection with Divine Mother. Life will always be full of problems, but if you chant the names of Divine Mother with devotion, Mother will comfort you throughout your life. Chant at least one name and you will be dialing Divine Mother's direct number! Amma says, "You can chant the *Lalita Sahasranama* only if it is your last birth."

On several occasions Amma has said that "one coat does not fit all." There are many paths for seekers to chose from. She gives us choices in our quest for the ultimate goal. For those who are not inclined to chant the divine names, She encourages selfless service and emphasizes the importance of meditation. Meditation is the greatest boon we can receive. One hour of meditation burns hundreds of bad deeds of previous births, so that over a period of several years there is no *karma* load. Amma repeatedly urges us to meditate during *brahmi muhurta.* Although meditation is really an art and our human bodies are not suited for it, Amma, due to Her infinite compassion for us, teaches us the technique of meditation with *mantra* and *pranayama.* And with Her grace and blessings, we are able to meditate.

Mantras and books are only maps and addresses to reach Divine Mother. It is through meditation alone that you can actually reach Her. What you enjoy in meditation has no boundaries. Be like Vishvamitra, and remain steadfast in *sadhana* in spite of all obstacles. Amma expects the best from us. Our faith must be as strong as Mount Kailash. Only a hundred percent faith will give us the connection with Divine Mother. Desires are snakes, so limit them. Cultivate *dharma.* She reminds us that life is a long play, an illusion, in which ego is our worst enemy. Amma tells us not to depend on Her physical presence, which would be like spoon-feeding, but to experience permanent comfort in life through purity and meditation.

"One must respect all *gurus;* all *gurus* are one," Amma says. All divine incarnations—Jesus, Rama, Buddha, are one. God comes to us in many forms, with many names. We see differences due to our own limitations. Amma encourages us to seek the blessings of all holy people.

We have a choice—we can either live in cosmic love or live in worldly intoxication. To develop cosmic love, chant the *Lalita Sahasranama*. Mental renunciation is the greatest virtue; it is much more important than physical renunciation. Be in the world, do your work, but mentally always meditate on Divine Mother. Amma reminds us that presently the universe lacks balance due to lack of love; therefore, we should develop cosmic love.

She teaches us how to pray and what to pray for, and that the longing for the Divine is not considered a desire which must be given up. Convert worldly desires into spiritual desires. Pray in silence, do not make a show of your devotion; keep it in your heart. Amma wishes all of us to become *paramahamsas.* She tells us, "Do not be anxious about anything; be like a stranger in the world."

Amma explains the spiritual meaning of various *stotras* and the benefits of chanting them. "You will realize one day that you are divine; you are the greatest Divinity!" She tells us many inspiring stories of devotion which touch our hearts. Without intense longing for God, one cannot sit in meditation. Superficial prayer and meditation are useless; they must both come from the heart.

Summarizing many points about *bhakti*, *dharma*, kindness, compassion and other divine attributes, Amma also cautions us that when we pray to Divine Mother for fire, She may give us water instead because She alone knows what is truly best for us. Amma affirms that we can attain *moksha* in this very life by meditating one hour daily. Her words are certainly fuel for spiritual inspiration, advancement and ultimate salvation. And as our lives become more enriched, year after year by Her grace, there seems to be a new purpose, a new mission to fulfill and we feel extremely blessed and fortunate to have Amma illumine our lives.

PRONUNCIATION KEY

All Sanskrit and non-English words (other than proper names and places) are in italics throughout the text. The only diacritical marks used in the text are " ā " and " ū." The words in Shlokas, Stotras and Kirtanas (i.e., Sanskrit quotations) have been spelled using the International Standard of Sanskrit Transliteration.

KEY TO TRANSLITERATION & PRONUNCIATION

Letter	Sounds Like
a	u in s**u**n
ā	a in f**a**ther
i	i in f**i**ll
ī	ee in f**ee**l
u	u in f**u**ll
ū	oo in f**oo**d
ṛ	ri in **ri**g, *or* roo in b**roo**k
e	ay in m**ay**
ai	ai in **ai**sle
o	o in r**o**se
ow	ow in c**ow**
ung	ung in s**ung**
ḥ	ha in a**ha**
k	k in **k**ite
kh	kh in sil**k h**at
g	g in **g**um
gh	gh in lo**g h**ut
c	ch in **ch**urn
ch	chh in cat**ch h**er
j	j in **j**ug
jh	dgeh in he**dgeh**og
ṭ	t in **t**on
ṭh	th in an**t h**ill

Letter	Sounds Like
ḍ	d in **d**ove
ḍh	dh in Go**dh**ead
t	soft t as in French '*tu*'
th	th in **th**umb
d	th in **th**e
dh	theh in brea**the h**ard
n	n in **n**umber
p	p in **p**un
ph	ph in u**ph**ill
b	b in **b**ird
bh	bh as in jo**b h**unt
m	m in **m**other
y	y in **y**earn
r	r in **r**un
l	l in **l**ove
v	v in lo**v**e *or* w in **w**orld
ś	sh in **sh**un - Amma often pronounces this as "sa" or "sya"
ṣ	sh in mar**sh**
s	s in **s**un
h	h in **h**oney
jn	ngy in si**ng y**our

DIVINE DISCOURSES

ॐ

SPIRITUALITY IS LIKE A DIAMOND

Embodiments of Divine Souls, Amma's Most Beloved Children,

I am so happy to see all of you today, children. There are very powerful vibrations here in this center. There is so much dedication from my son. He dedicates everything to his *Guru* and he wants to expand and evolve to the highest peak of *dharma.* So this center has very pleasant spiritual vibrations. I like it very much. I am so happy to see all of you once again here, my children. This is really a blessed evening.

Embodiments of Divine Souls, my children, spirituality is not a fish market. Spirituality is a diamond market. Only those who have inner beauty, inner vision, and inner richness will be able to understand the value of spirituality, the value of time, the value of their life and the value of the *Atman* in their life. Thus they will attain God-Realization. They are traveling in this eternal path and searching for the real Truth inside. Spirit is not outside. This is true for any spiritual seeker in the world, including *paramahamsas*, great sages, all the great *gurus*, *mahatmas,* and Lord Siva Himself. Lord Siva closes His eyes and sits in meditation. He is in Himself—Himself means the supreme Self, not the limited egoistic self. So when the spiritual seeker attains God-Realization, the supreme Self, he becomes everything in this universe. He becomes *sarvajna,* all knowing, *Omkara,* purity, the light of lights, Divinity, everything!

There is a beautiful Hindi song:

Dharatī jala aura agni pavana ākāśa
Nāśavanta yé carācara mein tū hī hai avināśa

Dharati, the Earth, is just a tiny particle in the cosmos. *Jala,* waters (all the oceans, lakes and rivers), *agni,* fire, *pavana*, the air, and ether—all the five elements will be destroyed one day. Only the soul is *avinasha,* indestructible. *Avinasha* is a beautiful Sanskrit word. It is beyond beautiful—soul is never destroyed. Soul is indestructible power. So children, your soul is indestructible, immortal. Our body is made up of the five elements; it is a mortal frame for the soul.

This human birth is a boon for you. In innumerable births—not just one, two or three births, but billions and billions of spiritual births—you have offered your prayers, *vedic* chanting of *stotras, yajnas, puja* and *japas* to God. Moreover, if you are able to sit in meditation for even a fraction of a second, it is because of the merits accumulated in your previous births. If you attain Self-Realization for even one fraction of a second, you attain Truth. This world is a dream, nothing but a dream. It is a long play lasting five, ten, sixty, seventy, eighty or ninety years. Do not get immersed in this play. Awake! Have *brahmic* awareness in your life. Open your third eye, the eye of knowledge. Do not see the world with the superficial vision of your physical eyes. In the spiritual level you go beyond the body, mind, and limited intellect and feel infinite joy.

Therefore children, meditation is the greatest boon. All the innumerable births in which you have meditated, performed penance or *tapas* and *pujas* have resulted in your meditating in this birth.

Many people do not understand the value of meditation. They think, "What is meditation? Why should we sit with our eyes closed, doing nothing?" We have innumerable thoughts, we are restless, we want to talk and work and sing and do something or the other. That is *kartritva,* doership. "I do this," "I," "me," "my,"—this is our problem. "I," "me," "my" has been our problem through innumerable births. It is the problem of the ego.

In meditation, all the snakes of thoughts—normal thoughts, good thoughts, bad thoughts, negative thoughts, unnecessary and useless thoughts—are gradually removed. When you meditate and repeat your *mantra,* the power of the seed letters in the *mantra* causes all these snakes gradually to come out of the pit of the mind and go away. One hour of meditation burns hundreds and hundreds of the bad deeds of previous births, all the bad *karma* load, and you have tremendous peace in your life. If you meditate regularly over a period of several years, there is no *karma* load at all. You have deep concentration and understanding, and glow with inner beauty. In silence you taste infinite joy. So spirituality is like a diamond.

Since you have performed penance and worship during innumerable previous births, in this birth you have the intense desire for God from childhood. You want to be one with God—that is the essence of the highest spirituality. Spirituality means oneness.

Ekamevadvitīyam Brahma nānyad asti akincanaḥ

There is only one supreme power in the universe—Mother Divine. She alone holds the entire universe in Her hand. She is the very source of all energy.

So how can you attain realization in this birth? Practice living in *dharma*. Cultivate *dharma*. Without *dharma*, there is no wisdom. *Dharma* gives inner purity and inner richness. The mind is nothing but a bundle of innumerable thoughts. Destroy all these thoughts by the regular practice of meditation.

In meditation, God talks with you, in prayer, you talk with God: We are always begging, "O Mother give me this, give me that, grant me this, grant me that." In meditation you hear the divine voice: "Proceed in your path. This is good. This is best for you. Do not tell lies. This is not good for you. Have awareness." You get direct messages from the Divine, the *Atman*.

Pranayama is the key to meditation. Without *pranayama* there is no meditation. The *kundalini*, which lies asleep in the *muladhara chakra,* is awakened by the power of *pranayama*. Gradually all the *chakras* bloom due to the vital energy of *pranayama.*

Every aspirant must understand the value of inner silence. The inner voice can be heard only in silence. That is why, in India, the older important spiritual centers emphasize only meditation and spirituality, not external practices. There are only five or six such *ashrams* now. In these traditional institutions, the emphasis is on meditation, inwardness, silence and pure spiritual values. Now innumerable new spiritual institutions have come up where spirituality is external. Without inwardness how can we attain God-Realization? If we are always walking, talking, singing, how can we attain Self-Realization? So silence and *pranayama* are the keys to meditation. By practicing both we attain *dharma* and true wisdom.

Wisdom means liberation from all of our immoral tendencies. We need one hundred percent devotion and faith in order to overcome the six inner enemies. All the pollution and dust must be vacuumed in order to get self-illumination.

Our strength must not be the strength of power and money, it must be the power of one hundred percent discriminative faith in God. Our strength must always be the strength of faith only—one hundred percent faith in God. Faith is a strong pillar of support throughout life. Without faith our devotion, meditation, spirituality, singing and chanting, all our words and deeds are a mere waste. Watch your words and deeds, watch your self. Meditate and attain *brahmic* awareness. If you have even one fraction of a second, use it to meditate on the Truth. Meditate to attain the supreme spirit, bliss, *Omkara.*

Ages and ages ago, in *Sanatana Dharma*—the very sound of the word *"dharma"* is so sweet—it was beautifully said, "Wake up from your long dream! Be always in wisdom." That is a very great *adesha,* command. Be always in wisdom, attain liberation from all immoral tendencies, particularly anger. So many seekers still have anger in their heart. Anger poisons our entire life. Get rid of it. If we have any illness in our body, we immediately go to a physician or holy person for healing. In the same way, drive out all your negativities by the practice of truth. Attain wisdom through *dharma.*

Without wisdom, even spirituality is sometimes restricted to limited rules such as: "Do not go there, do not see her, do not read their books." This is not wisdom. Cultivate pure devotion, true devotion, not show devotion. Do not show off your devotion to the world under any circumstances. Be a real *yogi,* have mental renunciation. Live a normal life outwardly, but have a rich inner spiritual life. Bloom the lotuses of divine attributes—silence, truth, wisdom, *samata* (equal vision), forgiveness, contentment, detachment and *dharma*—in the lotus pond of your heart. Sometimes there are no flowers in the pond, but when the rainy season comes, the pond is covered with lovely, fragrant lotuses in full bloom. The lotus is the seat of Lakshmi, divine light. So bloom the flowers of divine virtues in the lotus pond of your heart with the raindrops of devotion, wisdom and truth, and fill your life with the fragrance of Divinity.

There are twenty-four hours in a day. Keep one hour for meditation. If you have concentrated meditation for even one fraction of a second, I feel so happy! This is because you cannot get concentration in meditation without an intense desire for God. Burning longing for God gives you mental detachment. When you are attached to the world and its enjoyments you cannot have concentration. So your concentration depends on the intensity of your love for Mother Divine.

There are innumerable names for Divine Mother in the *Lalita Sahasranama*, the thousand names of Divine Mother. But Mother is attributeless, nameless and formless. Mother is indestructible power—do not limit Her to any particular form. She cannot be limited to a mortal frame. If we do that, it shows we have not gone beyond the mental stage. Mother is *Nirakara,* without form, *Nirvikara,* without *gunas, Nirbheda,* without divisions, *Bheda nashini,* destroyer of divisions. If you see divisions, Mother erases all thoughts of divisions from your heart—that is Mother's responsibility. Mother is *Ekarupa;* She has only one form. All forms are Her forms. All religions, all paths, all beliefs, all *mantras,* the entire cosmos is Her manifestation only. She is the main source of energy for all creation. So do not waste time, meditate on the Truth and attain oneness with Mother Divine.

In the beginning, Amma said to you that spirituality is a diamond market, not a fish market. Only an experienced jeweler can assess the true value of a diamond. Similarly, only a seeker with inner silence, inner beauty and inner purity can understand the value of spirituality. That is why saints do not have thousands of disciples, they have only five or six disciples in their *Gurukula pathashalas* (hermitage schools). Only those who are capable of understanding Divinity reside there. These disciples learn the Truth. The *Gurus* do not give the disciples any importance. They do not even look at them because they do not want them to be in body-consciousness all the time.

Those who are always in body-consciousness may not be able to continue for long on the spiritual path. They may give it up. Only those who have inwardness and an intense longing for liberation can wait patiently for years and years for the *Guru's* grace. This is because where there is patience, there only is real faith. Divine Mother is seated on the firm foundation of the pillar of faith, so your faith must be very strong.

In Sanskrit there is a name for the process of strengthening the foundation: *sthula nikarana nyaya.* A deep pit is dug in the ground and a strong pillar or thick pole is put into it. The pit is then firmly packed with mud and stones, so that nothing can move the pillar. Our faith must be as strong as Mt. Kailasa. Then all the problems and upheavals of life will not be able to shake us. We will always stay calm, and our problems will be like light balls of cotton, which are easily blown away.

Be always in *dharma*. Be always in wisdom. Be always in truth. Be always in honesty. These are universal *dharmas*.

In ancient India, the sages had very sweet feelings in their heart. They felt that the entire universe was one small family, a very cute family. In this family they included not only humanity, but also all of nature and all beings in the universe. They had the highest vision, for seeing Divinity everywhere in everything is true spirituality. So children, elevate yourselves to this vision of unity and oneness. This is Truth. Truth is more powerful than the sun, moon and all the planets. Truth is Mother Divine.

We need deep and lasting devotion to attain Mother Divine, but our devotion is not constant. We remember God only when we are faced with problems. Then we cry and pray to God for relief. As soon as our problems are solved, we forget God!

We should not pray only for the fulfillment of material desires. Desires are snakes. Desires arise due to the impurity of the mind. Desirelessness is the highest peak of purity, the highest peak of divinity. So be seated on the highest peak of divinity, children. Limit your desires, burn all the impurities of the mind and attain eternal peace. Understand the play of the mind—the mind is your first enemy. The ego is your greatest enemy. We have wasted our whole life in chasing after meaningless desires. We have come to the last few pages of the beautiful diary of life. Let us not waste these remaining pages. Even if only one line is left, fill it with *Om, Om, Om.*

Om is *Atman,* the supreme spirit, pure cosmic love, not just divine love. Mother's love is cosmic love—one hundred percent unconditional, equal love for all creation. Her education is cosmic education. When will you come to that college, children? In that college, we need one hundred percent marks from the students, not zeros!

Be always in *dharma,* attain the Truth. In Truth you will have inner vision. You will see divinity in every blade of grass, in each and every cell of this universe. Seeing divinity everywhere and in everything is true spirituality. Seeing divinity only in Amma is not amazing. It is not a great thing.

In innumerable births, Mother Divine gives so many beautiful dresses for Her small, little child. She thinks you are such a beautiful child. Mother decorates Her child with many ornaments and beautiful white clothes. She sends the baby to play. After five or ten minutes, this beautiful baby spoils her entire dress with ink, or mud or some juice. She returns crying and crying to Mother asking: "Give me one more dress. This dress is spoiled." Okay, Mother Divine gives another dress. Innumerable births are like innumerable dresses—each birth is a new dress. So how many dresses do you want from Amma, babies? This birth is another a new dress. It is also soiled with lies and material desires. We always expect material benefits from people in this world. In spirituality, there are no expectations at all. Spirituality is only giving, giving, giving; never expecting anything from anyone.

If you limit yourself to loving Amma, it is very sad. If you restrict yourself to Amma's words, her love, her name or this limited frame, you are to be pitied. Go beyond everything. Go beyond, beyond, beyond! Go beyond the world—even the *Vedas*—and attain the eternal peace and bliss of Self-Realization!

There are countless names for the *Atma*n, the Spirit—*Sarvajna,* omniscient; *Maha Purusha*, supreme Soul; *Ainashi*, indestructible and divisionless; *Chaitanya*, Consciousness; *Om,* primal sound; *Uhatita*, beyond imagination; *Ananda,* bliss; Devi and Deva—yet Divinity is nameless and formless.

Send anger permanently from your heart. I have thousands and thousands of letters from my children saying, "Amma, I still have anger in my heart though I have been meditating for forty years." You have meditated for forty years, still this anger is there? There are a thousand names of Divine Mother in *Sri Lalita Sahasranama.* One name is enough to burn all the impurities of our billions and billions of previous births, and even the worst sins. So keep chanting the divine names of Mother with one hundred percent faith.

This morning, several children said to me, "Amma, I have no discipline. What should I do, Amma?" Oh my babies, without discipline, how can we practice meditation? We must have self-discipline in life. Without discipline we miss our exits on the road of life and have to come back on the same road for fifty or sixty miles. We waste so much time and energy, and have to search for our exit all over again. So have awareness, have a definite goal; follow the map carefully.

Spirituality is supreme energy, the energy of the Divine. Burn all negativities with the power of the seed letters of your *mantra.* Always have positive thoughts and positive energy in your life. Then go beyond both positive and negative energies. Surely it is not your destiny to spend this life just eating, drinking, talking and wasting your life.

Beautify your entire life with positive thoughts, noble thoughts. Pray for the welfare of the universe, do good for others. Do not wish anyone ill. That is *amangala,* inauspicious. *Mangala* means auspicious. Always wish the entire universe to be happy, peaceful and prosperous. That is the meaning of the *mantra:*

Lokāḥ samastāḥ sukhino bhavantu

Be in harmony with all creation. Cultivate silence and attain supreme bliss. Only then will you become a real spectator in this long world-play of *maya.* Amma wants all her children to be spectators in this play. Do not become immersed in this play of *maya.*

Hari Om Tat Sat!

Let us do ten minutes silent meditation. This meditation is for universal peace. Let us keep in mind the innumerable orphan children, abused children, senior citizens and other people who are suffering in the world and meditate for their welfare.

San Francisco *1 May 1997*

ॐ

SRI LALITA SAHASRANAMA—THE THOUSAND PETAL LOTUS

Brahmā Viṣṇu Maheśwara jananī
Devī Bhavānī
Brahmānandā Maṇidvipa vāsinī
Devī Bhavānī
Brahma jnāna sukham dehī
Brahmānanda sukham dehī
Devī Bhavānī Lalitā Bhavānī

Embodiments of Divine Souls, Amma's Most Beloved Children,

The meaning of this song is that Divine Mother is the Mother of Brahma, the Creator, Vishnu and *Ishwara* also. She is *Sivakeshavadi Janani*: Siva and Keshava or Vishnu, and all the other Gods are Her children, for She is *Para Shakti, Adi Para Shakti. Brahmananda Manidwipa* means, "Manidwipa is the abode of *Brahmananda* or infinite joy, spirit and transcendental purity." Indestructible divinity is Mother's abode—that is *Brahmananda Manidwipa.*

We should make only one noble request to Amma: "Mother, grant me *Brahmananda sukham.*" *Sukham* means infinite spiritual joy, the bliss attained in meditation. We need only bliss from Mother. The key to *brahmic* bliss is in the hands of Divine Mother.

Mokṣa dvāra kavāṭa pāṭana karī

Moksha is salvation. To enter into the land of bliss, there is a beautiful door—the door of divine wisdom. "Mother holds the key to the door of bliss, and I want to enter into the land of bliss only."

Brahmananda sukham dehi: "I pray to Mother to give me *Brahmananda.*" *Brahmananda* means the bliss of pure Consciousness. By the way, this desire for bliss does not come under ordinary desires. This is a unique, noble and beautiful application to Mother. So the meaning of this song is very beautiful. Now we have Divine Mother's address. Where is Mother? Mother's address is *Brahmananda Manidwipa*. Who is our Mother? She is also the Mother of Brahma, Vishnu and *Maheshwara*.

Mother is *Srishti sthiti laya karini*: the cause of creation, sustenance and dissolution. She is *Sarva vyapini* omnipresent, and *Sarvajna,* omniscient. So pray to Her only for *Brahmananda sukham*.

Today we will talk about Divine Mother's thousand names—the *Lalita Sahasranama*. This is just a short introduction to the *Lalita Sahasranama.* These names are not from this Earth; they have descended from Manidwipa, the abode of Divine Mother. There are eight Devis called *Vasinyadi Vagdevatas,* the Goddesses of Speech. They approached Mother and spontaneously, without any conscious effort, they chanted these thousand names by the grace of *Sri Lalita Parameshwari*.

Lalita Parameshwari means *Adi Para Shakti* in Her small, limited form—very tender and very kind. Actually, "kind" does not describe Mother adequately. She is beyond kindness, beyond compassion, beyond inner beauty, beyond everything! That is Divine Mother. *Lalita Parameshwari* is even beyond motherly affection.

All these thousand names of Mother Divine are *advaitic*. There appears to be *dvaita* or duality at first, but when you meditate, you realize that all the inner meanings reflect Her all-pervasiveness and oneness. That is the essence of the very beautiful names of *Sri Lalita Sahasranama*. If you call Mother by any one name: Amma, *Sri Mata*, *Janani*, Devi, or any other name such as

Kamakshi, Bhavani, or *Lalita,* Mother's heart melts immediately. There is a beautiful *shloka* that describes how *Bhavani's* tender heart melts towards anyone in the world who calls out to Her:

Bhavānī tvam dāse mayi
Vitara dṛṣtim sakaruṇām
Iti stotum vāncan kathayati
Bhavānī tvam iti yaḥ
Tadaiva tvam tasmai
Diśasi nija sāyujya padavī

This is a very beautiful *shloka* about Mother *Bhavani.* One of Mother's sons, who is very innocent and ignorant, does not know anything about Mother. He has very little devotion in his heart, and he is always in worldly intoxication. But at one time he prays to *Bhavani:*

Bhavānī tvam dāse mayi vitara dṛṣtim sakaruṇām

"O Mother *Bhavani,* shower me with Your grace. I am a very insignificant creature." He continues, "Please just show me a little grace. Just bestow one tender look on me." He wanted to pray with the whole *shloka* but, because of his innocence, ignorance and lack of devotion, he could only say: *"Bhavani tvam."* He was able to say only these two words. Immediately Mother *Bhavani,* who has the entire cosmos in Her hand, blessed Her son with Her compassionate and kind look and gave him the wonderful boons of *salokya, samipya, sarupya and sayujya.* In these four stages Mother granted him the blissful state.

When you say *Bhavani* even once, it is enough for Mother. *Bhavani* means One who has created this world-illusion. *Bhavani* is the creator of *maya,* but She is beyond *maya.* Only She can remove the illusion and ignorance in the hearts of Her devotees, Her children, and uplift them to the attainment of Self-Realization. That is *Bhavani.*

So in this beautiful *shloka,* a son calls Mother *Bhavani* just once—without devotion, without knowledge and without meditation. and Mother immediately gives him salvation, *moksh*a—liberation from all immoral qualities. So when you call Mother Divine with one thousand names, what happens? What happens, babies? Mother's heart melts with compassion. When you call Her with only one of Her names, Mother feels so tender towards you—beyond tender. If you call Mother Divine with one thousand names, She melts like butter. So call Her daily with at least one name or ten names. Many children in the West are learning the *Lalita Sahasranama.* They listen to the cassette and gradually they are learning the names in the *Lalita Sahasranama: Sri Mata*, *Sri Maharajni*, *Srimat Simhasaneshwari*. They are so beautiful!

There are sixteen divisions in the *Lalita Sahasranama.* The first division is *Matri Devi Varnana*, the description of Mother Divine. It appears to be extolling Her appearance, describing Her outward beauty, Her jewels and crown, etc. However, that is not the real meaning. Mother's inner beauty, Her tender and very, very soft feelings and Her very loving responsibility toward this world are described in this section.

If there is a beautiful woman who is cruel and has no kindness in her heart, will anyone go near her? No one will ever go to her because of the hardness in her heart. Everyone will be afraid of her, no matter how beautiful she may be, or how rich she may be. The first canto actually describes Divine Mother's kind and compassionate heart. How is She? What is Her responsibility towards this universe?

Take an example: If you have any problem today, you come and cry before Amma. Amma comforts you today, but what about tomorrow? Tomorrow and the day after, you will have more problems, right to the end of your life. Life is full of problems. That is very natural. How will you face all these problems, that is the question. We need support in our inner life. True devotion is a very strong pillar; it gives us that support. Have faith, one hundred percent discriminating faith, and you will get a connection to Mother Divine. That connection will give you comfort throughout your life—not only for one moment. Mother will comfort you always. You will have a permanent connection with Mother Divine. Divinity is transcendental:

Purṇa sarvajna Satcidānanda Brahmānanda

Beyond the *Vedas,* beyond compassion, beyond beauty —She is the light of lights. She is everything. Mother is indivisible oneness. So children, when we chant all the names of the first part of *Sri Lalita Sahasranama*, Mother comforts us inside. We need inner comfort because, not only in this country, but all over the world, life is full of problems. There is so much anxiety, stress, and frustration because of our fast-paced lifestyle. We get no rest at all and we are under great mental stress. So all the children are crying and crying and always crying. We need comfort in our inner life.

One of Mother's names is *Krodhakara ankushojjvala***.** Mother holds so many weapons in Her hands. One of them is the *ankusha,* or goad, which controls elephants. There are elephants in Africa and India. An *ankusha* is an instrument with a very sharp point like a needle. The keeper pokes the elephant on the head with the *ankusha* to control it. The huge elephant is controlled with the small point of a needle! *Krodha* means anger. Anger is like a big elephant, a big African elephant. Mother controls that anger with Her weapon, the *ankusha* in Her hand and destroys it permanently in our life. This is the meaning of the *mantra.*

Krodhākārānkuśojjvalā
Manorūpekṣu kodaṇḍā

Panca tanmātra sāyakā
Nijāruṇa prabhāpūra majjad brahmāṇḍa maṇḍalā

When you meditate, all the innumerable billions of dark forces in your life are immediately dispersed by the illumination of Self-knowledge by the grace of Divine Mother.

Nijāruṇa prabhāpūra majjad brahmāṇḍa maṇḍalā

If you really want Mother, children, if you really need Mother, turn your back on meaningless worldly enjoyments. You must turn your back on them. Close your eyes, open your third eye and see the divinity of Mother, the inner beauty in each and every cell of this cosmos—not only on this Earth, not only in a particular religion, not only in a particular faith. Enjoy Mother's play—this long cosmic play. This is Mother's play; She plays with all these toys. Just as we enjoy playing with our pets, Mother likes to play with Her live toys. Life is just a long play, babies. Do not merge any more in this play. Meditate. Dispel the ignorance of illusion in your heart and open your third eye.

Open your heart; invite Mother Divine into your life. Have a rich inner life. Have one hundred percent beauty in your heart. Discipline is also very important for a spiritual aspirant. Without discipline there is no spirituality. Discipline teaches us detachment. With detachment we have dispassion and discriminative knowledge and we are always in endless transcendental bliss. There are no words to explain the state of bliss, to describe the land of bliss.

In the second part, *Bhandasura vadha*—Bhandasura means the ego—Mother kills our egoism. The third part is about *kundalini.* It is very beautiful. The fourth division is about the *Sri Chakra.* If you know the *Sri Chakra*, you know everything in the cosmos. The *Sri Chakra* is an enigma. The *Sri Chakra* is a vast ocean, the abode of

Mother Divine. Children, whatever is in the *Sri Chakra* is in the cosmos and also in our body. The *Sri Chakra* is also in our body. There are nine *chakras* in the body. *Yogis* or meditators compare the *Sri Chakra* to their body. They feel that Mother Divine is always in their inner life and they enjoy Mother in the form of silence.

Mother's language is silence. Mother's inner beauty is beyond comparison, beyond motherly love also. So a real seeker, a real devotee, a real aspirant always searches for Mother within. When we enjoy Divinity externally in this world, there is a limitation. However, when we enjoy Divinity inside, there is no limitation at all, and we taste real bliss. Knowledge about the *Sri Chakra,* with its many secrets, is contained in the fourth canto. The fifth part of *Sri Lalita Sahasranama* is *Yogini nyasa. Yogini* means how to practice *yoga,* meditation, and all those things. Innumerable subjects are covered in the *Lalita Sahasranama.*

These beautiful thousand names of Mother Divine contain the essence of all the four *Vedas*, the essence of all the *Upanishads* and *Agama* and *Nigama shastras. Agama-Nigama* refers to the scriptures that talk about a wide variety of subjects. The essence of all these—*Agama,* N*igama, jyotisha, nirukta* and *Vedanta*—is in the form of elixir in *Sri Lalita Sahasranama.* So my dear children at least call Mother with one name—the first name, *Sri Mata,* or *Sri Lalitambikayai namah,* the last name.

There are so many *sahasranamas* in the world, among them *Sri Rama Sahasranama*, *Sri Venkateshwara Sahasranama, Sri Siva Sahasranama,* and *Sri Vishnu Sahasranama.* Poets and other people have composed all the other *sahasranamas*. However, *Sri Lalita Sahasranama* is from Manidwipa. It did not originate from poets, but from the body of Mother Divine. That is why it is so powerful. Children, chant at least one *mantra* daily. You will be dialing Divine Mother's direct number! Call Mother, babies! Pray to Mother from the bottom of your heart with true devotion. Devotion is very essential. Without devotion there is no inner beauty in our lives. Without faith prayer is meaningless. So pray to God with one hundred percent faith and with one hundred percent pure devotion. Daily meditate for at least one hour.

Yesterday and this morning, I received so many letters from my children. Some of them mentioned so beautifully in the letters that they meditate for one hour every day, and some other children meditate for four hours daily. I am so happy to read these letters. All the children ask Mother for salvation. Whether this is possible or not is not the question. They pray to Mother for salvation—amazing, beautiful! Yes, and that is the real, noble desire we need at least in this birth, only one noble desire: "Mother give me salvation! You have the key with You. Give me salvation and liberation from all of my immoral qualities. Kill my anger; kill my lust, greed, jealousy, and destroy my attachments. I have so many bonds. Mother give me liberation from all bonds and open the door of wisdom." The door of wisdom leads us to the land of bliss.

The sixteenth and last chapter of the *Lalita Sahasranama* is about salvation. *Sivaya namah:* Mother Herself is Siva. *Siva Shaktyaikya rupinyai namah.* Siva and Shakti are merged in Her form. She is everything. All the innumerable *devatas* are small particles in Mother's body. Brahma, the Creator, is a small, tiny particle in Her *kumkum. Kumkum* is the red powder we use for the little *kumkum* dot on the forehead. The sun is in one of Her eyes, the moon in the other. And here, between the eyebrows, is *agni,* fire. She holds the whole cosmos in Her hand. She is everywhere as formless energy. So children, meditate on Mother Divine's energy. All your negative and positive energies will be destroyed. You will be elevated to the highest peak of pure supreme Consciousness, eternal bliss.

If you really want Mother, turn your back on all worldly intoxications. Be always in *dharma*. Let *dharma* alone rule your entire life, for where there is *dharma* there only is wisdom. Where there is wisdom there only is Truth. So be always in truth. In the *Lalita Sahasranama* Mother is in the form of Truth. *Satyayai namah—satya* means Truth. She Herself is Truth.

Divine Mother Herself is *nada*. *Nada* means *Om*. From *Omkara* emerge innumerable seed letters—*Ayim*, the seed letter of Saraswati, *Srim*, the seed letter of Maha Lakshmi, *Hrim*, the seed letter of Parvati, *Jagat Janani*. So all these seed letters are subtle forms of Mother Divine. There is great power in language. If anyone speaks your language, you are so happy. If anyone curses you with one little word, although it is just a small word, you see only the negative feeling behind it. If anyone praises you, you feel so happy because there is a positive feeling behind the words. Behind all the seed letters, there is divinity, purity and tremendous power.

You must pronounce the seed letters of a *mantra* in the correct way, because when we mispronounce Sanskrit *mantras*, the entire meaning changes. So we must take great care while chanting all the *mantras* in the *Lalita Sahasranama*, or the seed letters of the *Maha Mrityunjaya Mantra*, the healing *mantra*. We must be very careful to chant these *mantras* with one hundred percent correct pronunciation, rhythm and tone of voice. Therefore, children, first listen to the *mantras* carefully. Chant the *mantra* only after you have taken time to learn the *mantras* correctly. Enjoy chanting them, and chant them thousands and thousands of times!

Millions of *pujas* or ritual worships are equal to one *stotra*—only one *stotra*. Ritual worship performed externally while chanting *Om Sri Matre namah, Om Sri Maharajnai namah, Om Srimat Simhasneshwaryai namah* is physical worship. So millions of performances of such external worship equal one repetition of a *stotra* such as *Sri Lalita Sahasranama,* or *stotra parayana.* Thousands and thousands and thousands of *stotra parayanas* are equal to one verbal *japa* of a *mantra* such as *Om namah Sivaya* with a *japa mala,* or rosary beads. Thousands and thousands and thousands of verbal *japas* are equal to one mental *japa* or silent repetition of the *mantra;* and thousands and thousands and thousands of mental *japas* are equal to one meditation! Such is the power of meditation. This is mentioned in *Sri Lalita Sahasranama:*

Dhyāna Dhyāt̤r Dhyeya rupāyai namaḥ
Dharmādharma vivarjitāyai namaḥ

This *mantra* is so very beautiful, beyond beautiful. *Dhyana* is meditation, *dhyatri* is the meditator, and *dhyeya* is the final goal of meditation. This *shloka* says that *dhyana* is Mother and *dhyatri* is also Mother. *Mantra* is Mother in Her subtle form, and *dhyeya,* the final destination, supreme bliss, is Mother too. Divine Mother Herself is all of them!

"O Mother! You Yourself are the combination of these three—*dhyana, dhyatri* and *dhyeya.* Mother, due to the dark curtains of ignorance, I am not able to understand all these divine things. O Mother Divine! Grant me a rich inner life. I have so much poverty in my life—poverty in devotion, poverty in wisdom, poverty in knowledge, poverty in good thoughts and good deeds. Please grant me an inner life rich with noble thoughts, forgiveness, compassion, courage and detachment. Grant me all these divine virtues. Then only will I attain *dharma.* In *dharma* alone do we have wisdom. So Mother, grant me all the rich, divine inner virtues. You are the only giver. Where else can I go and whom else can I ask for these blessings? O Mother, please grant me all these divine virtues, beautify my inner life and then elevate me from ignorance so that I can attain wisdom and *dharma* in this birth."

This is the feeling in *Sri Lalita Sahasranama* in the *shloka:*

Dharmādharma vivarjitāyai namaḥ

Mother is beyond both *adharma* and *dharma—dharmadharma* means righteousness and unrighteousness. Righteousness is right, unrighteousness is wrong. She is beyond everything. O children, you have knowledge about this world. Understand the value of your life. Your life is a precious gift from God. Your life is a beautiful boon. At least in this birth do not misuse this gift. We have wasted our time in innumerable births due to ignorance—the same ego, anger, lust, greed, jealousy—all this pollution is still in us. We are always in this mud pond. That is also mentioned in the *Lalita Sahasranama:*

Samsāra panka nirmagna samuddharaṇa
panḍitāyai namaḥ

The six enemies are still in our heart. Our main enemy is egoism. So pray to Mother: "Kill my egoism, my *ahamkara,* O Mother!" When there is no *ahamkara,* no egoism, then only we have humility in our heart. Humility is the main enemy of egoism. So cultivate humility—humility combined with devotion. Where there is devotion we have knowledge. Where there is knowledge there only is humility. So children cultivate humility and mental detachment.

It has been said that he pride of renunciation is worse than the pride of wealth. The pride of wealth is not good; but the pride of renunciation is very, very bad—the very lowest state. Mental renunciation is a hundred percent good for a spiritual aspirant; it is very essential. So ask Mother: "Grant me true mental renunciation." When we have mental renunciation in our life, we have love towards God. Nothing else in this world attracts our mind. We find no enjoyment at all in the limited things of this world.

Those who have discriminative knowledge in their heart understand the value of devotion in this world play. They never get immersed in this little drama. So my dear children pray to Mother: "Grant me the boon of all the divine virtues—courage, dispassion, compassion, detachment, forgiveness, kindness, wisdom and truth." Only then will you attain *dharma* and have wisdom in your life.

So, Embodiments of Divine Souls, at least enjoy infinite bliss in this birth. That is Amma's wish for her children. The essence of spirituality is that you yourself become God. That is the essence of all spirituality—oneness with God:

Ekamevadvitīyam Brahma nānyad asti akincanaḥ

The *Lalita Sahasranama* is the first word from Mother's sweet and tender voice that expanded into the four *Vedas*. Children, these *Vedas* are vast and complicated. You cannot study or understand them all. However, we have their essence in the form of *Sri Lalita Sahasranama.*

What should we do now? We must cultivate compassion in our heart. We must cultivate purity, *dharma* and cosmic love in our life. Then we will have inner richness and our life will be beautified by wisdom. So divinize all your thoughts with divine attributes. Go beyond the cages of the body, mind, and limited intellect and attain immortality. This is the essence of the sixteen divisions of the *Lalita Sahasranama.*

Sahasra dala kamala means the thousand-petal universal lotus. This lotus is *Sri Lalita Sahasranama.* When will you bloom that flower, babies? Meditate seriously. At present there is no seriousness at all in your meditation. You meditate today and forget to meditate next day. Later, when you have some problems, you meditate again, but fail to do it regularly. You are not serious about meditation. So cultivate consistency in meditation; be serious. Cultivate *dharma*. Be a hundred percent honest and disciplined in your spiritual life. Honesty beautifies your inner life.

Children, meditate daily for one hour, an hour and a half, or two hours. How long you can sit depends on your interest. Pray with tears—pray from the bottom of your heart, not from the lips. Prayer is not a sound; it is a feeling, an inner feeling. How can we express our sweet, inner feeling in words? We pray externally because of lack of devotion. When we purify our heart and have a hundred percent devotion, all our prayers are in absolute silence.

Bloom your inner flowers and offer those flowers to Mother Divine, not these limited flowers. (Points to the flowers in vases around Her.) Do not hurt flowers. Do not cut flowers. They cry in pain, "O, this gentleman cut my head." These flowers are alive; in every aspect of nature there is life. So do not injure anyone or anything, not even flowers. Bloom your inner flowers. When you offer the thousand petals of the universal lotus, the *Lalita Sahasranama,* you will have perfect purity and self-illumination in each and every cell of your body. Moreover, you will experience infinite joy and bliss and your entire life will be filled with the fragrance of divine knowledge.

Just feeling the comfort of Amma's physical presence today or tomorrow is a process of spoon-feeding. Understand? When little infant babies cry, a spoon of milk or some food stops the crying. If the baby cries again, another teaspoon of sustenance is given. So this is spoon-feeding; it gives only a little temporary physical satisfaction and comfort. Amma wants her children to experience permanent comfort in their life. This is possible through purity and meditation. Meditation is a ladder to immortality. Expand your life from this mortal frame to immortality. Do not be bound to this mortal frame. Go beyond everything in the universe. Mother Divine is *Vedatita, Sarvatita,* and *Lokatita,* beyond the *Vedas,* beyond everything, even this universe; and She is *Uhatita*, even beyond imagination.

There are three natures in our mind. When the mind is in *tamas*, our food habits are *tamasic*—we are always eating, always sleepy, lazy, angry, jealous, greedy. When we are in *rajas,* we command people, we make demands on others, we stress people out—"Do this, do that!" So we become a big problem to society because of our dominating *rajasic,* nature. In *rajas* we have a great deal of pride, egoism, jealousy and ignorance. In *sattva* we are pure, we have devotion, humility and no egoism at all. Our thoughts and actions are always filled with *sattva* and we sing devotional songs. We are always in *bhava,* deep spiritual feelings.

In *vishuddha bhava* we are beyond duality. We feel, "I am one with Divinity, there is only oneness." In *vishuddha sattva* there is one hundred percent purity, no division at all—only divisionless, attributeless oneness! There is no consciousness of the body, mind or intellect and no awareness of this world either. In *vishuddha sattva* we feel this life to be a long play. These are stages in the spiritual path.

There are so many stages on the path of meditation. Children, do not waste time. Have *brahmic* awareness in your life. Awake, children! Wake up from this long dream. Get up early in the morning. Meditate on God for inner purification and liberation from all limited, immoral qualities and attain purity in your life. Where there is purity, there only is *dharma*. Purity is the gateway, the main entrance to *dharma*. So be always in pure *dharma* only. That is your Mother's wish for her little babies.

We have committed thousands and thousands of mistakes with our tongue. So purify your tongue and thoughts with the powerful seed letters in the *Saraswati Mantra*. When we meditate on the *Saraswati Mantra* we

have humility, knowledge, inner purification, concentration, stability, equal vision and inner beauty. All these divine qualities bloom in our life. The four seed letters in the *Saraswati Mantra—Om*, *Ayim,* the seed letter for Saraswati, *Srim,* the seed letter for Maha Lakshmi, and *Hrim,* the Devi seed letter—are the *mantras* for *Para Shakti*. So children, chant this *Saraswati Mantra* daily for the ability to speak good, sweet and gentle words. Speak softly and speak truthfully. Avoid lip service. Avoid lip *Vedanta.* It is not good. Do not commit any mistakes with your tongue. This is Amma's wish for her babies.
(Amma speaks in Telugu.)

Swamiji: This story is about Amma's father. Once he visited Mysore, the place where the Chamundeshwari Temple is located. As he was meditating, his *japa mala*, rosary, was taken away by a small girl who was adorned with all kinds of beautiful ornaments. He thought she was just an ordinary little girl. He tried to catch her, but she kept going up the mountain. He was six feet tall, and though the girl was a small child—shc was only five or so—he was not able to catch her. This is because She was the Divine Mother! After he had chased Her for some time, She went into a bush and disappeared. When he looked down, he saw the footprints of the Divine Mother, one in yellow tumeric powder and the other in *kumkum*, the auspicious vermilion powder—two footprints on the ground. He collected that holy dust in a small silver bowl and worshipped it throughout his life. Some of that sacred powder will be mixed in the *vibhuti* with which Amma will bless each and every one tomorrow as a special blessing. So tomorrow will be a very special day for all of us.

Jai Karunamayi!

San Francisco *2 May 1997*

ॐ

DEVI'S SELF LUMINOUS FEET

Om Śrī Cakra vāsinyai namaḥ
Om Śrī Lalitāmbikāyai namaḥ

Brahmā Viṣṇu Maheśwara jananī
Devī Bhavānī
Brahmānandā Maṇidvipa vāsini
Devī Bhavānī
Brahma jnāna sukham dehī
Brahmānanda sukham dehī
Devī Bhavānī Lalitā Bhavānī

Embodiments of Divine Souls, Amma's Most Beloved Children,

Yesterday we had a little introduction about Mother—Mother Divine—*Lalita Devi*. *Lalita* means beyond tender, beyond tenderness; beyond inner beauty; beyond all the divine attributes—attributeless. Mother is divisionless; Mother is indestructible power, the main source of energy, *mula shakti*—a very beautiful word in Sanskrit—the root source of energy for the entire cosmos. In this beautiful song we ask Mother: "Mother, for innumerable births—billions and billions and billions of births—I have been in illusion, in ignorance. I have kept my eyes closed. Even now I am immersed in the mud pond of selfishishness, anger, jealousy, lust and greed. In this birth, in this moment, in this fraction of a second, I beg You for liberation from all these immoral natures."

In one of the names in the *Lalita Sahasranama*, Mother is described as:

Antar mukha samārādhyā bahir mukha sudurlabhā

When any seeker thinks of Mother externally, there are limitations. In mental worship and in meditation an aspirant finds infinite joy. That joy is boundless—not like the joy of physical pleasures. When we go to temples and see the beautiful sculptures, perform *pujas,* sing *bhajans*, and have the blessed *darshan* of holy people, we enjoy these things a great deal. But there is a limit to this kind of enjoyment. In *samadhi* there is no limitation at all. You experience boundless, infinite joy. You taste and touch divine bliss in *samadhi.*

Antar mukha samārādhyā

"Mother should be meditated upon by turning inward," inside the temple of the body. There are four pillars for this temple. One of the pillars is wisdom; the second is cosmic love; the third, Truth and the fourth is *brahmic* awareness. Enclosed by these four pillars is the main shrine—the heart. It is a beautiful lotus with the divine fragrance of Truth and *brahmic* awareness. When you have spiritual wisdom and equal vision, Mother blooms within in the form of self-illumination. She is omnipresent, omnipotent and omniscient—*Sarvajna*. You enjoy infinite joy in your life in meditation only. That is very clearly stated in *Sri Lalita Sahasranama:*

Antar mukha samārādhyā bahir mukha sudurlabhā

There is limitation when you worship Mother in Her physical aspect or form. If you worship Mother mentally, all the inner flowers bloom and you have immense joy and immense concentration. You feel infinite bliss in each and every cell of your body, which is filled with divine elixir.

The *Lalita Sahasranama* is not a mere collection of ordinary words or *shlokas. Sri Lalita Sahasranama* embodies that tender love of Mother which is beyond tenderness itself. *Sri Lalita Sahasranama* contains the secret of *yoga.* The secret of all the *yogas* is in the essence of each and every name of Mother Divine in *Sri Lalita Sahasranama*. It is so beautiful!

Children, at present our feelings are very dry. This is true of all our worldly relationships. and friendships—in the home and in society. We have so much dryness, so much emptiness inside. Physically our life is one hundred percent colorful. We have all the facilities, every comfort in our life. But inside, we have a hundred percent emptiness. This emptiness is due to lack of love.

When you chant or sing the *Lalita Sahasranama*, and are able to understand the meaning of even one of the *mantras,* your heart will be opened. You will develop *brahmic* awareness and have wisdom in your life. You will feel divine cosmic love in your heart and have a direct connection with Mother Divine, *Adi Para Shakti*. This is not a physical connection. If anything is physical, it has a limitation. The eternal has no limitation at all. *Lalita Devi* is the eternal Mother, not the physical mother. Mother *Lalitambika* controls all the billions and billions and billions of galaxies in the entire cosmos!

We just chanted:

Om Śrī Cakra vāsinyai namaḥ

The *Sri Chakra* is the abode of Mother—*Brahmananda.* If you understand the *Sri Chakra*, you know all there is to know about the entire cosmos. The *Sri Chakra* is Mother's symbol, Mother's form and Mother's abode, *Brahmananda. Sri Lalitambika* is your eternal Mother—She is always in your heart in the form of your life:

Prāṇada Prāṇa rūpiṇyai namaḥ

She is your very life. Each and every being is *Lalitambika* only. Every grass blade, every small mud particle, all the sages and *devatas* including Brahma, all the planets, mountains and oceans, the kingdoms of flowers, birds and animals, all of mankind and the *Vedas*—the entire universe, the entire cosmos is filled with Mother's divine cosmic love! When we chant the *Lalita Sahasranama* we have a direct connection with Mother Divine.

The thousand names are nothing but the secrets of *yoga.* There are innumerable *yogas* in the *Vedas:* One of them is *karma yoga*—self*less* service. Where there is one hundred percent less self, there only is true service. Selfless service is really very difficult to practice—it is very hard indeed. But, once we understand *karma yoga,* we begin to enjoy selfless service. Children, the main essence of life is selflessness. The kingdom of wisdom is in our heart. The main entrance to this kingdom is selfless service.

Children, love everything in nature; love humanity, love the universe as your own self. Meditate, open your heart and see divinity in each and every cell of this entire universe. That is true spirituality. If you limit yourself to a particular sect, faith, or to a particular religion, you limit yourself to a frame. Spirituality is boundless. The entire cosmos is enfolded in Mother's divine love. That is *Lalitambika.*

So pray to Mother to bloom all your inner flowers: the root flower, the *svadhishthana* lotus, the *manipura* lotus, the *anahata* lotus—this is *anahata* (pointing to Her heart). When *kundalini* comes to the *anahata chakra,* we become so pure; we have so much purity in our heart—so much purity and inner beauty. All the divine attributes bloom inside: First we have truth, then wisdom and forgiveness, compassion, dispassion, dedication, discriminative knowledge and mental detachment. We have no bonds at all to anything in the world. We love each and every cell of this universe as Mother Divine. We become extremely pure. With each and every heartbeat we hear within the sacred sound, *Om, Om, Om, Om* in:

Prati roma kūpam

"Each and every pore of our body sings *Om,* because Mother is inside our heart." This body is Mother's temple—the real temple for Mother Divine. It has been said, *Deho devalayah.* In *Sanatana Dharma*, the human body itself is referred to as the temple of God. Children, see divinity in every human temple. Only then will you be able to see divinity in each and every being in this universe.

Have *brahmic* awareness in your life and love Mother Divine. Sing Mother's thousand names from the *Lalita Sahasranama.* Practice regularly—listen, listen, listen—listen to the cassette many times. Practice one *shloka* a day. Then you will be able to sing all the 182 *shlokas* containing the thousand divine names.

It is so beautiful. Mother is always in your heart. Your heart is opened by Mother's cosmic love. When the sun of knowledge blooms in our heart, there is no ignorance and all dark forces leave our life for ever.

It is because of selfishness that we have ignorance; ego problems and illusion. Root out the egoism permanently from your life; send it permanently from your heart. Kill the ego and invite Mother Divine into your heart by chanting Her beautiful thousand names which are sweeter than elixir. Keep Mother always in the secret place of your heart. Do not show your devotion externally. Appear to be an ordinary worldly person, but be a true seeker inside. Be a *yogi* inside, be a pure soul inside—that is very important for a spiritual aspirant. Have wisdom and have complete faith in Mother. Pray to Mother to grant you a rich and grand inner life. When we are in truth, life is a very grand; when we are in untruth, our life is filled with poverty.

Because of limited immoral qualities such as greed and jealousy, you are suffering from a lack of love for Mother Divine. Children, desirelessness is the highest peak of purity but it is really not possible to destroy all desires. So cultivate the desire for nobility; have the desire to understand the reality in life. Have a beautiful desire for Self-Realization, because the main aim of human life is to realize the the Self. Your Self is:

Prāṇada Prāṇa rūpiṇyai namaḥ

In *Sri Lalita Sahasranama*, *"Pranada"* means "One who gives consciousness to each and every soul, so that every soul is Her own manifestation." Self means the supreme Soul. *"Prana rupinyai namah"* means "Salutations to Mother in the form of supreme Consciousness, *Chaitanya." Chaitanya* is a beautiful Sanskrit word for Consciousness. This *Chaitanya* is everywhere in the universe—in the air, fire, waters, earth and sky. Mother Divine is the embodiment of *prana,* vital energy. Salutations to that form of Mother! Enjoy Mother Divine in each and every cell of this cosmos. Mother is not limited to this Earth. This Earth is only a tiny particle within Her, it is like a tiny atom, a very tiny little atom. Do not limit Mother to the *Vedas,* do not limit Mother to only your *puja* room or place of worship, to the pictures on your altar and other limited forms. Everything, whether good or bad, is Mother only. So elevate yourself, expand yourself and attain God-Realization!

Antar mukha samārādhyā bahir mukha sudurlabhā

This beautiful name says that if you worship Mother externally, you limit Her. But if you meditate on Mother with the powerful seed letters of *maha mantras* or by chanting Her divine thousand names from *Sri Lalita Sahasranama*, all the inner *chakras* will begin to bloom.

There are 72,000 *nadis* in our body. There is a very subtle and fine nervous system in our heart, lungs and brain, in the medulla oblongata. There are so many junction points in these subtle nerve channels. When you chant the *Om Mantra* 108 times the entire nervous system is stimulated. This brings awareness into our life: The repetition of *Om, Om, Om* erases the consequences of all the bad deeds in our life, all the *karma* load. The powerful seed letters of the *maha mantras*—the *Saraswati Mantra,* the *Maha Mrityunjaya Mantra,* the names of Divine Mother from *Sri Lalita Sahasranama*—destroy all the negative *karmas* or deeds from the root. Then you have immense peace, concentration, self-confidence, and willpower. These qualities begin to bloom in your life. Once you enjoy inner peace, you gradually attain *dharma*, the highest righteousness.

Dharmādharma vivarjitā

Mother is the embodiment of *dharma;* She is also beyond *dharma.* When you attain *dharma* you touch Mother's feet. The entire cosmos is under the lotus feet of Divine Mother. Salvation is under Her feet. Imagine all the entire billion parts of the cosmos under Her feet, just like small atom particles. All the planets are illuminated by the rays of light that emanate from Her feet. Divine Mother's lotus feet give lighting to the whole cosmos! The sun illuminates the moon; both the moon and sun light up the Earth. But the sun is not self-illuminated—it gets its light from Mother's divine lotus feet. Not only one sun, all the billions of suns in the universe are so illuminated:

Sūrya koṭi sama prabhā

"Mother's divine feet shine with the radiance of billions of suns." And all the billions of suns get their lighting from Mother's feet! Mother's lotus feet are decorated with the sound of the *Vedas:*

Sinjāna maṇi manjīra manḍita Śrī padāmbujā

"Mother's lotus feet are decorated with tinkling anklets." There is a beautiful Telugu song which says that Mother's feet are decorated with the sound of the *Vedas.*

She wears beautiful anklets of gold set with gems. The musical sound that emanates from these anklets is really the sound of the *Vedas.* So when Brahma, Vishnu, Siva, the *rishis* and all the holy ones offer their salutations to Mother, they hear the sound of the *Vedas* emanating from Divine Mother's sacred feet. That is *Lalita Devi.*

O my infant babies, meditate on the Divine Mother! Offer your entire life like a small grass flower at Mother's lotus feet. Pray: "O Mother, even though I have committed billions of mistakes, You have the heart to forgive me. Grant me a pure life, a rich inner life so that I may live in *dharma.* I want to attain salvation in this birth." It is important to remember that the longing for the Divine is not considered a desire which must be given up.

So children, the *Lalita Sahasranama* is not an ordinary *parayana —parayana* is chanting a *stotra*. It contains many secrets about *yoga. Sri Lalita Sahasranama* is the essence of all the *yogas*, the elixir of *yogas.* When you listen to it and chant it, when you meditate even on one name of Divine Mother, you will attain God-Realization—of this there is no doubt. Only a person for whom this birth is the last, will chant the names of Divine Mother, *Lalita Devi.* Only such a one will worship Mother inside.

Worship Mother always inside, children. Make your heart a hundred percent clean; purify the heart. Anger is not sweet or good; it is the door to hell. Lust is the second door to hell. Jealousy is the third door to hell. So do not enter those doors. Salvation is the door which leads to Mother—*moksha dvara.* The key is with Mother only. Pray to Mother: "Give me the key to salvation, O Mother! My sweet Mother, You are beyond sweetness. My life is a boon from You. Please purify my life, because I can't purify myself. You alone can purify me with Your kind, tender look." *Lalita Devi* is the tender Mother—beyond tenderness. *Lalita* is *"lalitya,"* which means "softer than butter—very tender." Mother's look is so tender. *Madhura vachani*—Her words are so tender, beyond tender; Her heart is beyond tender. Everything about *Lalita Devi* is tender beyond words.

Nijāruṇa prabhā pūra majjad brahmāṇḍa manḍalā

The entire cosmos is filled with the tender orange-red radiance which emanates from Divine Mother's self-illumination.

Sindūrāruṇa vigrahām trinayanām
Māṇikya maulī sphurat
Tārānāyaka śekharām smita mukhīm
Āpīna vakṣoruhām
Pāṇibhyām alipūrṇa ratna caṣakam
Raktotpalam bibhratīm
Saumyām ratna ghaṭastha rakta caraṇām
Dhyāyet Parām Ambikām

Aruṇā karuṇā tarangitākṣīm
Dhṛta pāśānkuśa puṣpa bāṇa cāpām
Aṇimādibhir āvritām mayūkhair
Ahamityeva vibhāvaye Bhavānīm
Dhyāyet padmāsanasthām
Vikasita vadanām padma patrāyatākṣīm
Hemābhām pīta vastrām karakalita lasad
Hema padmām varāngīm

Sarvālankāra yuktām satatam abhayadām
Bhakta namrām Bhavānīm
Śrī Vidyām śānta mūrtīm sakala suranutām
Sarva sampat pradātrīm

Mother *Lalita Devi* is truly beyond tenderness, beyond all attributes. She is both formless and with form. She is described as:

Dhyāyet padmāsanasthām

The meaning usually given by commentators for this *shloka* is very different from its true *yogic* meaning. There are so many books explaining the *Lalita Sahasranama.* But we must see *Sri Lalita Sahasranama* with a yogic view, not in the ordinary superficial way. The meanings of the names in *Sri Lalita Sahasranama* are different from the *yogic* point of view. If you open your heart and meditate on Mother Divine, She Herself will bless you amd reveal the real meaning of Her thousand names. Now we have some books with commentaries—they do not really describe Mother—they give only the grammatical and literal meanings.

Dhyāyet padmāsanasthām

The meaning in your book is: Mother Divine is seated in *padmasana.* She is sitting in a *padma—"padma"* means "the lotus." Mother is sitting in the thousand-petal lotus, in *padmasana.* That is the literal meaning. But the *yogic* meaning here is completely different.

Dhyāyet padmāsanasthām

"O my spiritual aspirant, meditate on me in *padmasana."* What happens when you sit in meditation in *padmasana?* Your backbone is straight and the entire nervous system is stimulated. When you chant the *Om Mantra* once, your entire energy flows along a track from the tip of your toe to the *sahasrara.* The seven flowers of the *chakras* bloom immediately when you sit in *padmasana,* the lotus posture. Thus the spiritual meaning of *dhyayet padmasanastham* is "Meditate on me in the lotus posture."

Vikasitavadanam: The literal meaning of this word in the *shloka* is generally explained in books as: "Divine Mother's face is beautiful as a lotus and glows with a lovely radiance." The spiritual, *yogic* meaning of *vikasitavadanam* is: "When a seeker meditates, his face blooms with infinite joy." Because Mother is inside, Mother's radiance shines in your face. It is not your face, it is Mother's face. *Vikasitavadanam* is the blooming radiance of divine glory.

The entire *Lalita Sahasranama* is *yoga:* the secret of *yoga*, the essence of *yoga,* the elixir of *yoga* only. One of Mother's names is *Sarva vyapini*—all-pervading and divisionless. Mother is oneness, and oneness with Mother is the essence of *Sri Lalita Sahasranama.*

My dear sweet children, embodiments of *dharma*, embodiments of Soul, do not waste your time in this worldly intoxication. If you really want Mother, turn your back on worldly enjoyments. Pray to Mother in your heart. Make this human body a fit temple for Divine Mother. Offer your entire life like a small flower at Mother's divine feet. Dedicate your entire life to Mother. What is there in your hands? Nothing is in your hands, only unhappiness. In all the many billions of *janmas*, births, you have experienced suffering, pain, problems, unhappiness, depression, and so many other misfortunes such as illness, mental weakness, anger and jealousy. Mother's abode is peace, Mother's abode is infinite joy—endless, boundless bliss. When will you return to your Mother's home? Come back to your Mother's sweet home. Meditate and climb the spiritual ladder and attain Self-Realization, *Brahmananda.*

In the beginning of our program we sang the song:

Brahmānanda sukham dehī Manonmanī

When a seeker goes inward, he becomes divine. When he is always outward, he is worldly. So children close your physical eyes and open your third eye. Enjoy Mother Divine in each and every cell of your body. Listen to the inner voice. Try to understand the inner Reality. Have *brahmic* awareness in your life. Always chant the names of Divine

Mother. Listen to the names and gradually chant them along with the cassette and then sing them. We have so much stress in our lives. When you listen to Mother's names all the stress is released immediately from your life. The impurities are burned by Mother's purity. Mother is pure; Mother is pure Consciousness. It is only Mother who pervades this entire universe. Mother alone sustains this entire universe. Mother is *Sarvajna,* omniscient. Mother is the embodiment of divine love only. So cultivate cosmic love for Mother and attain Self-Realization.

Love Mother, do not love these changing material things. Mother is unchanging, so love only Mother, babies. All of our other relationships in this world involve change. There is nothing permanent about them—only Mother is permanent. If you have that awareness in your life, you will understand the reality and silently love Divine Mother in your heart. Keep Mother in your secret place. Do not show the universe your love for Her. Continue to wear your ordinary clothes, go to work, be in *samsara*, in your family, in this world—but be not in the world mentally. Be not in this *samsara*, be not in this worldly intoxication, be always in spiritual *dharma*.

The *Lalita Sahasranama* is beyond *dharma*, beyond the *yogas* and beyond cosmic love. *Lalita Devi* is *madhura vachani*—Her words are so very sweet and tender. *Mridu madhura hasini*: Sometimes we laugh loudly, but Mother's laugh is very soft and tender. *Mridu* means very tender, a slight smile, not a broad smile, not loud laughter. Everything about Mother is soft and tender.

Children listen to, chant, sing and always think about Mother's names: *Sri Mata, Sri Mata, Sri Mata, Sri Maharajni, Sri Maharajni, Sri Maharajni; Srimat simhasaneswari*—daily chant one name a week. After some months you will be able to sing the entire *Lalita Sahasranama.* Mother Herself comes and helps you when you try to approach Her—that is Her nature and Her responsibility. Why are you concerned about your knowledge of Sanskrit? (Laughter) That is not your problem. That is Mother's problem. If you really want Mother, She Herself takes the responsibility. She sits in your heart, opens your heart, and She Herself teaches you the *Lalita Sahasranama.* So many children all over the world really don't know anything about Sanskrit, but they sing the *Lalita Sahasranama.* This is because Mother takes responsibility for Her children. If you really want to learn the *Lalita Sahasranama*, one day She will come, She *must* come, no doubt, and She is the teacher, She is the *Guru.*

Devī nāmam madhuram Devī rūpam madhuram

"The form of Devi, the form of Mother Divine is so sweet." *Madhuram* means sweet—beyond sweetness, elixir.

We enjoy sweet elixir in the form of Mother Divine. Her name is so very sweet. We want to enjoy that sweetness. We have committed so many mistakes with our tongue. When we chant Mother's divine names, all our sins are burnt by the fire of Divine Mother's purity. So always chant Her names and do not commit mistakes with your tongue. Chant the *Saraswati Mantra.*

All our words must always be spoken smoothly, gently, softly and truthfully—like gems, pearls and rose petals. Do not injure anyone's feelings with your words. Do not use harsh words, children. Do not injure anyone's feelings. Do not scold anyone. And whatever you speak must always come from truth only. So always chant Divine Mother's names.

Devī nāmam madhuram

"Namam" means "Devi's names," the thousand names of Devi—beyond elixir, beyond sweetness!

Devi rupam—the divine form of Mother—the whole cosmos is like a tiny atom particle in Mother's form! I cannot imagine Mother's form. My Mother's form is sweeter than elixir. Mother is really formless and nameless, but for the sake of Her children, She takes on a form. This is the second line.

Devi dhyanam madhuram means meditation on Devi is more than elixir—more than sweetness.

Devi padam madhuram: Her lotus feet are more than elixir. They are your sweet treasure. Mother's feet are beyond the cosmos.

When we talk about Devi, we never say: "Devi's feet." We always say: "Devi's lotus feet." The lotus blooms in the morning and closes by evening, but Devi's feet are self-luminous, divine, and thus far beyond the lotus flowers of this world. So meditate on those lotus feet. Always keep Mother's lotus feet in your heart. Your heart will become so tender by the touch of Divine Mother's lotus feet, and you will always feel cosmic love in your heart.

Sarvam Devi madhuram: Whatever you enjoy in this world is nothing but Mother only, only Mother's love. We love to sing this song for it expresses beautiful feelings towards Mother Divine.

Meditate on the treasure of Mother's divine feet; keep that treasure close to your heart and merge with your eternal Mother in meditation. Salvation is under Mother's feet. *Moksha* is under Mother's feet. So all the *devatas*—Brahma, Vishnu, *Ishwara*—and the great sages—Vishvamitra, Vasishtha, Vamadeva, Shuka, Sanaka-Sanandana and others—also meditate on Devi.

May this be your prayer: "O my Mother, grant me salvation. Even though I have committed billions of sins, You have the heart to forgive your children and elevate them to the highest peak of *dharma,* purity, wisdom, truth, and equal vision—*samata* or balance." Equal vision is when you see divinity in both good and bad. Mud and gold are the same to you, you see no difference between cities and caves. All things are the same; everything is equal. When you attain this highest knowledge, you will enjoy Mother Divine in your life.

So this is *Sri Lalita Sahasranama* with its innumerable *yogic* meanings. Next time, if we have the opportunity, we will discuss the *Lalita Sahasranama* some more. For now chant Mother's names daily. Learn the names one line at a time until gradually you know them all. There are 182 *shlokas* in the *Lalita Sahasranama*—in 182 days, you will know the entire *Lalita Sahasranama!* Isn't that Mother's responsibility? No problem, babies. (Laughter)

All the dry feelings, all the negative feelings, all the negativity in your life is burned by the fire of Divine Mother's cosmic love. So children, pray to Mother for true devotion; pray to Mother for wisdom; pray to Mother for liberation from lust, jealousy, anger and greed—all these limited immoral natures. Go beyond this mortal frame and merge with your eternal Mother; and enjoy infinite joy in your life. Meditate! Meditate! Meditate!

Once again, in this beautiful song—*Devi namam*—the name of Divine Mother is sweeter than elixir, beyond elixir. The form, the divine form of Mother is tender—beyond beautiful, beyond tender, beyond everything. There are no words to express the beauty of Her form. So we just feel Mother's lotus feet here on our forehead at the *ajna chakra*, and on the crown of our head. Let Mother bloom the thousand beautiful petals of the *sahasrara* lotus. Let this lotus bloom fully, and always keep Divine Mother's lotus feet on your head.

In India people only worship Mother's feet. While they wash Mother's feet and offer curds, milk, honey *ghee* and fruit juice—the *panchamritas*—cardamoms, and so many things including tender coconut water, they chant the *Sri*

Suktam, the *Purusha Suktam*—all the hymns of the *Vedas*—and pray to Mother. That is elixir. After that they drink the *tirtha,* the sanctified holy water. But babies, it is not possible for all those rituals to be performed here, so imagine Mother's feet on your head because Her divine lotus feet illuminate the entire cosmos.

Sing Mother's glory. Meditate on Mother's divinity, Her cosmic love. Then all the dry feelings, the emptiness, will be replaced with contentment. You will begin to feel: "O, I have my Mother. She is always here, She is always here, She is always here." And gradually you will feel: "She is always in my entire body—each and every cell is filled with my Mother's divine love." You will feel Mother's divine elixir inside your body temple. All the inner flowers will bloom in your meditation. You will experience *samadhi.*

Without dispassion there is no detachment. With detachment we have faith and devotion. In devotion we have wisdom. When you attain wisdom you attain *dharma.* Where there is *dharma,* there only is Mother Divine. So pray to Mother Divine for the attainment of *dharma* and for Her *darshan*—Her *real darshan.* See the Reality. Do not limit Mother to particular forms. Mother is everywhere. She is the embodiment of *dharma.* So give your respect to each and every *sadhu,* holy person. Even if someone is a small *sadhu,* show him respect. If you give me one percent respect, give a million times more respect to all holy ones. Go and get their blessings. Take only the good things, spiritual things, from them. Seek always only spirituality, not external things. Do not find faults anywhere in this universe. Never injure anyone's feelings, particularly in spirituality. If you do not like their opinions or attitudes towards spirituality, do not say anything. Be in silence. Do not say anything negative—never injure anyone's feelings under any circumstances. Be in your own belief and meditate. See your *Guru*, see your Divine Mother everywhere in the universe—that is real spirituality—and attain the true *dharma,* attain the *Lalita Sahasranama.*

Ajā Kṣaya vinirmuktā Mugdhā Kṣipra prasādinī
Antar mukha samārādhyā Bahir mukha sudurlabhā
Trayī trivarga nilayā Tristhā Tripura mālinī
Nirāmayā Nirālambā Svātmārāmā Sudhā sṛtiḥ
Samsāra panka nirmagna samuddharaṇa punḍitā
Yajna priyā Yajna kartṛ Yajamāna svarūpiṇī

When any of Her children are in the mud of this worldly intoxication, Mother helps them and guides them on the high path of *dharma.*

Samsāra panka nirmagna samuddharaṇa paṇḍitā

The word *pundit* generally means a person learned in the *Vedas.* But there is only one true *pundit* in the cosmos, that is Mother Divine. She elevates Her children from the illusion and ignorance of this *samsara* and uplifts them to *dharma.* That is Mother's responsibility. So children, love Mother only, meditate only on Mother, sing only Mother's name, live in this world for the sake of Mother's love. Love each and every cell of this universe like Mother Herself. See Mother Divine everywhere in the universe. Elevate yourself, expand yourself, meditate and attain the eternal *dharma* in your life. That is Mother's blessing for all Her infant babies.

We will now meditate for ten minutes for universal peace.

Swamiji: It is the greatest *yoga*, the greatest *kundalini yoga,* when we chant these thousand names of Divine Mother. Our hearts will be melted. Amma always says that we must have cosmic love, we must develop cosmic love. This can be cultivated and attained when we chant these powerful *bijakshara mantras. Sri Lalita Sahasranama* is called *mantra shastra.* All the thousand names of Divine Mother are beautiful *bijaksharas,* seed letters, which when chanted, stimulate our spiritual energy right from our toes, as Amma was saying, up to the *sahasrara.* So very powerful are these *mantras* that the spiritual energy rises, travels upward and reaches the *sahasrara.*

Apart from teaching meditation, Amma was giving a great deal of importance to the chanting of these thousand names of Divine Mother, so you can imagine how great the names are. Amma was also saying that Divine Mother is with form and without form. One of the *mantras* Amma quoted was:

Antar mukha samārādhyā Bahir mukha sudurlabhā

This name means that by mere external worship we cannot understand or reach Mother. She can be reached by cultivating inner beauty and by inner worship. Inner worship is nothing but meditation. The *Lalita Sahasranama* is the greatest *yoga* and this *Sahasranama,* as Amma was saying yesterday, was not composed by an ordinary poet or even a *rishi*—*rishi* means a sage—but it has descended to us from Manidwipa, the abode of *Lalita Parameswari.* So it is the greatest gift for mankind. Patanjali Maharshi has given the world the greatest boon of *yoga shastra,* but this gift is even beyond *yoga.* We cannot really say that the *Lalita Sahasranama* is a *yoga* because Amma always says it is beyond *yoga.*

Amma was talking about Mother's divine lotus feet. I can recall that recently, just before Amma's present visit to the U.S., Amma was explaining the *Lalita Sahasranama* in India. Amma was saying that the sacred feet of Divine Mother cannot be compared to the lotus. We always have the habit of referring to them as "the lotus feet of Divine Mother." But the lotus flower is very ashamed on hearing this, because the lotus itself sees the Divine Mother's feet and thinks: "See how ugly I am compared to the feet of Divine Mother. I am not beautiful at all. Why are they comparing me to the divine feet of Mother?" However, none other than the Divine Mother Herself can explain the divinity, the greatness and the love of Divine Mother!

I would like to share the story of another incident with all of you. Before we came here, just one-and-a-half months ago, we had a one-day meditation retreat which spanned twelve long hours. This is because Amma not only teaches us but She also makes us practice, which is very important. So the day was divided into nine sittings of meditation, one-and-a-half hours each. There were nearly one hundred people meditating throughout the day. In the last round, Amma also was sitting with all of them.

After the meditation was over, to the surprise and amazement of all—and some of the Western devotees were also present—Amma was just sitting with both Her feet down on the floor when we saw nectar coming out from Amma's feet. The nectar, the elixir was overflowing from Amma's feet and everyone had the chance to see it. One of Amma's American sons photographed that incident. The people who were there that day were very blessed.

The reason I want to share this is: When the divine ones come down to this Earth, they don't say that they are God or that they are divine. We have to understand this ourselves. With each and every word, expression and kind look they elevate us and remind us that this is divinity. But in spite of that we are entangled in illusion, and that is why we are not able to understand divinity even though it is right in front of our eyes. You have had the rare opportunity of being with Divine Mother these four nights here in this city. You are all very fortunate indeed.

Amma: Four nights are not enough, *nanna*.

Swamiji: The U.S. is a very big country and if we stayed in every town for ten days, it would take us one whole long year to travel everywhere. In India, right after the day we leave, devotees call us and ask: "When are you going to come back?"(Amma laughs softly.) And this in spite of being with Mother all the time for the rest of the year. Yesterday Amma was saying that however much we see, however much we enjoy, there is no limit. We are not satisfied at all. And even if the material things of this world could satisfy us, we can never get enough of Divinity. We still want to enjoy more; we still want to see more; we still want to listen to more!

As Amma was speaking, what I felt and what many people feel is—it's not just Amma's message or Amma's discourse—it is Amma's singing that enchants us. Amma's words are like a soft, melodious song. Tonight Amma was interspersing Her discourse with melodious songs, and everyone was completely absorbed. They were in a different world, in a different heaven. I think you all experienced this.

Many people have been asking about the meditation retreat in India. It will be held in Bangalore, where Amma has Her *ashram*. It is a very beautiful city in southern India with a good climate similar to what you have in California—very pleasant and not at all hot. There is another *ashram* in Penusila—that is in another part of South India. It is in the mountains near the city of Madras. It is in a remote place, not near any village or city—completely in the interior, in the forest. When you go there you are cut off from the world. No television, no newspapers, no phone calls—you don't know what is happening in this world.

Amma: There is no stress at all because of no newspapers. (Laughter)

Swamiji: Amma has selected that place for the main *ashram.* It was the place where Amma did *tapas,* meditation, for over ten long years for the welfare of mankind.

Jai Karunamayi!

San Francisco *3 May 1997*

ॐ

MENTAL RENUNCIATION IS THE GREATEST VIRTUE

Namaḥ Śivābhyām navayauvanābhyām
Paraspara sliṣta vapudharābhyām
Nagendra kanyām Vriṣa ketanābhyām
Namo namaḥ Śankara Pārvatībhyām

Om śaraṇāgata dīnārta paritrāṇa parāyaṇe
Sarvasyārti hare Devī Nārāyaṇī namōstute

Om praṇatānām prasīdasya Devī viśvārti hāriṇī
Trailokya vāsinām iti lokānām varadā bhavām
Om taccham yorāvṛṇī mahe

Ghātum yajnāya ghātum yajna pataye
Daivī svastir astu naḥ svastir mānuṣebhyaḥ
Ūrdhvam jigātu bheṣajam śam no astu dvipade
Ṣam catuṣpade

Amma's Most Beloved Children, Embodiments of Divine Soul,

I am very pleased to see all of you. Children, in this world, love is lacking in our lives and there is so much suffering. Our affections and our relationships are always changing, forever changing. Changing things are impermanent—only Truth is permanent. So how can we attain the permanent, unchanging Truth in our life? We can live in only two ways—one is in cosmic love—equal, unconditional love for all creation—the other, in ignorance and in world-intoxication. When we attain *dharma*—*dharma* means righteousness—we attain wisdom.

The main aim of our life is to live in *dharma* and to attain Self-Realization. How can we realize ourselves? By practicing meditation. Meditation is nothing but purification of our egoistic self. We are now limited to this mortal frame, the body. We are always at the physical level. The second level is mental. The mind is always full of negative thoughts. So *dhyana,* meditation, gives knowledge. *Dhyana* leads to the vision of Truth. When will we attain the vision of Truth, children?

Meditation is a fire. Purify your entire life with the fire of meditation and attain *jnana.* Only then will you have the vision of Truth and Divinity. In the mental level we have mostly negative thoughts. So much negative energy is working in this world. By meditation you will overcome this negativity and attain peace and divinity in your life.

There is a third level—the intellectual. We know so much about this world. However, divine knowledge is beyond the intellectual level. Divinity is beyond everything. There are a thousand names of *Sri Lalita Devi* in the *Lalita Sahasranama.* So many children know about the *Lalita Sahasranama*—the thousand names of Divine Mother. In that *Lalita Sahasranama,* Mother is described as *Vedatita,* beyond the *Vedas; Lokatita,* beyond this world; *Uhatita,* beyond our power of imagination; *Sarvatita,* beyond everything, including body, mind, and intellect! Divine Mother is beyond everything. Only one who attains *dharma* and wisdom will be able to understand the sweetness of the Spirit, the *Atman,* in his life.

My dear children, embodiments of *dharma,* you are not this body; you are not anything physical. Your self is Soul! You are *dharma*. But you are in this body cage. We limit ourselves in these three cages—the physical, mental, and intellectual. Go beyond these cages in meditation. Meditation is just like a fire. In the *Vedas* meditation is called a fire—there are so many types of fires. Anger is one kind of fire and hunger is another kind of fire. Meditation is the fire of *yoga*. Burn all the impurities of innumerable births in this pure fire of *yoga* and purify each and every cell of the body with meditation. Chant *Omkara*, chant your *mantra,* and attain God-Realization! This is the main aim of life. So have a definite aim in your life. We must have a definite aim.

What is our destiny? Our destiny is to attain the Spirit, the *Atman,* and the land of bliss. In Sanskrit it is called *ananda bhumi,* the land of bliss. The main entrance to this land of bliss is righteousness. Where there is righteousness, there only is wisdom; where there is wisdom, there only is discriminative knowledge; where there is discriminative knowledge, there only is Truth and where there is Truth, there only is bliss. We connect with them one by one.

Babies, you are already on a good path. Many of you have so much spirituality in your hearts. Stay in your path and be in this world—but be not in this world mentally. Be always in the Spirit only. Enjoy bliss all the time—in waking, dreaming, sleeping and natural *samadhi*. And in all the four states, you must enjoy bliss by living in *dharma. Dharma* is very, very powerful. There are no words to describe truth or *dharma* or wisdom. We must experience them.

Meditation is the path to the experience of the highest *dharma* in life. *Dharma* is righteousness. There are many divine attributes mingled in *dharma.* There is only one great virtue for the spiritual aspirant. What is that great virtue, children? For a spiritual aspirant there must be one greatest virtue in this world. What is that virtue?

(Silence…)

Amma: Please be free with Amma. You are nothing but my flesh, blood and soul.

Audience: Love....humility.... surrender....compassion.... selfless service.... peace.... patience....

Amma: Mental renunciation is the greatest virtue for a spiritual aspirant. Without mental renunciation, how can we attain peace, bliss, humility or *dharma?* Therefore, the virtue of mental renunciation is the greatest jewel for a spiritual aspirant. Adorn yourself with that jewel immediately. Be in this world physically, but have mental renunciation, for it is the greatest virtue—a very dynamic virtue. So children, attain mental renunciation.

Meditation leads you to immortality and tranquility. Meditation purifies your entire life—it purfies not only this birth, but all the innumerable births in which you have been searching for the Truth. There are so many thorny paths, slippery steps, so many ups and downs in our lives. We are searching, searching, searching for the Truth. This life is a boon—the greatest boon from Divine Mother. So children, utilize at least this birth and attain *dharma.* Amma always expects wisdom from her children, for it is the greatest virtue for a spiritual aspirant.

Divine, spiritual attributes are a must in the life of a spiritual seeker. The first one is true devotion for God—not just a superficial display of devotion. Devotion is the main foundation for spiritual life. Devotion makes our life so sweet. With devotion we melt. Even if our heart is like a stone, when we chant Divine Mother's names, our whole heart melts and is filled with the nectar of divine cosmic love! So devotion is very important. Also, our devotion must be full of faith—one hundred per cent faith. Faith leads us to Truth.

Truthfulness is also very important. It is through truth that we attain wisdom. Wisdom means knowledge and the vision of Truth. When we attain the vision of knowledge, we understand the value of life, the value of time, the value of everything in life. Then we have liberation from anger, jealousy, greed, lust, and all the various little immoralities in our nature. Children, these are the small weeds that cover divine love.

There is a beautiful tree in our heart—the cosmic tree. However, the weeds of anger, lust and jealousy—all these weeds have covered the cosmic tree within for innumerable lifetimes. So remove these weeds with the power of the seed letters of your *mantra* and gradually drive out all the six inner enemies. Our main problem is our egoism, our selfishness. Kill this selfishness immediately. Do not kill animals, do not kill insects, do not kill anything in this world. Kill your first enemy, which lives in your heart as the ego. We have egoism because of selfishness, and because of the ego we become limited. We are always in the body cage. Come out of this cage and attain beautiful wisdom.

When you attain liberation from the cage of egoism, you will have purity in your life. So fill all your thoughts with pure devotion. Only with devotion can we have humility. Humility, nobility and purity give us inner beauty and lead us to a pure, divine life.

So my dear babies, meditate daily. Practice meditation early in the morning. In India, usually people meditate during *Brahmi muhurta,* which is between 3:30 and 4:30 a.m. Here you have so much work and so you are always tired. You work hard continuously like machines simply to attain a little happiness. Children, from now on, spend at least one hour in meditation in the morning—from 5:00 to 6:00 a.m. or from 5:30 to 6:30. Pray to God: "O Mother! Grant me a grand inner life. Grant me peace, grant me true devotion." If you have devotion, you have everything. Now we have devotion, but we also have weeds in our hearts. Because of these weeds our devotion is always covered and suppressed. So remove the weeds from your heart, meditate and merge in peace. Merge in divine cosmic love. Attain the highest *dharma*. What is the highest peak of purity in life, children?

Audience: Silence.

Amma: Is Amma bothering you with questions? (Laughter)

Audience: Love…

Amma: What is the highest peak of purity in life?

Desirelessness is the highest peak of purity. It is impossible not to have any desire in this world. So have a desire for devotion, have a desire to attain *dharma,* have a desire to attain wisdom, have a desire to attain Truth. Convert your worldly desires into spiritual desires. Then these desires will beautify your entire life. When we attain humility—humility is so beautiful—when we attain humility, this body becomes a temple for God. This temple has four pillars: The first pillar is righteousness; the second is wisdom; the third is selflessness; and the fourth is Truth. In this temple of the body, the heart is the holy inner shrine. Your soul is the idol of the presiding deity; the main entrance to this temple is purity and divinity. So open the doors of the temple of your heart. Always have *brahmic* awareness; be always in *dharma*—righteousness is correct, unrighteousness is wrong. Selfishness is wrong selflessness is always sweet. Be always in selflessness.

When we attain *dharma,* there is no self at all—self means the small, egoistic self. Meditation and pure devotion burn all the black curtains of ignorance. We attain true humility and divine cosmic love. So children, taste that bliss. Taste the Spirit in your life. Amma is asking her babies: "Why are you always tasting bitterness in this world? Why are you so unhappy, with so many depressions and so many disturbances in your life? Why are you always unhappy because of this changing material world?" Divine Mother is unchanging Truth. So attain the unchanging Divinity—Mother Divine.

There are a thousand names of Divine Mother in the *Lalita Sahasranama.* Why do so many people all over the world chant *Sri Lalita Sahasranama?* We are all in this materialistic world with dry feelings. Our entire life is without real love. We just talk to people superficially, saying "Hello, hello." This is not permanent. All our relationships are changing. Today we are friends, tomorrow we are not. Everything is impermanent. That is why we have so much unhappiness in our life. We are suffering from lack of pure love. The chanting of the *Lalita Sahasranama,* the thousand sweet, elegant names of Divine Mother, develops divine cosmic love in our heart. We have a permanent connection with Mother Divine.

Mother Divine, with Her thousand hands, is always seated on the thousand-petal lotus in the *sahasrara,* the cosmic lotus. (Amma points to the crown of the head). So the *Lalita Sahasranama* is nothing but divine cosmic love. *Sri Lalita Sahasranama* is indeed the essence of all the *yogas.* There are innumerable *yogas—karma yoga, bhakti yoga, jnana yoga, dhyana yoga, prema yoga.* The *Lalita Sahasranama* is beyond love also—it is divine cosmic love. It is known as the beauty beyond all beauties, the light beyond all lights, knowledge beyond all knowledge, love beyond all love—cosmic love. Children, only those who attain this cosmic love will taste the bliss, the Spirit, and always be in infinite joy. So children, taste that bliss and experience that infinite joy by practicing meditation.

Many people do not understand the value of meditation. They think: "What is there in meditation? We have no taste for just closing the eyes and sitting without doing anything." Meditation is not suitable for everyone. Only those for whom this is their last birth, will close the eyes and sit in meditation, and pray to God in the temple of the body.

Devo devālayaḥ jīvo Deva sanātanaḥ

This body itself is the greatest temple for the great Spirit—our spirit, our *prana. Prana* means vital energy. One who meditates in the temple of the body will attain the Truth—God-Realization—in this very life.

So how can we attain immortality, for we are always in this mortal frame—in the physical, mental and intellectual levels? How can we attain the highest state of purity, without any desire? We have so many enemies in our hearts. How can we destroy these enemies? How can we drive them out permanently? By practicing truth and righteousness, and by chanting Divine Mother's name we can enjoy bliss and peace in our life. By chanting Divine Mother's names, and meditating on your *mantras,* and on Truth, you will gradually experience all the ignorance leaving your heart. You will enjoy peace within. First you will enjoy the peace inside, and then you will be able to see Divinity everywhere in the universe.

A seeker who has true devotion, discrimination, faith and inner silence is able to understand Reality. This understanding leads to immortality. Only when you have inwardness can you see Divine Mother everywhere. So babies, be in this world physically; be not in this world mentally. A small boat or ship is always floating in water. No problem. If the water enters into the boat or ship, then only is there a problem. So be in this world—be a worldly person outwardly, but be a *yogi* mentally. Be a *hamsa,* a swan. Be a pure devotee inside. Offer your entire life to God.

Bloom your inner flowers, the *chakras.* When we meditate on the root *chakra,* the *muladhara chakra* gradually blooms, and when that happens we have no worldly desires. We are inward, withdrawn, and everything in this world seems tasteless.

When we attain the *svadhishthana chakra* in meditation, all criticisms, unnecessary talk and constant thoughts about our bondages are destroyed.

When we reach the *manipura chakra,* knowledge shines like the sun. All the fog of ignorance dissolves and the sun of *jnana* shines brightly, bringing wisdom.

When the *kundalini shakti* comes to the heart *chakra*, you have humility, a hundred per cent purity, true devotion, equal vision, balanced mind and stability—in Sanskrit these are called *samata.* Gold and mud appear to be the same; cities and caves are the same; good and bad are the same—everything is the same. A throne encrusted with the nine precious gems, or a seat of stone are the same—everything is the same—because you are able to see divinity everywhere.

Go inside and see the Spirit within. Always think about the pearls, not about the shell, the mother of pearl. In this heart *chakra,* known as the *anahata chakra,* the *Om nada,* the *Omkara*, is heard continuously within. Each and every cell of your body sings *Om* without your knowledge. You are always in divine intoxication, in purity, and there are no words at all to describe this state. You are in silence, in absolute silence, enjoying the *Om Mantra* inside. The 72,000 *nadis* of the subtle nervous system sing the *Om Mantra* throughout the body. There is so much purity and silence—no thoughts, no negativity, nothing in your hearts—and you enjoy perfect peace and bliss.

When you attain the throat *chakra,* which is called the *vishuddhi chakra,* whatever you speak will be very tender. You will never injure anyone's feelings in this world under any circumstances. All your words will be sweeter than elixir. Normally we commit thousands of mistakes with our tongue. We speak harsh words, abuse and criticize others due to the pollution of desire in our hearts. But children, when we attain the *vishuddhi chakra,* we become a hundred per cent pure. The different levels of speech, *para vak, pashyanti, madhyama* and *vaikhari* are mentioned in the *Lalita Sahasranama* as Divine Mother's names. In all these levels, you are always absolutely truthful. Whatever you speak comes from Truth. It happens like that.

When one attains the *ajna chakra,* it is so beautiful! The *nada*—the *Omkara* sound—ends there. Beyond this point there is no sound. When the third eye opens at the *ajna chakra*, the knowledge of the entire cosmos unfolds before you. You can see all the suns and moons. There is not one sun, there are innumerable suns in the cosmos. This Mother Earth is like a very tiny atom. You will not be bothered by differences of religions or castes or anything else. All humanity will belong to your own soul. The bird kingdom, the animal kingdom, the oceans, rivers, mountains, all nature, trees, even grass blades and mud particles—everything will be a tiny atom in your own Spirit. Your Spirit will come out of the body and touch the whole cosmos! The entire cosmos will be in your vision. You will see that your Self is wisdom, your Self is truth, your Self is time—past, present and future—everything. Your Self is benediction, your Self is indestructible power, your Self is divisionless, your Self is purity, and your Self is oneness. When we attain to this highest peak of realization, there are no differences; there is only oneness. Your Self is activating the entire universe. Everything belongs to your Soul only. There is no jealousy, no limitation at all.

Now our feelings are limited. Sometimes there is no true wisdom in spiritual people also. Those who attain the highest peak of realization have no limitations at all. In realization there is only boundless, limitless joy. So enjoy that state children.

When you reach the *sahasrara kamala,* each and every petal of the thousand-petal lotus gradually blooms and you merge with Divinity. You become *Brahman,* supreme Consciousness. Therefore, in meditation only can you reach the highest supreme Consciousness and taste infinite joy in your life and attain immortality.

So children, meditate. The fire of meditation burns all impurities and fills our life with perfect purity, inner richness and inner beauty. Now we are suffering from so much poverty—poverty in devotion, poverty in purity, poverty in inner beauty, poverty in wisdom, poverty in knowledge, poverty in divinity. So divinize your thoughts, chant Divine Mother's names and meditate for purification. Have only one desire—and it really cannot be counted as a desire—a desire for Self-Realization. Be in your path. Do not look back.

If you really want Divine Mother, turn your back on worldly objects. You must turn your back on worldly enjoyments. If you really want Mother, you must turn, turn, turn, your back on these limited little worldly enjoyments, and have pure devotion for Divine Mother's lotus feet. The whole cosmos is under Mother's lotus feet. So children, imagine the billions of universes under Divine Mother's feet! They are illuminated by Mother's feet only.

My dear babies, meditate on Truth. Fill your life with divine cosmic love. Start the day with love, fill the day with love, and end the day with cosmic love. Always chant Divine Mother's names for the attainment of love. We have some natural treasures in our life. What is the greatest natural treasure, babies?

Audience: Silence.

Amma: Contentment is the greatest natural treasure in our life. Now we have no contentment at all, because of this worldly *maya. Maya* is very subtle. *Bhavani, Sri Mata,* is the creator of *maya,* She Herself is *maya,* and She is also the destroyer of *maya.* So pray to Mother to destroy *maya*—the selfishness, egoism and all limitation from your life. Pray to Her for purity through devotion. Only purity gives peace of mind, equal vision, forgiveness and compassion. Go beyond compassion—compassion is an ordinary thing. Mother Divine is beyond compassion, beyond motherly love. She is the light of lights; She is beyond all the lights in this world. So children, attain that self-illumination in your life. Meditate, meditate and surrender. Surrender to Mother. Surrender to Divine Mother.

When Mother is in Her v*ishva rupa—vishva rupa* means Her universal form, *Karanguli nakhotpanna Narayana dashakritih*. *"Kara"* means "the hand;" *"nakha"* means "Her nails;" *"utpanna"* means "from which are born." Narayana is Vishnu, and *"dashakritih"* means "the ten *avataras* or incarnations of Lord Vishnu." With just a little gesture of Her hand, the *dashavataras,* the ten forms of Vishnu are created from Her fingernails! That is Mother Divine! The whole cosmos is like a dust particle on Divine Mother's lotus feet. The *Vedas* sing of Her:

Duradhigama nissīma mahimā Mahā Māyā
Viśvam bhramayasi Para Brahma Mahiṣī

O Mother! The *vedic pundits,* learned scholars, and even the great sages such as Vishvamitra, Vasishtha, and other *maha rishis* are not able to understand your *lila. "Lila"* means "play." Even Brahma, the creator, is not able to understand Your play, for You are *Duradhigama nissima mahima.* These beautiful words in Sanskrit mean: "You alone know about Yourself." No one can ever know anything about You. Even the creator, Brahma, Siva or Keshava (Vishnu), can never know You, for You are *Siva Keshavadi Janani*—You are the Mother of Brahma, You are the Mother of Vishnu, and You are the Mother of Siva. You are the Mother of the ant too! The ant is such a tiny insect. Divine Mother is the Mother of Brahma as well as the ant. There is no Mother for Mother!

These words are so very beautiful. Because Mother alone knows about Herself. *Maya* is very subtle; *maya* is bondage—we are always thinking about our family. We chant their names—my, my, my, my, my, me, my, my, me, my, my daughter, my son-in-law, my grandson—this is our continuous chant. So this is the pollution of our tongue.

Children, go beyond these bondages. In our innumerable births we have had innumerable families. We have been chanting all these names in all those births. So from this day on, stop chanting the names of your family members, your daughters and daughters-in-law. Go beyond this limited point of view, and always chant Divine Mother's names, which are full of elixir. They are even beyond elixir. So sing Mother's glory, let Mother's name be ever on your lips and your tongue and in your heart. Make your body a temple for Mother, so that Mother always sits in the thousand-petal *sahasrara kamalam.* Seat Mother in your heart and in your *sahasrara.* Mother is not always in the root *chakra.* She is traveling:

> *Śaṭkārāngana dīpikām Siva satīm*
> *Śaḍ vairi vargāpahām*

So sometimes Mother is in the root *chakra,* sometimes in the heart *chakra.* When Mother is in the heart *chakra,* we have *sattvic* thoughts and pure devotion, and we are in silence. That is how we know that She is in the heart *chakra.* During meditation, sometimes you experience bliss—then Mother is in the *ajna chakra.* When you attain to the highest Spirit in your meditation then that is *ananda bhumi,* the land of bliss. So when Mother grants you the land of bliss, She opens the door of wisdom. She opens the door of *dharma,* She opens the door of purity, and you attain the highest peak of divinity in your life.

Children, try to understand the essence. This is the essence of spirituality. You are already in a good path, the spiritual path. Your path is so sweet. Devotion, wherever it may be, is so sweet. Keep whatever belief you have and remain in that belief only. Chant your own *mantra.* Give your respect to your *Guru* and go everywhere. Go and pay your respects wherever there is spirituality. Take the blessings of all holy people.

In meditation you burn all impurities. When you chant any *mantra* once, the power of the *mantra* destroys all impurities. The *mantra* may be *Om,* or *Om namah Sivaya,* or *Om Sri Lalitambika,* or *Om Sri Bhagavan,* or the *Rama Mantra,* the *Krishna Mantra,* the *Siva Mantra,* the *Soham Mantra,* or any *mantra* that your *Guru* gave you as a *prasada* at the time of *diksha,* initiation. Initiation is a new birth for our spiritual journey.

The dark forces of ignorance and illusion have surrounded us in all our innumerable births. When you get initiation, it is a new birth for you. So give great respect to your *Guru,* meditate on your own *mantra,* and attain your eternal Mother. Eternal Mother is beyond everything. So babies, meditate on the Truth. Always sing the glory of Divine Mother, and always dwell in divine peace.

Always give your selfless service to all without any expectation from anyone in this world. If we expect anything, we get pain. If we expect nothing, we can just give our service and stay behind the curtain. Be always behind the curtain—that is so rich. That is real selfless service. Selfless service is the essence of spiritual life. Therefore, where there is no selfishness, but one hundred percent selflessness, there alone is real service. Children, selfless service to all beings in the whole world is the greatest *yoga.* So walk towards your eternal Mother and come back to your sweet home. This world is not your home. Here we always have so many problems such as ego, jealousy, arguments, unhappiness, depression, etc. Come back to your Mother's sweet home, the abode of *Omkara,* the abode of peace, and the abode of indivisible eternity.

Mother is indivisible and indestructible. Mother is purity; She beautifies this universe with Her cosmic love. So my dear babies, meditate. Meditate and purify your life. Surrender, surrender, surrender to God. Ask Mother: "O my Mother, even though I have committed billions of mistakes, You have the heart to forgive. So forgive me and grant me true devotion, right understanding and true knowledge." With right understanding and knowledge you will go beyond all limitations and attain the highest peak of *dharma.*

Sri Lalita Sahasranama is nothing but the greatest *dharma.* Through righteousness we attain the true inner beauty of Divine Mother—the land of bliss—and taste wisdom and purity in our life. So children, daily chant Mother's divine names—even one name is enough to purify our heart and dissolve the fog of ignorance and illusion inside. There is so much illusion—it is all melted by divine wisdom. When the sun of the knowledge of Truth shines, there is no darkness or ignorance in our heart. So meditate on the Truth.

Meditate on Mother Divine and pray for wisdom, pray for bliss. Say: "O Mother, grant me right understanding and knowledge, grant me true devotion. I have a little devotion, very little devotion—not one hundred percent, not even one percent, only one quarter percent of devotion. So at least grant me one percent devotion. That is enough—just one percent devotion. I am always intoxicated with this worldly *maya.* You are the creator of *maya,* so show me the right path, give me right understanding and knowledge. Then only can I attain your lotus feet. O Mother, please grant me the greatest of virtues, mental renunciation."

Mental renunciation is much more important than physical renunciation. Be in this world, do your work, but mentally always meditate on Mother Divine. Purify your heart with true prayer. Prayer must always come from the bottom of our heart, not from the lips. How can we express our love and devotion for Mother in words? It is not possible. However, we can offer our love from the bottom of our heart, and offer our entire life to Divine Mother like a *prasada,* an offering. Burn all your impurities in the form of lighted camphor and offer that beautiful light to Mother!

When I come to the U.S., flowers are blooming everywhere, but their life is very limited. Such small, cute flowers, so beautiful! In their limited life, some flowers bloom for forty or fifty days only. Some big trees have thousands of flowers and all the flowers fill the world with beauty. In our eighty or ninety years of life, how many flowers have we bloomed, babies? None. In *Sri Lalita Sahasranama* it is said that there is one beautiful flower that Mother likes best:

Caitanya kusumārādhyā Caitanya kusuma priyā

Mother likes the worship of cosmic Consciousness—not physical or even mental worship. She likes the worship with the flower of meditation. *Chaitanya* means cosmic Consciousness. That is the beautiful, transcendental flower She likes. So offer the flower of transcendental cosmic Consciousness at Mother's lotus feet—not these flowers, fruits, bananas, mangoes or grapes. There is a *phala* or fruit in our life—the fruit of liberation from the six inner enemies: anger, jealousy, hatred, lust, selfishness. So Mother wants the *mukti phala,* the fruit of liberation, for Her children. *Mukti phala* means *jivan mukti,* liberation in this very life from all the six inner enemies. She wants Her children to be in wisdom. That is what Amma expects from her children.

"Chaitanya kusuma" means "the beautiful inner cosmic flower, the fragrant flower of pure Consciousness." That fragrance is peace, endless peace. Now we have some peace, but after a while it is gone. Here, as we meditate together, we are in peace, but this is also limited.

When we attain *dharma,* wisdom, liberation from the six enemies, and liberation from egoism, we attain eternal peace. The cosmic flower blooms in our life. We enjoy the fragrance all the time, every minute. Mother is always with us, but we are not able to understand this because of *maya,* because of the black curtains of ignorance that cover our eyes and heart. Destroy the black curtains with pure devotion. Meditate on Mother with pure *bhakti*. Dwell in devotion, wisdom, and peace.

Therefore, children, pray to Mother always with tears. Sit alone in your meditation room. We are always alone. In our billions of births, we have always been all alone. Our relationships in this world are only physical; they do not last. The relationship of the soul with your Mother is permanent. Understand that relationship and have a beautiful connection with Her by chanting Divine Mother's elixir names.

In the *Lalita Sahasranama*, Mother is called *Sri Mata*: "O my Mother, You are my Mother, my soul Mother, You are nothing but my flesh, blood and soul." This is true. When you attain God-Realization, you will understand the meaning of these words, not now. This is because there are many levels. As we are always in the physical level, we cannot understand the meaning of these words.

So babies, meditate, meditate, meditate. Surrender, surrender, surrender to Mother Divine. And pray to Mother to grant you right understanding and divine knowledge. Then only will you be able to open your third eye and have a vision of Divinity in each and every cell of the cosmos. So do not limit yourself to a particular faith, a particular frame, or a particular anything. Evolve and expand, that is the nature of the soul. Evolve yourself, elevate yourself, and expand yourself. Dwell always in your sweet universal Self. That is the only wish Amma has for her babies.

There is so much pain in this world. Pray for the welfare of others also. There are so many abused children. Last year and the year before, so many children came here, and many others wrote to me. They are constantly crying. Children everywhere are so sweet. We should never abuse children. We do not have the right. We must give love to everyone in this universe. Senior citizens go through so much pain. One day we will also become the senior citizens of this country. Then what will be our position? So give your love—not your mercy—give your true love and service. That is your responsibility. You take so many things from nature, but you never give anything in return. When we love nature, we become wise. So give your love to this Mother Nature—not ordinary love, not pity, but cosmic love.

Meditate on Mother Divine and chant Her thousand names. Then your heart will be filled with divine cosmic love. Let the love overflow from your heart. Then only can you give love to the whole universe. My children, this is your responsibility towards society. You must give your love to all, to everyone, without any discrimination. In the *Vedas,* in *Sanatana Dharma,* it is said: *Vasudhaika kutumbam,* the entire universe is one family. "*Vasudha*" means "the universe," "*eka kutumbam*" means "only one family." So India is a worship room, U.S. is a hall, Germany is a hall, Japan is a hall, China is another hall—so many halls and verandahs are there. At the physical level you may say this is my country, that is your country; you belong to a particular belief, I belong to a particular belief; I belong to this holy *Guru* or you belong to that holy *Guru.* Do not see the *Gurus* at this level. This is only the physical level.

When we attain the highest peak of *dharma,* everything belongs to our soul only—even the bad and negative things. This is *dharma*. *Dharma* alone rules this entire world. So let *dharma* rule your entire life. That is Truth. Without *dharma,* rules of correct conduct, there would be chaos in life. If there are no road regulations, what happens to the traffic? There have to be rules for traffic. So have *dharma* on the road, *dharma* in the office, *dharma* in life, *dharma* in meditation, *dharma* in family life—have *dharma* everywhere. Let only *dharma* rule your life!

Hari Om Tat Sat!

Portland *5 May 1997*

ॐ

PRACTICE MIND CONTROL

Dhyāyet padmāsanasthām vikasita vadanām
padma patrāyatākṣīm
Hemābhām pītavastrām karakalita lasad hema
padmām varāngīm
Sarvālankāra yuktām satatamabhayadām
bhaktanamrām Bhavānīm
Śrī Vidyām śānta mūrtīm sakala sura nutām
sarva sampad pradātrīm

Sakunkum vilepanām alika cumbi kastūrikām
Samanda hasitekṣaṇām saśara cāpa pāśānkuśām
Aśeṣa jana mohinīm aruṇa mālya bhūṣojjvalām
Japā kusuma bhāsurām japa vidhau smared
Ambikām

Om śaraṇāgata dīnārta paritrāṇa parāyaṇe
Sarvasyārti hare Devī
Śrīman Nārāyaṇi namōstutē

Om praṇatānāma prasīdasya Devī viśvārti
hāriṇī
Trailokya vāsinām iti lokānām varadā bhavām

Om namaḥ Śambhave ca Mayobhave ca
Namaḥ Śankarāya ca Mayaskarāya ca
Namaḥ Śivāya ca Śivatarāya ca

Om śānti śānti śāntiḥ

Embodiments of Divine Souls, Amma's Most Beloved Children,

Yesterday we spoke a little about Divine Mother's glory. Today I want to talk to you about the control of mind through regular meditation. There is a beautiful saying in the *Vedas:* "Search for true knowledge in your self." Knowledge is not outside. Peace, divine knowledge and everything is inside, inside the soul. So search for Divinity within. When we meditate we understand the beauty of purity, peace and divine knowledge in our life. So search for divine knowledge.

What is knowledge? What is the real meaning of knowledge? We have knowledge about so many worldly things. We have a great deal of knowledge in terms of education and degrees. But divinity is beyond worldly knowledge, and divine peace is beyond everything in this world. So how can we attain the greatest divinity, the real peace and bliss in our lives?

Let us take the example of Jesus and his knowledge. There is a beautiful scene in the life of Jesus which reveals the essence of His life. Out of the innumerable scenes depicting Jesus' life, this scene is particularly beautiful—it is beyond beautiful. There were two robbers who were also being crucified along with Jesus. They were taunting Jesus in the lowest way, but Jesus prayed for them. This is knowledge: When these two robbers were criticizing and abusing Jesus, He still loved them and prayed for them—for their peace and for their salvation. He who attains divinity is always in the state of perfect purity. Purity is the gateway to divine knowledge.

Jesus is so pure. There is so much beauty is in His heart. Each and every cell of His heart is purified by divine cosmic love. Since the flower of cosmic Consciousness is blooming in His heart, He sees divinity everywhere in the universe. So there is no question of His criticizing the robbers, or responding at their level. He is far above all that. This is knowledge. So babies, be in this knowledge. If anyone scolds you or criticizes you, they are doing it out of ignorance. So do not respond in kind. Be always in pure consciousness. Be always in knowledge. Have forgiveness in your heart. Forgiveness is divine. This is knowledge. So what is knowledge? How can we attain that highest state of knowledge? By practicing meditation.

Here is one more example. This is also very beautiful, it is about Buddha. You know Buddha. Buddha is beyond compassion, beyond motherly love, beyond everything, because He Himself is God. There were some people who, because of their ignorance, wanted to kill a small lamb. They were very ignorant people. At that time Buddha offered: "I will sacrifice my life. You can kill me, but do not kill this baby lamb." This is knowledge. This is the beauty of knowledge. So be in this beauty, babies. Be in this knowledge. When anyone attains knowledge, he is like Buddha, or Jesus—He is God.

Amma always refers to all of you as "Embodiments of Divinity." You are not this body, mind and limited intellect. You are the embodiment of *dharma* or righteousness, the embodiment of divine love, the embodiment of purity. Your soul has so much purity. It is just blanketed by some dust because of the pollution of this *maya*, worldly intoxication. When we meditate, all this dust vanishes and we get so much clarity in our life. We are purified and search only for divine knowledge.

How can we control this mind? The *Saraswati Mantra* is particularly effective. Ages and ages ago, during the time of the *Ramayana*, long before this present age of *Kali yuga*, five thousand years before *Dvapara yuga,* before *Treta yuga*, before *Krita yuga,* Lord Rama descended on this Earth. Divinity always descends to this world to uplift *dharma.* Divine Mother's only work is to comfort Her children and to uplift *dharma.* God elevates His children to the beautiful state of divine bliss. What other work does the Divine have in this world? God does not come here to construct buildings, or anything else. This world is really just a beautiful play. When you open your third eye, you will understand and enjoy this divine play.

So ages before, in the time of the *Ramayana*, Rama as a small boy was living in a *Gurukula pathashala.* A *Gurukula pathashala* is a hermitage school. The great sages all had little hermitages in the woods where they taught such things as *dharma*, the *Vedas*, family values, human values, the values of society, how to rule the country and many other things. Sri Rama was in His seventh year when He went to the *Gurukula pathashala*, the hermitage school of Vasishtha Maharshi, His *Guru*, to be educated there. His *Guru* gave him the *Saraswati Mantra* as part of His education. In the television series, *"Ramayana,"* Vasishtha Maharshi is shown sitting near a six foot statue of Mother Saraswati. The pupils pray to Mother:

Yā kundendu tuṣāra hāra dhavalā
Yā śubhra vastrāvṛtā
Yā vīṇā vara daṇḍa maṇḍita karā
Yā śveta padmāsanā
Yā Brahmācyuta Śankara prabhṛtibhir
Devaiḥ sadā pūjitā
Sā mām pātu Sarasvatī Bhagavatī
Niḥ śeṣa jādyāpahā

This beautiful *shloka* is a prayer to Mother Divine as Saraswati Devi, Goddess of Knowledge, in which the seeker asks for divine knowledge. It has been there from that time, ages ago. Even now students chant this *shloka* in in every school in India.

This is a universal prayer in India today:

Niḥ śeṣa jādyāpahā

"Please remove my ignorance completely. Mother, destroy all ignorance and bloom the beautiful white lotus, the divine flower of cosmic Consciousness within me. Mother give me the pure knowledge about Yourself, about Divinity."

Gradually when we meditate with the seed letters of the *mantra*, all the blankets on our *chakras* are removed, the dust on the *chakras* is wiped away and they become clean. Our heart becomes so tender, so very tender, and we attain peace in our life. Gradually our third eye opens and we attain bliss.

Devotion is very important. Without devotion all we do is wasted effort. So children, have devotion. Be in your belief. Meditate on your *mantra*. Meditate on your *Guru*. And offer your entire life to God like a *naivedya prasada,* like an offering of food or pure water to God. This is very important. Without this devotion we will have dry feelings even in our spirituality, and no wisdom at all. We will become selfish and think: "I know everything." This is also one sort of egoism. So kill the ego permanently and be always in your Self. Taste bliss in *bhakti*. Taste real, eternal peace in your *bhakti*. Attain the highest *dharma* in your life. Meditate only on the Truth and be always in divine wisdom—that is divine knowledge.

Daily practice meditation with *mantra* and *pranayama. Pranayama* is the key for meditation. Without *pranayama,* there is no concentration. *Pranayama* gives you immense concentration in meditation. *Pranayama* gives a hundred percent oxygen to our body. The *chakras* are infused with vital energy and we develop so much inwardness in our meditation. That is why *pranayama* is the key to meditation.

The quality of your meditation also depends upon the *mantras* you use. In India a large number of people meditate on the *Gayatri Mantra*, the *Om Mantra* or the *Saraswati Mantra.* Some meditate on the *Rama Mantra,* some on the *Namah Sivaya Mantra* and some on the *Narayana Mantra* as their main *mantra. Devi Mantras* are very secret: the *Shodasakshari Mantra,* the *Panchadashakshari Mantra,* the *Navakshari Mantra,* the *Bala Mantra,* the *Bala Tripurasundari Mantra.* These *mantras* are never printed in books as they are very secret. They are given directly by the *Guru* to the disciple. These are the *mantras* used all over the world for meditating.

So children, your meditation depends on your *mantra* and your interest. This is mentioned beautifully in the Shankara philosophy:

Manuṣyatvam mumukṣatvam
Mahā puruṣa samṣrayaḥ

"The human body, intense longing for spirituality and *Sri Guru*—these three combined are called *yoga.*" Without this human body, you cannot meditate. This body is a temple. We need this temple. Because of your previous births with good *samskaras* and lives filled with devotion, you have purity and devotion in this birth. This leads you to your *Guru* and to *moksha*, salvation. Without these *samskaras*, being in this human body—just eating, walking, and talking—means living in the same illusion with no meaning at all in our lives.

Meditation on your *mantra* leads you to *mokshatvam.* the desire for liberation. *Moksha* means salvation which you achieve through inwardness and by *maha purusha samshrayah,* the greatest grace and protection of the *Guru.* He initiates you into a *mantra* with the powerful combination of seed letters. There is a very powerful *mantra* called the *Shakti Panchakshari Mantra.* We all know the *Siva Panchakshari Mantra, Om namah Sivaya.* However, there are some special seed letters for meditation only, which are like powerful fuse *mantras.* They are used only for meditation, never for audible chanting. One such *mantra* is the *Siva Shakti Panchakshari Mantra.* It has all the seed letters of the *Om namah Sivaya Mantra,* and also contains an extra, very special *bijakshara* for *Shakti.*

So the *Gurus* grace their children with these secret *mantras.* All the *Gurus* take on so much responsibility. They do not simply give a *mantra* to their disciples and leave the rest up to them—a true *Guru* never does that. They take full responsibility for their disciples. They make them sit and meditate and they take responsibility for every aspect of their disciples' spiritual progress. The disciples always have a connection with their *Guru.* This is what is meant by *Maha purusha samshrayah.* So children, only when all these three—the human body, a desire for spirituality and the grace of the *Guru*—are combined, do you attain the highest bliss in your meditation.

Sadhana is very important for the spiritual aspirant. *Sadhana* means the daily practice of meditation, without any interruption. Do constant *sadhana*, but not with blind belief, without any knowledge about the *mantra.* We must understand that meditation involves many things—not just closing the eyes and sitting still. This is not enough. We need some knowledge. This is the responsibility of the *Guru.* He explains the importance of meditation and the meaning of the *mantra.* He leads you to the highest peak of bliss. Practice meditation daily early in the morning for one hour, one-and-a-half hours or two hours and also in the evening—one hour, or one-and-a-half hours. But we have no time. What can we do? Try to sit in meditation for at least ten or fifteen minutes every morning.

In meditation only we have immense concentration. The black curtains of ignorance burn only in meditation. We get self-confidence and immense wisdom through meditation. Meditation purifies our mind and heart—it purifies our entire life. The power of the seed letters of our *mantra* gives us so much knowledge that without our knowing it, all our words come from the divine Truth only. This is knowledge. So search for this knowledge. Search for divine knowledge, not ordinary knowledge.

Our *samskaras* from innumerable births lead us in this birth also to the right path of divine knowledge. In this slippery path there are so many ups and downs, thorns, stones and many sharp glass pieces. They injure us. Go beyond all these things and attain the highest *dharma* in your life—the highest *dharma.* Start the day with divine cosmic love. Yesterday when we were discussing the *Lalita Sahasranama,* we discussed how Divine Mother says: "Bloom the flower of cosmic Consciousness, that beautiful lotus." Amma likes only that flower. She loves that lotus of cosmic Consciousness so much!

When you meditate, this flower, *chaitanya kusuma,* the flower of cosmic Consciousness, blooms in your heart, and your heart opens. You taste the Truth! When you attain Truth in your life, you attain real wisdom. You have inner beauty, peace, and liberation from all these immoral natures—anger, jealousy, greed, hatred. Only when we have liberation from these immoral tendencies do we have wisdom in our life. So children, Amma expects from you the greatest wisdom, the greatest wisdom of Truth.

Attain the divine virtue of wisdom by meditating daily without any interruption. Meditate with your *mantra.* Sometimes when we meditate without using the *mantra,* we experience depression. Seekers say to me: "How do I attain God? Although I have meditated all these years, nothing has changed. I have not attained peace in my life. I see no use in this meditation. I have given it up. I have given up my devotion also. I have no faith at all."

Therefore *mantra* is very important. Without *mantra* there is no meditation at all. Yet continuous chanting of the *mantra* still keeps our mind working. So meditate on the *mantra* five times and then leave a gap. Sit in silence for five or six minutes. If your mind begins to wander here and there, meditate on the *mantra* mentally five times. If you have concentration, a hundred percent concentration in meditation, there is no need to continue with the *mantra.* But if your mind becomes restless, thinking of worldly matters, again take the *mantra* vibration inside and focus your mind between the eyebrows. This is the place of our third eye. So meditate here, concentrate here. (Amma points to Her forehead.) Focus your mind and again chant the *mantra* mentally, not verbally, five times and then be silent. This silence is real meditation.

Meditating without a *mantra* leads to depression. The *mantra* destroys thoughts, the innumerable billions of thoughts, good and bad, and we become thought-less.

Dhyānam nirviṣayam manaḥ

"Freeing the mind from all sources of thoughts is real meditation." So we need *mantra.* Meditation is a ladder from this mortal world to the immortal world. *Mantra* is very important. Climb the ladder of meditation with the help of the *mantra,* and attain immortality and infinite joy in your life. Thus we now understand that *mantra* and *pranayama* are very important for the spiritual seeker.

Do not always seek miracles. Be always in peace. Dwell always in peace, meditate on the Truth, and practice silence. Do not disturb holy people; be silent in their presence. One hour of meditation burns hundreds and hundreds of the bad deeds of previous births, all the bad *karma* load, and you have tremendous peace in your life. If you meditate regularly over a period of several years, there is no *karma* load left. So children, meditate. Search for divine knowledge. Attain the greatest *dharma.* Attain the highest peak of bliss in meditation. Bloom all the flowers of cosmic Consciousness and offer your entire life to God. Be always in Truth. Be always in wisdom. Without Truth there is no light at all in our life. Mother is Truth. She is the light of all lights.

Understand the value of divinity, the value of time, the value of your life. This life is a boon from God. Utilize this boon. Offer your life to God like a flower. This is called *mantra pushpa* in Sanskrit.

In India we have so many *pujas,* where devotees offer many flowers in worship. At a *puja,* such as the *Sri Chakra puja,* devotees worship the Divine Mother for as long as eight or nine hours at a stretch. They close their eyes and, continuously, without interruption, they sing all the hymns and *mantras* very beautifully.

At the end of the *puja*, the devotees close their eyes and mentally think of the heart lotus, the white lotus. The knowledge of the inner consciousness blooms and they mentally offer the inner lotus to Mother Divine without any outward show. This flower of inner consciousness reaches Mother's divine feet—of this there is no doubt. Only this flower reaches Mother Divine. So offer that flower, children. Mother likes only that flower.

Caitanya kusuma ārādhyā Caitanya kusuma priyā

Chaitanya kusuma is the beautiful, beautiful flower of cosmic Consciousness. This flower is beyond beauty, its fragrance is everlasting. The fragrance of this flower is permanent peace. The world is always changing. There is no permanence at all in this world. Everything changes after some years. The only permanent thing is Divinity. So your only aim is to attain that Divinity at least in this birth.

We have wasted innumerable births, and are now wasting our entire present life just for meaningless worldly enjoyments. We never cry for God. We never think seriously about God. Our meditation is also not serious at all. Just now we sat for a five minute meditation—there was no seriousness. Our meditation is only for five or ten minutes. Even if you sit in meditation for ten or eleven *hours,* that is also a baby meditation. (Amma laughs.) Yes, it is a baby meditation! If you have just ten or eleven minutes of real concentration in that meditation, Amma is so happy. That ten hours, eleven hours meditation is also a baby meditation because all the thoughts are still inside—anger is inside, lust is there—all those things are still there inside. All the weeds are there still. When we send them permanently from our heart and when all the blankets of ignorance are removed from the *chakras,* only then will the inner flowers bloom. Then after all the inner flowers bloom, the final lotus—the lotus of cosmic Consciousness—will gradually start to open. Each of the thousand petals will unfold very slowly.

So think seriously, babies. Meditate seriously. We are not serious in our meditations. Try to meditate seriously. Pray to God with tears. Pray in the early morning. At midnight, if you wake up, meditate at that time. Sit alone and pray to God for purification: "O my Divine Mother, O God, grant me the right understanding and knowledge about my Self. I want real understanding. I do not have true knowledge now. I really want true knowledge about my Self. I want to attain divine bliss at least in this birth. So please grant me this boon."

God has given you so many things. How can you thank Him? In the world, if anyone offers you anything you say: "Thank you, thank you so much." Is it enough to thank Divine Mother or God? No. God is beyond thanks. If you commit millions of mistakes even in this minute, Mother has the heart to love you and forgive you. That is the nature of Mother Divine. That is the beauty of Mother. So babies, understand the real beauty of Divinity and attain that divine beauty in your life. There there are so many babies who love Mother, whose hearts melt at the thought of Mother Divine.

Mokṣa dvāra kavāṭa pāṭana karī

The key is with Mother, in Mother's hand. So ask Her continuously, bother Mother: "O Mother, give me, give me, grant me, grant me salvation." Bother Her so that She opens the door and you reach the land of bliss—*ananda bhumi*. You attain the highest *dharma,* bliss and peace in your life. That is the essence of spirituality.

Children, open your hearts. Open your hearts. Fill your entire heart with divine cosmic love. Let only *dharma* rule your entire life. And search for divine knowledge. Search inside, not outside. Do not search in books or anywhere else—always inside, in your meditation. *Experience* that divine knowledge inside, for you cannot get it by reading books or by listening to discourses.

We must experience Divinity in our Self. So children, Amma wishes all her children to attain the highest peak of bliss in their lives. Bliss is *samadhi. "Sama"* means "balance;" *"dhi"* means "you are always in the blissful state of pure Consciousness." That is the natural state of *samadhi:* natural *samadhi* means always being in a state of God-Consciousness. Jesus is always God, not only sometimes. Ramana Maharshi, Ramakrishna Paramahamsa and many other holy people are always in the godly state because they are naturally established in supreme Consciousness—they are always in the highest bliss. They do not experience the first three states—waking, dreaming and deep sleep. Those states are for ordinary people. *Samadhi* is our natural state, so be in that state. Amma expects all her children to be at that highest peak. Be seated in *Omkara. Omkara* is your home. So abide always in *brahmic* awareness.

We are so unhappy in this world because of our desire for material things. When we attain *samadhi* we have permanent happiness in our life. Our bliss is permanent. We are always in the *brahmic* state. Krishna, Rama, Jesus, Buddha, Ramana, so many holy incarnations were in that natural state—not for a little while, but all the time, under all circumstances. So children, be seated in that highest *dharma*. Go beyond all these holy people also. Go beyond Buddha, go beyond Jesus, go beyond Rama, go beyond Divine Mother and be seated here, on Mother's head. And play there. You have that right. You are Her children. You have that right. So bother Mother. "O Mother, grant me, grant me, grant me *moksha!*"

Sometimes children want to go on a picnic, so they ask their mother for one or two dollars. If their mother says: "No, no, not now," they continue to bother her: "Give me, give me, give me, mmm….mmm….mmm…." So the mother gives five or ten dollars. Yes, when you ask Mother for only one dollar, She gives you ten! That is the beauty of Mother. Mother is beyond motherly love. So children bother Mother Divine: "Grant me bliss!"

There is a beautiful song in Telugu:

Rāvammā Ammā Rāvammā
Rāja Rājeśvarī Rāvammā
Nirmala jīvana sudhālu tonakagā
Śānti tīramuna mammu cherpagā
Rāvammā Ammā Rāvammā

"*Ravamma*" means "Mother, come, come, come!" "*Ra*" means "come." Where is Mother? She is everywhere—in you, in your friends, in everything. Mother is *Sarvajna,* omniscient. She is omnipresent and omnipotent. She is divisionless. Mother is oneness. But because of the curtains of illusion, we are not able to see Mother Divine everywhere in the universe. So we call Mother: "O Amma, Amma!" This *raga* is called *chakravaka*—a very soft *raga*, very tender *raga*. In this soft *raga*, the aspirant calls: "Amma, Amma, come, come, come!" The moment he utters the sound "a," which comes before "ma," Amma is immediately woken up from Her highest throne, Her *simhasana,* in Manidwipa, the abode of *Omkara.* All the planets are like lotuses—Venus is one lotus; the Earth is one lotus; Saturn is like a beautiful blue lotus; the sun is a diamond lotus and the moon is a silver lotus. Mother steps on all these beautiful lotuses, one at a time, as She hurries to see Her child.

The devotee prays to Her: "Amma you gave me so much purity in every birth. Each birth is like a set of new, white clothes. Every fresh, valuable dress you gave me, I spoilt with ink, some juice, or with mud. Again you gave me more dresses—so many billions and billions of births. I spoilt all the dresses, and wanted one more dress from You. I will spoil this birth also because of my ignorance. O Mother, come, come! Come, Amma. Be seated always in the temple of my heart. Purify my entire life with your pure love."

Nirmala jivana—"nirmala" means "pure;" *"jivana"* means "life;" *"sudha"* means "nectar." The song means, "Fill my heart with the nectar of your pure cosmic love. So, Amma, again and again I bother you. I know my Mother never gets irritated."

It is difficult to translate some Sanskrit words into English. For instance, there are three hundred words for mother in Sanskrit, while English has only five or six—woman, girl, lady. For the word beautiful, there are so many Sanskrit words—*saundharya, lavanya, shobha.*

Mother never gets irritated with Her children. We get irritated with people. If they repeat themselves, we get so irritated and we think: "Why is he bothering me?" You bother Mother for billions of births, but Mother never feels irritation. See Her beauty. This is knowledge. So search for true knowledge, babies. Search for wisdom and see

Mother's beauty everywhere, first in your life and then in the entire universe.

So the meaning of this beautiful song, *"Ravammma...."* is: "Amma give me the nectar of Your divine love. I want to experience it in *samadhi."* If it is physical love, I say: "Children, I love you." But that is so limited—I touch you, put a mark of *vibhuti* or *kumkum* on your forehead, and I comfort you. In *samadhi*, you enjoy the bliss that is beyond everything. There are no words to explain that bliss. So that is what you need in your life—that blissful state. We need the experience of *samadhi*. So children seek the real *samadhi* and meditate with purity on Mother Divine. Achieve inner beauty.

This is in the *Lalita Sahasranama*. Do not look at the English commentaries. The English commentaries on the *Lalita Sahasranama* only explain the literal meanings of the words. Do not touch those literal meanings. If you really want to understand the thousand names of Divine Mother, chant at least one name everyday: *"Sri Mata, Sri Mata."* One day *Sri Mata* will open your heart and give you the right understanding and knowledge about *Sri Mata*. Do not look at the meanings in English or even in Sanskirt books. They are very limited. So children, babies, meditate.

You can compare these books about *Sri Lalita Sahasranama* to a map. Suppose we have a map of Portland, or a map of the Rose Garden. We never see the beauty of the real roses in that garden, we see just the map. All our books are like that map. If you want to see and enjoy the beauty of the rose garden, you must go there and see the roses. In the same way, *mantras* and books are only maps about Mother's address. The *Gayatri Mantra* is one such address. In the *Bhagavad Gita,* Lord Krishna gives so many addresses. In the Bible Jesus gave so many addresses: "This is me. This is me. This is my level." There are so many addresses—the *ashvattha vriksha,* the sacred *pipal* tree, symbol of wisdom, is Krishna; Arjuna himself is Krishna.

So when you chant one particular *mantra*, one day you connect with the real Divinity. You realize, "The *Gayatri Mantra* is my self, my inner Self." If you only connect on the physical plane, it is superficial. So meditate. You must meditate on the Reality, the Truth only. *Dharma* is so pure. *Dharma* is very powerful. Without *dharma,* there is no universe at all. *Dharma* only rules the entire universe. Divine Mother *Lalitambika* is the embodiment of *dharma,* divinity, purity, and energy. She is the source of energy. Without Mother's energy:

Śivaḥ śaktyā yukto yadi bhavati
śaktaḥ prabhavitum
Na ca Devam devo na khalu
kuśulaḥ spanditumapi
Atas tvāmārādhyām Hari Hara
Virincādibhir api
Praṇantu stotum vā kathamakṛta
puṇyaḥ prabhavat

This is a beautiful *shloka* from the *Saundarya Lahari.* This verse by Adi Shankaracharya is beyond beautiful, beyond divinity: "Mother, without Your energy, even Brahma, the creator, cannot move—He cannot move even one foot. Without Your consciousness, without Your permission, even Lord Siva cannot move; and Vishnu cannot move either. Everything in this universe becomes still without Your consciousness because You are the very source of energy for everything in the cosmos, including all the Gods and Goddesses. O Mother, grant me the ability to sing about Your glory and Your beauty."

"Akritapunyah prabhavati" means, "How can I pray, without Your permission, how can I sit in front of You,

Mother?" This beautiful *shloka* says that if Mother wishes, you can meditate, and you can attain *Brahma jnana* in a fraction of a second. If She does not wish it, you will remain in this worldly intoxication, searching for unnecessary material pleasures, counting your money, wanting meaningless things. You will focus on filling your stomach, sleeping, walking, and using unnecessary words—the pollution of the mouth. All these things have no meaning at all. You will have no fragrance of peace, no enlightenment and no experience of infinite bliss in your life. You will not attain immortality in this birth also. Everything is in Mother's hands only. *Akritapunyah prabhavati*—"Only if You wish it, I can meditate. If You do not wish it, I will stay in this illusion, *maya.* So Mother, help me, teach me and elevate me." This is the prayer in this beautiful verse.

There are so many *shlokas*. Chanting these *shlokas* brings awareness to our heart. So also with *Sri Lalita Sahasranama.* Even if you do not know the meanings of the *mantras*, just chant them and the divine nectar of Mother's love and affection will fill the vessel of your heart and overflow from it.

So children meditate on the Truth only and attain divine knowledge in your life. That is Amma's wish for her babies.

Srī Mātā Jai Mātā Srī Mātā
Tana mana prāṇa mé Srī Mātā
Pavana gagana mé Srī Mātā
Nayana nayana mé Srī Mātā
Aṇuva aṇuva mé Srī Mātā
Janana maraṇa mé Srī Mātā

This song describes how Amma pervades the vital energies. "*Tana*" means "body," "*mana*" means "mind." The mind is not stable—it always goes up and down. It gives us wrong information. (Amma and audience laugh.) *"Pavana"* means "air;" *"gagana"* is *akasha,* "the sky." *"Pavana gagana me Sri Mata"* means "Mother is in the air and sky, the galaxies, everywhere." *Nayana, nayana me Sri Mata*—Mother is in everyone's eyes. You can see Mother Divine in every eye. *Anuva, anuva me Sri Mata—Sri Mata* is in the soil, in each and every dust particle. And *janana marana me Sri Mata*—Mother is there with you at your birth, and again in death Mother comes to you—always, always, always. Only Mother comes to you in death. This song has such beautiful inner meanings.

So babies, merge with your eternal Mother. Merge with your eternal Mother. She is pure Consciousness, the Divine. She is called *Siva Shaktyaikya rupini.* Siva is nothing but Mother only. Shakti is both Mother and Father. They are only one, pure Consciousness.

That pure Consciousness is *Lalitambika.* This is very clearly mentioned in the *Lalita Sahasranama.* All the names and meanings are nothing but the nectar of *yoga. Sri Lalita Sahasranama* is the essence of *yoga*—it is also beyond *yoga.* Sing at least the first name, *Sri Mata* every day. Chant Mother's glory and offer your life, your entire life to Mother Divine!

Hari Om Tat Sat!

Portland *6 May 1997*

ॐ

DIVINE MOTHER'S ADDRESS

Om namaḥ Śivāya namaḥ Om (4x)
Om namaḥ Śivāya namaḥ Om Om Om (4x)
Durgā Bhavānī namaḥ Om Om Om
Durgati nāśinī namaḥ Om Om Om
Kailaśa vāsinī namaḥ Om Om Om
Ātma nivāsinī namaḥ Om

Embodiments of Divine Souls, Amma's Most Beloved Children,

In this beautiful song, we have Amma's address: Amma is *Atma nivasini,* always inside in the *atma.* She is in Mt. Kailasa—*Kailasa nivasini*; Kailasa is so far away. She is *Durgati nashini*—through innumerable billions of births, even if Her child has committed billions and billions of mistakes or sins, if he just chants *one* name of Divine Mother, Mother will destroy the entire *karma* load at once. If we just pray from the depths of our heart, Mother is so happy, She burns all the impurities and gives realization to Her children.

So Her address is *Atma nivasini*—here, in your heart. The heart is the real temple for Mother Divine. There are four pillars for this human temple. In *Sanatana Dharma* it is said:

Deho devālayaḥ jīvo Deva sanātanaḥ

All humanity, every human being, is a temple for Mother Divine. This is a beautiful temple, with four pillars—compassion, wisdom, truth and purity. The main entrance gate of this temple is selfless service and wisdom. Where there is wisdom, there only is selfless service.

In this beautiful song, we feel Amma is always in our heart in the form of *prana,* energy, life—all these are innumerable names for Mother Divine. *Prana* is vital energy.

There are innumerable junction points of subtle nerve channels in our body, so many *chakras* which bloom—the *muladhara, svadhishthana, manipura, anahata, vishuddhi, ajna,* and finally the main *chakra,* the thousand-petal lotus of the *sahasrara.* So children, pray to Mother Divine with silence, discriminating and one hundred percent faith. You have Her address:

Ātma nivāsinī namaḥ Om

"Namah" means "surrender, surrender, surrender, total surrender to Mother." Mother is the primal energy. Without Mother, there is no sun, moon, fire, air, anything in this world. Mother is the basic energy for the entire cosmos.

We have faith sometimes—if things are going positively for us, we have faith. If we have some physical problems, or anything negative happento us, we lose our faith in God. We say, "Rcmove all the pictures, idols and everything. I no longer believe in God." This is not ignorance but childishness. Mother forgives Her children for all their mistakes. That is Mother. Mother is beyond compassion. We cannot describe Mother's divine love in words. That is Mother's beauty.

So children, meditate on the lotus feet of Mother Divine with pure devotion. Wake up early in the morning, and start the day with a beautiful prayer to Mother. Gradually by praying to Mother, the rock of our heart melts and becomes softer than butter. So children, pray, pray, pray to God, pray to Mother. Always pray from the bottom of your heart. Use some *mantra,* meditate—prayer is a ladder to attain God-Realization.

The keys to Self-Realization are prayer, meditation, *mantra japa*, worship—all these activities. You can follow any belief. But we need a hundred percent purity in our life. All spiritual activities—meditation, prayer, *mantra,* chanting—beautify our entire life, and then we have immense concentration, equal vision, and inner beauty. Inner beauty is very important. When you follow the spiritual path, you gradually develop humility in your heart along with innumerable divine attributes such as nner purity, righteousness, truth, faith in God, selfless service, surrender to God, equal vision always, a balanced state of mind, faithfulness, truthfulness and honesty.

Now there is so much poverty in our life—poverty in wisdom, poverty in devotion, poverty in divine knowledge, lack of faith in the Divine, poverty in discrimination, poverty in so many things. We have knowledge about worldly things. This knowledge is not enough to attain God-Realization. There is no peace of mind at all in our life, no bliss. We are suffering from lack of love and so much emptiness inside.

Our external life is so colorful. See the flowers in the garden? Everywhere flowers are blooming. There is so much beauty. But inside, we have so much emptiness. Why this emptiness? Because of ignorance. Why this ignorance? Because of illusion. Why this illusion? Because of egoism. Why this egoism? Because of selfishness. So our selfishness leads our life to egoism. Egoism is our main enemy. Do you know who is the enemy of egoism? Humility is our ego's main enemy. So cultivate humility, cultivate dispassion and detachment in your heart, and gradually attain pure Consciousness in your life.

Children, this will not happen after only one day of meditation. We must practice regularly, and then only will we attain the highest Spirit, the *Atman,* in our life. So chant Mother's name, always chant the divine names, and be always in divine bliss.

Contentment is also a natural treasure. Without contentment, our life has no meaning at all. So have contentment—cultivate contentment. How can we cultivate contentment, children? How can we cultivate contentment in our lives?

(Amma takes answers from those gathered.) Wisdom… .*nanna?* Meditation—beautiful! *Nanna?* Compassion... .surrender.…beautiful responses! Friendship.…*nanna?* Acceptance.…silence—beautiful! Realization.…

Devotion is the main basis for contentment. Without devotion, there is no silence at all. Without devotion, we never attain contentment or peace of mind. Devotion is elixir, nectar. So devotion is the main basis. Children, cultivate devotion and have humility. When we have devotion in your heart—it leads us to path of divine knowledge. This divine knowledge leads you to contentment. Then you have peace of mind, equal vision, a balanced mind, purity, and an inner richness in your life. Now there is no richness inside. Richness is only there externally, in clothes, jewels and all those things. But inside—miserliness, hatred, jealousy, anger, so many negativities. They are weeds. Jealousy, hatred and anger are black curtains covering our entire life. There is no richness inside. So when we pray and meditate, and practice any spiritual activity in any belief, all these black curtains, these curtains of innocence and ignorance, are burned by the purity of our devotion.

The main gateway to divine wisdom is purity. Children, practice devotion, a hundred percent devotion, and purify each and every cell of your body with divine cosmic love. Cosmic love is nectar. Divine cosmic love is peace. Divine cosmic love purifies the entire universe. Divine cosmic love is righteousness. So cultivate righteousness and cosmic love.

In the *Lalita Sahasranama,* the thousand names of Mother Divine, the first name is *Sri Mata. "Mata"* means "Mother," but here She encompasses three aspects: first

Mother, second Father, and third the teacher, the *Guru.* Mother particularly encompasses the aspect of *Guru mandala rupini*. The main *gurus* are first, Brahma, then Vishnu, and *Ishwara*. This *Guru mandala* is just like the *rudraksha* beads in a *japa mala.* All these *gurus*—the sages such as Vishvamitra and Vasishtha, Brahma, Vishnu—are like beads. The main bead is Mother Divine. Do you know about the central bead that is called the *meru? "Meru"* means "the peak"—the main bead is Mother Divine.

As *Ma*, Mother, She gives so much love and compassion. She is beyond motherly love and compassion also. So motherly love and compassion are not the correct words to describe Mother Divine. They limit Her. She is beyond, beyond, beyond all these things. Mother is beyond the *Vedas*, beyond all feelings, beyond this world, beyond even meditation, and beyond peace also. Children, when you call Mother even once in this birth with pure devotion, Mother's heart melts and you attain peace, bliss and knowledge. You attain the highest peace of bliss in your life.

If you have *brahmic* awareness you enjoy Mother's play in your life. Children, always have *brahmic* awareness, attain Self-Realization and enjoy Mother's divine world play.

This world is so beautiful, and Divine Mother is so beautiful. More and more and more beautiful is our soul. Children, attain God-Realization. Have *brahmic* awareness in your life. Open your third eye. Enjoy Mother's play each and every minute of your life.

In the *Vedas*, *Sri Mata* is described like this: "From the beginning of this universe to the end of this universe, many generations of children through innumerable births, have committed billions and billions of mistakes and sins. If at least in one of their births, at least one time, only one time, without devotion also, without knowledge also, without purity also, they sing Mother's name, all their births are purified."

Children, you have no sin at all. Amma calls you "Embodiments of *dharma,* embodiments of divine souls." You are not this body, mind and limited intellect. You are beyond all these things. You are the embodiment of Divinity. You are supremely pure. Your soul is pure. The soul is the light of lights. My dear children, be always in the highest consciousness of bliss. That is your natural state. We are always in this lowest physical consciousness filled with suffering, problems, unhappiness, depression and illusion. When you attain your natural state, you are always in transcendental bliss. So attain that state! That is your natural state. Be always on that highest peak of transcendental bliss! Become pure swans, *paramahamsas.* Enjoy this bliss each and every minute of your life. That is the meaning of your life.

The main aim of human life is realization of your soul, the Self. This is *maya.* You understand more than Amma, because (laughs) this *maya* is subtle. *Maya* has two legs—the ego of "I," "me," and "my," and bondage. So go beyond the bondage of *maya* and attain pure bliss and divine cosmic Consciousness. That is your natural state. Be a pure *paramahamsa,* a divine swan. Be always on that highest peak of bliss.

So children—meditate. Regular practice without any interruption is very important for a spiritual aspirant. So meditate daily for your spiritual progress, and attain inner beauty in your life. This enriches your entire life with cosmic blooming.

My dear babies, we have committed millions and millions of mistakes with the tongue. The *Saraswati Mantra* purifies our tongue. Do not speak ill of anyone, say no more words of hatred. Do not even speak about worldly things. Speak only about Divine Mother. And be always in silence. Be in this world like an ordinary person, but mentally be like a *yogi*, be like a *paramahamsa.* Do not show your devotion under any circumstances to this world. That is not important. Amma will know what is in your heart. That is enough. So do not show your devotion to this world.

Be always a pure *yogi* inside, a pure soul. Have pure devotion, attain perfection. Perfection is always without duality. There are no two perfections at all. Only God is perfection. If there are two perfections, there is some limitation. Children, whatever you enjoy physically has a limitation. Whatever you enjoy inside in meditation, in silence, in bliss—that is boundless. So attain the highest, boundless, transcendental blis in your life. Amma wishes all of her babies to be always in that highest bliss, as real *paramahamsas,* not small ducks in small mud ponds. (Laughs)

Devī nāmam madhuram
Devī rūpam madhuram
Devī dhyānam madhuram
Sarvam Devī madhuram

The Sanskrit word, *nama,* and the English word, name, are very close. *Nama* is also the word in Hindi. *Namam* means any name, but when we sing Divine Mother's name, we enjoy the elixir inside—nectar so much sweeter than elixir. Mother's name is like nectar—beyond nectar.

Devi rupam—Mother is really formless. Mother is bliss, Mother is divisionless, Mother is independent, Mother is everywhere, Mother is omnipresent, Mother is omnipotent, Mother is omniscient. Mother is indestructible power. How can we describe Mother in form? She has descended in a small, tiny form to comfort Her children. So (laughs) that is Mother's inner beauty. *Devi rupam madhuram:* Children, any form—Rama, Krishna, Jesus, Buddha, innumerable forms—is a form of Divine Mother only. All these holy persons who descended to this world belong to one Divinity—oneness, oneness, oneness. So in this beautiful name *Devi rupam—rupam* means all the innumerable births, all the innumerable forms, are Mother's forms, and each one is so sweet, sweeter than elixir.

Sarvam Devi madhuram: We enjoy this supreme sweetness in waking, dreaming and deep sleep, in every state. Amma, You are always here in our heart temple. We enjoy Your Self all the time. This is the meaning of the song. It expresses a beautiful feeling.

Why is *Devi dhyanam madhuram,* babies? Why is meditation on Devi *madhuram?* Because Mother is absolute Truth. All of these lives, innumerable lives, are a dream. Even one minute of our meditation is Truth. That is Truth. The world is an illusion; it is only a dream, only a dream. Our name, fame, earning money, everything is a dream; it is ignorance, *maya.* When you meditate for even one fraction of a second in your life, that is Truth. It is *madhuram,* beyond nectar.

Devī pūjā madhuram
Hṛdaya nivāsam madhuram
Devī pādam madhuram
Sarvam Devī madhuram

So many children know about the life history of Bhagavan Ramakrishna Paramahamsa. In the *Gospel of Ramakrishna,* it is described how he meditated on Siva, Vishnu, Rama, all these Gods for many years. The key is with Mother. So He meditated, meditated, meditated and meditated, and one day he was crying, crying like a baby, "How can I attain God-Realization?" Mother appeared before Him and said, "The key is with me. Pray, pray to me." And when Paramahamsa Ramakrishna prayed to

Amma, and meditated on Amma, the blanket here, in the *ajna chakra,* the third eye, was removed by His *Guru,* Totapuri, and he attained pure Consciousness, the transcendental bliss in meditation.

So the key is with Mother! Children, pray to Mother. Mother is the embodiment of the *pancha bhutas.* The *pancha bhutas* are the five elements—air, fire, water, ether, and earth.

Dharatī jala aura agni pavana ākāśa
Nāśavanta yé carācara mein tū hī hai avināśa

This earth, water, fire, air and sky, after millions and billions of years, they will all disappear. But the Divinity, Mother Divine, pure Consciousness, is attributeless and *avinashi,* indestructible. So your Self, your soul, is indestructible.

Devī dhyānam madhuram

Why is meditation sweet? Because we are in Truth, Truth. We meditate on the Truth. Truth alone can stand without any support of this world. So meditate only on the Truth, babies. Meditate, and attain God-Realization.

I am so happy to see all of you here, children, in Seattle. I love you, children, I love you.

We'll chant *mantras* now. The *Saraswati Mantra*, the *Mrityunjaya Mantra*, and also one more *mantra*—the *Gayatri Mantra*. Okay? The last is a new *mantra.*

The *Gayatri Mantra* is a very powerful combination of seed letters. When we chant the *Gayatri Mantra* once in our life, we have liberation from all the immoral natures.

(Amma chants *Om.*)

Om is chanted very slowly, very softly and gently, sweetly. *O-o-o-o-m.*

No, no, no, that was not melodious. Close your lips so that the *"m"* sound merges in the *sahasrara.* So, very slowly….

(Amma chants *Om* and then the *Saraswati, Mrityunjaya*, and *Gayatri Mantras,* followed by all present.)

Let us do a silent meditation for five minutes. This meditation is for universal peace.

Hari Om Tat Sat!

Seattle *8 May 1997*

ॐ

MOTHER IS THE GURU OF BRAHMA, VISHNU AND ISHWARA

Prātaḥ smarāmi Lalitā vadanāravindam
Bimbādharam prathula mauktika śobhi nāsam
Ākarṇa dīrgha nayanam maṇi kuṇḍalāḍhyam
Manda smitam mṛgamad ojjvala phāla deśam

Om Tat puruṣāya vidmahe Mahādevāya dhīmahi
Tanno Rudraḥ pracodayāt

Om bhūr bhuvaḥ suvaḥ tat savitur vareṇyam
Bhargo devasya dhīmahi dhiyo yonaḥ pracodayāt
Āpo jyotirasomṛtam Brahma bhūr bhuvassuvarom

Om taccham yorāvṛṇī mahe
Ghātum yajnāya ghātum yajnapataye
Daivī svastir astu naḥ svastir mānuṣebhyah
Ūrdhvam jigātu bheṣajam
Śam no astu dvipade śam catuṣpade

Om śaraṇāgata dīnārta paritrāṇa parāyaṇe
Sarvasyārti hare Devī Nārāyaṇi namōstute

Embodiments of Divine Soul, Amma's Most Beloved Children,

This is a beautiful *shloka* about Mother Divine. There are some *shloka*s and *ragas* that are sung in the morning. One morning *raga* is called *bhopala raga.* In the afternoon there are some *ragas* like the *Revati,* which is a fire *raga,* with very beautiful melodies. In the evening there are other *ragas.* As we relax and listen to these *ragas,* with all the powerful seed letters in the *shlokas,* we are drenched in the nectar of Mother Divine. When you meditate or just listen to a *mantra,* or just chant Mother's name, even if you have no devotion or knowledge, you will attain the highest bliss of divine peace in your life.

In the *Lalita Sahasranama,* and in the *Pancharatna shlokas,* Divine Mother is praised as the ighest Divinity. Brahma, all the *devatas,* all the Gods and Goddesses, are in a queue, a very long line. Millions of *devatas*—the Sun God, the Moon God, the creator of all the planets, the *rishis,* all the greatest sages—are waiting in line for Divine Mother's blessings. At the same moment, Divine Mother is always in everyone's heart! Mother's love fills all these hearts. They overflow with joy, infinite joy, from praising Divine Mother with these *shlokas.* So they are always immersed in divine nectar.

Cosmic love is nectar. Divine cosmic love is very powerful energy. Divine cosmic love is *Omkara;* divine cosmic love is bliss; divine cosmic love is the only real righteousness. So children meditate on Truth and always dwell in divine cosmic Consciousness. Enjoy the taste of infinite joy in your life. Meditate and bloom all the *chakras* in your body. Open the heart *chakra!*

In *yoga shastra,* the heart *chakra* is called the *anahata maha chakra.* When each and every petal of the heart lotus opens, we attain one hundred percent purity. When we reach that *chakra,* we enjoy silence inside—we never want to speak unnecessary words, have unnecessary friendships or do any unnecessary things. Even our walk becomes very smooth and graceful, as if we were flying in air; it is really very lovely. When the heart *chakra* blooms, whenever we meditate, we experience the joy of absolute silence within. Real meditators love silence only, not disturbance. Even if thousands and thousands of people are around us, we are in our own separate world—in a world of bliss.

So children, invoke Divine Mother's grace in your life, and be always in that grace. And meditate on the Truth. Be always in the highest Consciousness. This is the truth, the only truth in our life.

In the *Bhagavad Gita,* in the *Bible* also, we are taught that doubt is not good. Doubt misleads us. We are so unhappy with our doubts. Faith leads us towards God. So have faith, discriminating faith in your heart, and meditate on the Truth. Only then can you have oneness in your life.

Righteousness alone rules this entire universe. So when we understand the value of truth, we see that it is like a gem. It is often difficult to follow truth a hundred percent in our life, but it is possible. Sometimes it is really difficult, but gradually, as we practice speaking the truth, we understand the greatness of righteousness and truth. Truth alone can stand without any worldly support. That is the power of truth. It beautifies our entire life. Truth is the beauty of beauties, the light of lights. Divine Consciousness is the only truth. So children, be always in truth.

Whatever faith or belief you have, continue on the same path, chant your own *mantra,* meditate on your own *Guru.* This morning in our *yajna,* we sang a song:

Mānasa bhajare Guru caraṇam
Devī caraṇam praṇamāmyaham

In *Sri Lalita Sahasranama,* the thousand names of Divine Mother, Mother, or Devi, is called *Guru mandala rupini.* There are innumerable *Gurus* in this world. I respect all of these *Gurus.* You also must give your respect to all, even small, cute *Gurus.* True *Gurus* are always only one. Sometimes children ask Amma: "Amma, is Ramakrishna Paramahamsa great?" or, "Is Ramana Maharshi great?" (Laughs) "Is Shirdi Baba great?" or "Is Aurobindo great?" Oh children, Truth is absolute. All these *Gurus*—Sri Ramakrishna Paramahamsa, Ramana Maharshi, Aurobindo,

Shirdi Sai Baba—they are all only one. All are one. Never measure, never measure with your mind, with your tiny mind, the highest cosmic Consciousness of these true *Gurus.* According to your need, they come in different forms.

So if you need Amma, Amma comes again and again and again. That is the part *Gurus* play. All *Gurus* are the same *Guru*, so do not measure, under any circumstances, who is great, and who is not great. All are the same—one Divinity. All true *Gurus* are only one; they are only Truth.

Mind information is not correct information. Today the little mind says,"He's my best friend." Tomorrow—"He's not good." This is the kind of information given by the mind. You try to measure the highest spiritual Consciousness of all these divine people with your mind, not even with your intellect. This is not good, this is not good, this is absolutely not good.

So children, give your respect to everyone in the universe. Go everywhere like a honeybee. Take the elixir, the nectar from all *Gurus.* Do not see the oysters—only see the pearls. If you take one drop of nectar from every *Guru,* you will have so much nectar in your life! This is best. Why are we criticizing others? That is not good. So go to all holy people, take their blessings, see your *Guru* in them, see Divinity in them. See Divinity everywhere—in the bad, also. That is true devotion. Elevate yourself to that highest peak, and meditate.

From the beginning of the universe, Brahma, Vishnu and *Ishwara* are *Gurus.* But Divine Mother is the *Guru* for *Ishwara*. Mother gave the *mantra* to *Ishwara*. And Divine Mother is the *Guru* for Vishnu, as it was Mother who gave the *mantra* to Vishnu. And Mother also gave the *mantra* to Brahma. The *rishis*—Bharadvaja, Atri, Angirasa, Sanaka Sanadana, and all the great sages—received *mantras* from either Brahma, Vishnu, or *Ishwara*. The *mantras* given were—*Om namah Sivaya* from Siva, or *Om namo Narayana* from Vishnu, who received them from Mother Divine. So *mantras* come to us from the Trinity, who received them from Mother Divine.

Mother is *Guru mandala rupini.* She is beyond everything. She is not just a *Guru*—She is the main source of energy for all these *Gurus.* Without Mother, there is no Brahma, Vishnu or *Ishwara*, nothing—this universe is not there at all! So Mother is the main source of energy; Mother is the source of love; Mother is the source of nectar—Mother is everything. Mother alone pervades this entire universe. Mother only sustains this universe.

So meditate and become a beautiful model—a spiritual model—for this world. That is Amma's expectation of you. Amma never expects any material benefit from you. But she wants her children to be in that highest *paramahamsa* state. "*Paramahamsa*" means "the great swan." The swan, in his natural consciousness, is always thinking about the beauty of the Divine—he has supreme Consciousness. So be always in supreme spiritual Consciousness. Become a spiritual model for this universe.

So babies, it is really difficult to follow truth, but it is possible. Practice truth, practice *dharma,* cultivate *dharma,* and meditate on Mother. In *Sri Lalita Sahasranama* it is said in the *phala shruti*, the section at the end which describes the benefits of reciting *Sri Lalita Sahasranama:*

> *Nāma sahasra pāṭhaśca yathā carama janmani*
> *Tathaiva viralo loke Śrī Vidyācāra vedinaḥ*

"If it is your last birth, then only will you be able to meditate on Mother Divine." When you chant Mother's name, Mother Herself comes and sits in your heart in the form of the light of divine Consciousness.

Divine Mother is nameless, and *Nirakara*, formless. She is beautiful self-illumination. *Nirbheda*—there are no differences at all, only oneness. And She is *avinashi. Avinashi* is a very, very beautiful Sanskrit word. Everything is destroyed in this universe, but Mother is *avinashi,* eternal. After some billions of years, earth, air, fire, sky, everything is destroyed. After two hundred million years, there is no sun at all. The sun goes into a black hole. Without the sun, there is no moon. Without the sun and moon, there is no Earth either. Everything depends upon sunlight—the sun sustains the entire universe. It is said in the *Vedas,* Mother's divine energy alone is energizing the entire universe, and Mother is the only source of energy for the whole cosmos.

So if this is the last birth for you, then only will you chant the name of Mother Divine with the powerful seed letters. Children, make this birth your last birth. Mother is *nirakara* and *avinashi.* Indestructible divine cosmic Consciousness is Mother Divine! All the five elements—sky, air, fire, water and earth, even the sun and moon—after some hundreds and billions of years, will all be destroyed, but divine Soul is indestructible.

Really, the world is very beautiful. Human beings are also very beautiful. More beautiful is our life, more and more and most beautiful still is our soul. So children attain God-Realization by practicing mental renunciation and attain the highest righteousness in your life. Meditate always on the Truth. Practice *dharma.* Let *dharma* rule your entire life. Meditate only on the Truth. Doubts always mislead you. This is mentioned in the *Gita,* the *Bible,* in all spiritual, religious scriptures. Do not follow doubt.

Righteousness leads you to the highest peak of purity. Be always in righteousness. Righteousness is knowledge, righteousness is wisdom, righteousness is the purity of purity itself. So children, follow only righteousness in your life, and meditate on Mother's divine lotus feet.

Whenever you start your spiritual practice—meditation or worship or prayer, anything—first you must pray to your

Guru, and then do *Ganesha Prarthana,* pray to Lord Ganesha:

Om Śuklāmbara dharam Viṣṇum
śaśi varṇam caturbhujam
Prasnna vadanam dhyāyet
sarva vighnopa śāntaye

If you know the *shloka,* chant it. But first chant:

Om Gurur Brahmā Gurur Viṣṇu
Gurur devo Maheśwraḥ
Guru sākṣāt Para Brahma
Tasmai Śrī Gurave namaḥ

At that time, imagine your *Guru's* sacred feet here, in your heart. And the second *shloka* is a prayer to Sri Ganesha.

You must pray to Lord Ganesha to destroy all obstacles. If you pray to Ganesha, your mind will be steady and you will have a hundred percent concentration in your spiritual practice. So pray to Lord Ganesha with the *"Shuklambara dharam" shloka.* If you do not know the *shloka,* just pray *Om Ganeshaya namah.* That is easy:

Om Gaṇeṣāya namaḥ Vighneṣvarāya namaḥ

Just call Lord Ganesha. He understands your language. (Laughs) He never misunderstands.

And third, pray to Mother Divine. The main key is with Her, in Her Hands. Without praying to Divine Mother, even if one does everything else correctly, there will be no awareness of Consciousness at all. This is mentioned in the *Vedas.* At the end of every canto, it is repeated that the key is with Mother alone. So always call Mother. Call Her, pray to Her. Bother Mother—"Mother, give me, give me, grant me, grant me Self-Realization"—because the key is with Mother. Mother is *Guru mandala rupini.* She is beyond

Gurus, beyond motherly love, beyond light, beyond fire. Even fire is purified by Mother. That is the beauty of Mother!

Mānasa bhajare Guru caraṇam
Devī caraṇam praṇamāmyaham

So children, the *Guru's* lotus feet are in your heart. *Pranamamyaham*—make your salutations to Mother Divine not with your hands, but mentally. Sit and offer your salutations to Mother with your astral body. Under Divine Mother's feet is the entire cosmos! We offer our salutations to Mother's lotus feet because the key is with Mother; She alone can illumine our hearts with *brahmic* awareness. So offer your salutations to Divine Mother's sacred feet.

Nirmala hṛdaya virājita caraṇam

"Nirmala" means "pure—beyond purity, beyond even one hundred percent purity." Where there is purity, there only are Mother's divine feet. So if there is complete purity in your heart—no lust, no anger, no jealousy—Mother's feet are always in the lotus of your heart.

"Virajita" means, "Mother constantly lives in your heart." Her feet are always in the beautiful white lotus of your heart.

Sakala carācara vyāpaka caraṇam

"The entire cosmos and all the planets are under Mother's feet.

Bhava sāgara uddhāraṇa caraṇam

"Bhava" means "illusion, *maya." Maya* is very subtle. In *maya* we have egoism, selfishness, greed, jealousy, hatred, and so many confusions in our life. This *bhava,* this *maya,* is greater than the seven oceans. The seven oceans are small, very small compared to *maya. Maya* is a million times more vast than the seven oceans. So we cannot cross

this *maya* without someone's help. Mother's divine feet are like a ship. So get on the ship, surrender to Mother's lotus feet— surrender, surrender, surrender, and have faith.

Without faith, prayer is lifeless. A prayer is lifeless when you just say it with the lips, not from the bottom of your heart. With faith, prayer is very powerful. So pray to Mother Divine with a heart full of faith. You will attain the Ultimate!

Where is our self? We are very insignificant before Divinity, very insignificant. So children attain the highest *dharma* in your life, and always—whether you pray five minutes, ten minute or even one minute—pray to the Divine from the bottom of your heart. That is very important. And pray with faith. Without faith our prayers, our meditations are really meaningless and powerless.

Before the Spirit, Divine Mother, our mind and intellect are powerless. So dwell always in the Spirit, the *Atman*. Meditate on the Truth only, and attain the greatest *dharma* in this birth.

We have twenty-four hours in a day. Spend twenty-three-and-a-half hours on your office work, on your life problems, but pray to Mother Divine for at least half an hour. If that is not possible for you, pray for at least ten minutes, or five minutes, or even one minute. In one minute we have sixty seconds. If one minute is also not possible for you, call *"Ma, Ma, Ma!"* while driving, That is also enough.

Without *bhakti,* without devotion, without knowledge, even with fear, if you call, "Amma!" She is so satisfied. That is Mother's beauty. Sometimes, in the *Vedas,* She is called "the mad Mother." (Laughter) "Mad Mother" does not mean that She is crazy. Mother is not crazy. (Laughter) There are no proper equivalents for Sanskrit words in English! (Laughs) She's really a very innocent Mother, so simple and so pure inside. Children always forget Mother.

If they remember Mother at all—this beautiful, innocent, simple Mother—Her heart overflows with joy, and She is so happy: "O, my son called me. He called me!" She gets so overjoyed by just one call.

So children, if you have no time, at least when you drive, call Mother for one second. *"O Sri Mata!"* That is the first name of Mother in *Sri Lalita Sahasranama—Sri Mata*. What is the meaning of *Sri Mata*? There are innumerable meanings, five hundred meanings for *Sri Mata*. One meaning describes Her as the mad Mother—mad not in the ordinary sense, but because of Her inner beauty She is so simple in Her heart that She behaves like a mad mother, with excessive love towards Her children—far beyond compassionate love. So that is the beauty of Divine Mother.

Children, without prayer, there is no purity at all in our life. So many people are in illusion in this *yuga*. The *Kali yuga* is the *yuga* of illusion. Many people think they are very clever and say: "We have everything. We have good jobs, education, degrees. We have no need for prayers and God. We don't need God. Why should we pray to God?" They never even go to see holy people, and their criticism of the holy ones is really shameful.

If a person never calls to Divine Mother in his whole live, even without devotion—his life is lower than the life of an animal—much lower. So children, even without devotion, call Mother at least once. Do not go backwards in your development. This human life is a boon. The human body is a temple—*deho Devalayah. "Deho devalayah"* means "this human body is a temple for Mother Divine." So open your heart. Let your heart lotus bloom inside into cosmic Consciousness, and offer your entire life to Mother Divine.

There are so many religions in this world. All roads lead only to one supreme Reality, to the highest ultimate of bliss. When we forget the Divine, our entire life is a series of zeros. If there is no "one" before the zeros, they have no value. If "one" is there, the zeros become ten, a hundred, a thousand, ten thousand, a hundred thousand! Likewise, if Mother is in your life, you have everything.

When Mother is angry:

Rogān aśeṣān apahamsi tuṣṭām
Ruṣṭā tu kāmān sakalān abhīṣṭān....

"Roga" means "illness." If Mother wishes, any illness—mental or physical, any chronic problem—She just removes it with a single glance. Belief in God is beyond medicines, and beyond worldly thinking also. Amma, if You wish, it will happen in one fraction of a second.

Ruṣṭā tu kāmān sakalān abhīṣṭān

"Though I have nothing in this world, if You wish it, I will have everything—job, money, wealth, name, fame, everything in the world." That is Your boon so that I have fulfillment in my life.

Ruṣṭā tu kāmān sakalān abhiṣṭān
Tvām āṣrtānām navipannarānām
Tvām āṣrtā hyāśrayatām prayānti

When anyone surrenders to Mother Divine, his life is fulfilled one hundred per cent. He never says, "no" to anything, only "yes, yes, yes!" Because of his inner fulfillment, he is able to give everything to others.

If Mother is angry with us because of our *ahamkara,* ego, She sucks away our energy and we are left with nothing in life. Our entire life is filled with darkness, without a trace of happiness. Even if we have wealth, millions of dollars, large buildings and houses, cars, and everyone's friendship, we still feel emptiness inside, because we have no contentment or energy. Mother is the main source of energy. Never forget this point, babies.

So pray to Mother for contentment and divine knowledge. Have only two goals—the first, knowledge; and the second, cosmic love. These are very important for every spiritual aspirant. So open your third eye, and attain divine knowledge. That is the first goal, and the second is cosmic love. Only cosmic love conquers this entire universe. Cosmic divine love is bliss; it is Spirit; it is transcendental; it is *Omkara;* and divine cosmic love beautifies your entire life.

So cultivate cosmic love. Pray to Mother for fulfillment in your life. She is *purna. Purna* means complete fulfillment. Without Mother's grace, nothing can happen in the world—even an ant cannot move!

"If You never give permission to Brahma, the Creator, there is no creation at all. Only if You will it can Vishnu or *Ishwara* do anything in this world. Everything is in Your hands, O Mother! You are the source of divine energy. Grant me many boons—grant me wealth, health, peace, everything. Whom else can I go to and ask in this world? I always bother my Mother only."

So bother Divine Mother. Pray, pray to Mother with pure devotion. Pray to Mother for salvation. Pray to Divine Mother for divine energy, for support. If Mother supports your life, you will have no problems. If there is no support from Divine Mother, even if the whole of mankind supports you, you will have no strength. Her power is such that one touch from Her finger is enough to make the whole world collapse! If She turned the Earth like this, (gestures with Her finger) the entire Earth would collapse under Her divine touch!

Man's power is like a very tiny atom before divine energy. Truth is divine energy, righteousness is divine energy, purity is divine energy, wisdom is divine energy. Sometimes we have no wisdom with regard to money. We want so much money. But I have a daughter in Bangalore who set a good example. She is a beautiful daughter. I love her so much. She is a daughter with wisdom. Once a poor man was suffering with kidney problems, and needed a kidney transplant. So he asked her for help, for some money. By some money, I mean a hundred dollars or so. But this girl took the entire responsibility for him, and she spent five thousand dollars for the poor man. Now the entire operation is over and he is happy. But this daughter has wisdom. She never spoke about the matter, not even to her mother or to me.

So be always in that kind of wisdom. To worship God in the form of man is great. I like worship in the human temple. If this daughter had asked her mother or father, they would have said, "No, do not spend too much money. Just give him ten dollars or so." This man had asked for contributions from everyone. But this daughter had wisdom. If you want to do anything good, do it without telling anyone. I like that kind of wisdom. Be always in wisdom. If you ask, "Should I do this?" the immediate answer will be "No, give only one dollar." On hearing this advice, we at once lose our wisdom. If anyone loses wisdom, it is not good. Wisdom is very important for spirituality.

So we need wisdom in our thoughts, in our deeds, in everything. My babies, be always in wisdom like my daughter in Bangalore. Be ready to give even your life for others. That is wisdom. Today, or tomorrow, or the day after tomorrow, we must leave this body. What meaning is there in life if we do not help others? So be always in wisdom. Cultivate courage. It is very important. In the *Rig Veda* it is said that courage leads you to *abhih. Abhih* means fearlessness. Where there is oneness, there is no fear at all. Where there is duality, there only is fear.

Have no fear about anything. Be always fearless. When you attain *dharma,* you enjoy fearlessness. If there is duality, there is fear. In oneness, everything is *Atman* only. *Atman* is infinite beauty, the beauty of beauties. When you attain bliss in meditation, you experience the oneness in the universe. That is wisdom. To attain Self-Realization is real wisdom.

So have wisdom in your words and deeds. Be not anxious, be not a slave to your feelings, or to others' feelings either. Do not be like that. When we listen to others, their feelings immediately influence us. This is not good—it is not spirituality. Be like my daughter. I like her very much. She took the entire responsibility for helping a poor, sick man, but she never said a word to Amma. This man himself came and told Amma all about it. See her beauty. She never boasted about herself. This is real worship of Divine Mother, this is true worship. I like this kind of worship, with silence and sacrifice, for anything, for anyone. This is real spirituality.

O my embodiments of the Divine, my most beloved, beloved, beloved children, be always in wisdom. Be always in truthfulness. Be honest and meditate on the Truth. Live your life with righteousness and attain the highest purity. That is your Amma's only wish. And be like a swan. Go beyond Jesus, go beyond Buddha, go beyond Amma, go beyond Divine Mother also! Be seated on the highest peak of pure Consciousness. That is my wish. Sit here; sit here, with your mind centered in the *sahasrara*. (Amma points to the crown of the head.)

Beautiful! So do not be a slave to others' feelings, listen to your own heart, and follow the feelings of your heart. If you practice *dharma* or meditation, your *sadhana* becomes your best friend. In *sadhana,* all these black curtains of illusion are destroyed, and you have purity within. From that place of purity, you receive all the instructions you need. So have intuition and listen your heart.

Mānasa bhajare Guru caraṇam
Devī caraṇam praṇamāmyaham
Nirmala hṛdaya virājita caraṇam
Sakala carācara vyāpaka caraṇam
Bhava sāgara uddhāraṇa caraṇam

Children, be compassionate like Jesus. All the great souls have tender hearts, very tender hearts. Be like Buddha in kindness—be all kindness. Be like Divine Mother *Lalitambika* with a pure and tender heart. Cultivate all these divine attributes—equal vision, inner beauty, and silence. Silence is the language of Mother Divine. Practice silence, meditate, and have true devotion. Cultivate righteousness, forgiveness and detachment.

Detachment brings real inner peace to our life. Because of attachment we have so many mental bondages—so much tension, anxiety, impurities and ego problems. The problem of ego is due to our attachment to our family, our friends, and to this world. So always cultivate mental detachment and transcendental cosmic Consciousness. It is so beautiful. Be always in transcendental cosmic Consciousness, in the highest bliss, in oneness with Divine Mother. Mother's beauty is attributeless. She is *Vedatita,* beyond the *Vedas*, beyond *dharma,* righteousness. So cultivate these divine natures, divine virtues in your life and merge with Mother Divine.

Hari Om Tat Sat!

Portland *8 May 1997*

ॐ

MOTHER'S DAY—"SRI MATA IS YOUR TRUE MOTHER"

(Amma asks if anyone wants to sing a song for Mother's day. A devotee sings an English song:)

Please hold my hand….
Touch me and hold my hand O Mother Divine
Let Your eyes console me
Mother Divine please let the darkness part
Please hold my hand O Mother Divine
In the pleasure, in the pain
I am calling out Your name
Take me home to You Mother (2x)
Please hold my hand O Mother Divine

Amma: Does anyone else want to sing, *nanna*?
(A devotee sings a *bhajan:*)

Devī Bhavānī Ammā Karuṇamayī Ammā
Dayā karo Ammā Kṛpā karo Ammā
Jaya Mā jaya Mā Jaya Devī Bhavānī Ammā
Jaya Penuśila vāsinī Ammā
Vijayeśwarī Bhavānī Ammā
Ammā Ammā Ammā

Amma: Amma has been here three months now, so she's America *nivasini*, not limited to living in Penusila, correct? (Amma laughs.) Come please, come, son.
(Devotee sings song for Mother:)

Manda hāsa vadanī manoharī
Vijayeśwarī Mātā Ambā Vijayeśwarī Mātā
Jagat Jananī śubha kariṇī Vijayeśwarī Mātā

Ambā Vijayeśwarī Mātā Īśwarī Ambā
Maheśwarī Ambā

Swamiji: *Jai Karunamayi!*

In the *Lalita Sahasranama* in the very first verse, Divine Mother has been praised as *Deva karya samudyata. Devatas* are celestial beings. This name means that Divine Mother has taken form to help and to elevate the *devatas*. But this time the Divine Mother has taken the form of Sri Karunamayi, our Amma, Vijayeswari Devi, and it seems to us that this time She has manifested for *manushyas*—not for *Deva karya*, but for *manushya karya*—to help and elevate human beings from the level at which they are.

I am sorry! Amma is saying that some sages may have come to this Earth to elevate human beings, but Amma's children are not human beings, they are sages. (Laughter)

Amma: Angels and sages.

Swamiji: I mean angels and sages! See what a compassionate heart Amma has, because She is calling us angels and saying that we are *paramahamsas*, great swans. We know that we are nowhere near that stage, but Amma always sees the purity only. Amma is always teaching us that we are really like pure swans when we come to this Earth, but we are soiling ourselves when we come in contact with this worldly life. So the teaching is very clear.

And Amma says that you are *hamsas*, you are swans, you are purity, you are pure soul—so elevate yourselves. I am calling you divine souls and angels, so live up to these names—be angels, be divine!

In this meditation retreat we have all been very fortunate to be able to meditate in Amma's presence. Amma is very close to us, so the vibrations are very strong. Whatever we ask for, Amma will bless us, because Amma is *kalpa vriksha*, the wish-fulfilling tree.

Recently an Indian came to a program at a devotee's home in San Francisco. He wanted Amma's blessings before going into a new business venture. There were four thousand people competing for a particular post, and he thought he had no chance of being chosen. But out of the four thousand people his name was called out, and he was told that he was being given the opportunity. He was really amazed and very surprised because he had never thought he would get the post. When they called out his name, he was asked to say a few words. He was speechless—he went to the dais and said, "It is by the grace of my Mother that I have got this opportunity." Then he offered *pranamas* to everyone and sat down.

He took Amma's blessings just before he went to the meeting. This shows us that if Amma wishes, She can turn the world upside down! This is just one small example.

And the other incident is about a young doctor from New Jersey. He had been trying to get a job, but he was not able to get anything in spite of his qualifications. He was a highly educated young man. He came to Amma, and when he was taking Amma's individual blessings, he was weeping a lot. He told Amma, "For the last eight years I have been trying to get a job, without any success." Amma said, "Why are you worrying about this? It is a very small matter. Don't worry at all. Everthing will be solved." After the New York program we were on the West Coast, and within two weeks he called me and said, "I don't know what has happened. It is the greatest miracle!" He told me that he had applied for a high post in a hospital for which eight thousand other doctors had also sent applications, but he was selected! He said it was a wonder!

So we can see how Amma makes possible that which is impossible. These two examples are about material benefits, but when we come to Mother we must ask for spiritual elevation—we must not be entangled in worldly affairs, or attached to worldly things. When we pray to Amma with complete surrender at Her lotus feet, and ask

Her for the experience of the bliss of supreme Consciousness, Amma will surely give it to us. So we have to ask for the right thing. Always ask Amma, but ask inside—you need not talk to Amma. Whenever you sit in meditation, pray to Amma and She will give you that elevation and bless you. I am sure of this. *Jai Karunamayi!*

(Amma sings)

Om Śuklāmbara dharam Viṣṇum
śaśi varṇam catur bhujam
Prasnna vadanam dhyāyet
sarva vighnopa śāntaye

Om Gurur Brahmā Gurur Viṣṇu
Gurur devo Maheśvaraḥ
Guru sākṣāt Para Brahma
Tasmai Śrī Gurave namaḥ

Om sarva mangala māngalye
Śive sarvārtha sādhake
Śaraṇye Trayambike Devī Nārāyaṇī namostute

Om śaraṇāgata dīnārtā paritrāṇa parāyaṇe
Sarvasyārti hare Devī Nārāyaṇī namōstute

Om Śrī Vidyām jagatām dhātrīm
Sṛṣṭī sthiti Layeśvarīm
Namāmi Lalitām nityām
Mahā Tripura Sundarīm

Om Hrīmkāra āsana garbhitānala śikhām
Sauḥ Klīm kalā bibhratīm
Sauvarṇāmbara dhāriṇīm vara sudhām
Dhautām trinetrojjvalām

Vande pustaka pāśānkuṣa dharām
Sragbhūṣitām ujjvalām
Tvām Gaurīm Tripurām Parātpara kalām
Śrī Cakra sancāriṇīm

Amma's Discourse:
Embodiment of Divine Souls, Amma's Most Beloved Children,

Today is Mother's Day, a very auspicious day on which you remember your mother. You are in front of your real Mother. Today we will chant the first *shlokas* in the *Lalita Sahasranama.* Many prayers are chanted in India before beginning *Sri Lalita Sahasranama.* It takes two hours to sing these prayers. But Mother does not need many prayers. If we just call *"Lalitambika!"* with deep love, Mother comes. That is the beauty of *Lalita Devi*, Her tender heart and tender pure love. Everything is tender. Tenderness is *Lalitambika.*

So, my children, let us start *Sri Lalita Sahasranama* today. We will chant five or six *shlokas* and learn them.

Śrī Mātā Śrī Mahārajnī Śrīmat Simhāsaneśwarī
Cidagni kunḍa sambhūtā Deva kārya samudyatā

(Amma chants the names one at a time, and the devotees repeat them after Her. This continues for several minutes.)

Swamiji: The *Lalita Sahasranama* starts with *Sri Mata.* Only Amma can explain this name, because many a time, I have heard Amma explaining this single name *Sri Mata* for days together! And to tell you briefly, I can only say that *Sri Mata* means Amma. Just imagine Amma—that is all I can say about *Sri Mata.* Amma is beyond everything, because in Amma you find everything. *Lalita Sahasranama: "Sahasra"* means "a thousand," and *"nama"* means "names"—a thousand names of the Divine Mother.

Actually there are many, many *sahasranamas* for all the Gods and Goddesses—aspects of Devi such as Lakshmi, Saraswati and Gayatri; and for Gods like Lord Siva, Lord Ganesha, Lord *Subramanya*, and Lord Vishnu. There is a *sahasranama* of a thousand names for each and every God! The main difference between all these *sahasranamas* and the divine *Sahasranama* of *Lalita Devi* is that in all other *sahasranamas,* the same name may be repeated, but in *Sri Lalita Sahasranama*, there is no such repetition.

Another important difference is that other *sahasranamas* have been composed by great sages, great *rishis*, but this *Lalita Sahasranama* was not written or composed. It was chanted spontaneously by the eight *Vag devatas,* divine energies that emerged from the Divine Mother's body. So, in one word, no ordinary person can praise Divine Mother because She is beyond imagination. No one can explain Her divine beauty that is beyond words.

Even the great Adi Shankaracharya, who has written commentaries on many other holy texts, did not write one for *Sri Lalita Sahasranama* because of the greatness of this beautiful work. Amma is saying that Shankaracharya was a highly intellectual person. Actually, he was beyond intellect, as he was an incarnation of Lord Siva Himself. That is why, at the tender age of seven, he became well-versed in all the *Vedas* and *shastras.* Just imagine how great he was, and what a brain he had.

(Amma speaks in Telugu)

Swamiji: Many of the *shlokas* and *stotras* in praise of Divinity that we chanted just now were composed by him.

Amma: Not one or two hundred *shlokas,* but thousands! Shankaracharya composed thousands and thousands of *shlokas* praising all the Gods and Goddesses. His compositions are full of rhythm, beauty and good rhyme. He is the author of the *Viveka Chudamani, Vishnu*

Sahasranama, Bhaja Govindam, and the *Saundarya Lahari.* He wrote countless commentaries on the *Vedas, Upanishads,* the *Bhagavad Gita* and the *Brahma Sutras.*

Swamiji: Amma is saying that there will never be another Shankaracharya. Whatever he spoke was *Veda.* He lived on this Earth only for thirty-two years, that is all. And in these thirty-two years, he composed, he wrote and he traveled throughout India on foot. When he came to this Earth, his life span was destined to be only seventeen years, but the Gods, seeing his knowledge and intellectual power, asked him to extend his life. No one knows what happened to him, whether he gave up the body or whether he entered into *samadhi.* Many say that he never left the body or the Earth. He went to the Himalayas and merged with Lord Siva.

Amma: Adi Shankaracharya's inner beauty and knowledge cannot be expressed in words. Shankaracharya is a priceless gem of India.

Swamiji: Without Adi Shankaracharya there is no philosophy at all for India.

Amma: No philosophy at all.

Swamiji: No philosophy, you can say very definitely.

Amma: In America, for the last twenty years they have been teaching the *advaita* philosophy, Shankaracharya's *Veda* philosophy, in several universities. I receive so many letters from university students, from Boston and from other universities. They say, "Oh! Shankara is always with us. When we learn the Shankara philosophy, we are full of hope because he teaches that we are soul—we are eternal souls. We never die, we are always in bliss." The Shankara philosophy gives people so much hope, it is very beautiful.

Swamiji: So this Adi Shankaracharya who was very well-versed in knowledge, who was *Saraswati putra,* the son of Saraswati Devi, and was able to interpret each and every *shastra,* did not touch *Sri Lalita Sahasranama.* This is because the *Lalita Sahasranama* is very delicate, very tender, and he was a highly intellectual person. He thought that if he tried to explain this sacred *stotra,* its tender beauty, its softness and delicate love might be lost due to his intellectual approach. That is why he never touched it.

There are no good commentaries on *Sri Lalita Sahasranama* other than the one by Bhaskaracharya. But many a time when Amma speaks on this beautiful subject—I have been listening to Her talks for the last eighteen or nineteen years—it is very new to me! Every time Amma explains the greatness of these beautiful names, it is different.

Once Amma said that She would explain all the meanings of the names in the *Lalita Sahasranama* within eleven days. The first day Amma spoke about the introduction—how this *Lalita Sahasranama* was composed, and the benefits of chanting it. And later that day, Amma started explaining the first name, *Sri Mata.* Each day Amma gave a two-hour discourse. For seven days She continued to explain the first name, *Sri Mata!* So you can imagine how great this one name, *Sri Mata,* is.

Amma: To sing always the *Sri Mata. Jai Mata, Sri Mata* song—that is enough. *Sri Mata* will give you a beautiful connection with Herself.

Swamiji: When Amma asks me to talk about *Sri Mata*, I feel I am not capable. Even when I translate for Amma, I feel I cannot convey the real meaning of Her words. The words I use, the tone of my voice, cannot convey the true feeling. The inner feeling is very important, and a person's words and tone can change it.

The second name is *Sri Maharajni*. I would like to tell you what Amma said about this name. *Sri Mata* is a very easy name. It is easy for even Western people to pronounce it. As I just told you, in a word, *Sri Mata* is our Mother—our Amma, our Karunamayi Amma. *Sri Maharajni* means a queen, seated on a royal throne, very far from us. People have been saying that when they sit like this near Amma, as at this retreat, they feel very close to Her. But once we go to large halls for our public programs, Amma will be on the dais and we will be sitting in chairs, far away from Her. There may be a thousand people present, and we will not be able to talk and laugh with Mother as we are doing now.

Sri Maharajni means Divine Mother is the universal Empress, who is sitting on the throne of the universe. We can't approach Her in that form. So always pray to Her as Her own child, for She is your true Mother, *Sri Mata*.

Amma gives an example: You may have children of your own, and you may be working in an office in a very high position. At home you play with your children very affectionately, but when you are in the office, and the children come there, you cannot act in the same way. There is this kind of difference between *Sri Mata* and *Sri Maharajni*. When the father is busy at a meeting, the child is not allowed to go there, or to play with him as he does at home—there is a lot of distance. That is why Amma has said many times, approach Mother as *Sri Mata* only, not as *Sri Maharajni*.

Amma is *Maharajni* in the second *mantra,* not in the first *mantra*. Lord Siva meditates on only one *mantra*. He says,"I do not know all the nine hundred and ninety-nine *mantras*. I know only one *mantra*, *Sri Mata*." This is mentioned in *Sri Lalita Sahasranama* in the *purva pithika,* the prelude. Lord Siva Himself says, "I do not know all the meanings of the names in the *Lalita Sahasranama*. I experience only one *mantra*, *Sri Mata*. That is enough for me."

Srimat simhasaneshwari means She is seated on the throne of the universe. The next name is *Chidagni kunda sambhuta*. When the Divine Mother descends on Earth, She can take any form She likes. "*Sambhuta*" means "manifested from," and the *chid agni kunda* is the *homa* fire, the fire of consciousness. That is, Divine Mother manifested from the fire pit of a *homa*. The word *chid agni* also indicates the spiritual energy *kundalini*. As *kundalini* She awakens, rises and ascends to the *sahasrara*. She was awakened from the *homa* fire, as the *kundalini,* for *Deva karya,* to bless and grant boons to the *devatas,* celestial beings. And now we feel that this time it is not for *devatas,* it is for *manushyas,* human beings. This time the Mother has descended for us.

In order to realize, in order to experience the love of Divine Mother, this *mantra* also says that you yourself have to become a *devata*. You must not be at the human level—you must become a God. Then only can you understand the greatness of Divine Mother! That is the inner meaning of this *mantra*.

Amma gives a beautiful example: If we ourselves have education and knowledge, then only can we understand the knowledge and education of another. Only two doctors can understand each other's medical talk. Ordinary people cannot understand it, because the very language is different. Similarly, unless you elevate yourself to godly consciousness and become a *devata,* you cannot understand Divine Mother. So that is the qualification we need.

Amma: Yes, the qualification means inner purity. How can we attain inner purity? Simply by chanting the name of Mother Divine mentally, we immediately attain purity in our life. We attain purity at once because Her name purifies everything. The sacred and powerful seed letters in *Sri Lalita Sahasranama* purify billions of our past lives. Mother is called *Papa agni shamani*, one who destroys the fire of sins. All the countless sins which we have committed have to be burnt. The Divine Mother's grace is the *agni*, the fire, which can burn them all—not only the sins of this birth, but of innumerable past births.

We are suffering because of the heavy load of all the *karmas* of our past births, and this load has to be reduced. The Divine Mother alone can reduce the heavy *karma* load which we have been carrying, and which makes our heart heavy.

These are not the words or feelings of any sage. This is said in the *Vedas*—this is the feeling of the *Vedas,* this is the essence of the *Vedas,* this is the truth of the *Vedas*. This is no one's personal feeling. Only Divine Mother can destroy all our sins when we chant Her name only one time—one time—from the bottom of our heart with tears. When you call Mother, Mother comes immediately and sits in your heart, and She opens your heart. She removes all the obstacles, all the *karma* load, and all the negativity, and elevates Her babies to the highest purity.

One who has purity in his life attains God-Realization. It is very easy to chant all the *mantras,* but meditation on the *chakras* is very difficult. By chanting Mother's divine name just once, all the *karma* load inside is burnt and we have so much contentment and peace and infinite joy, and we attain realization in this birth.

Nāma sahasra pāṭhaśca yathā carama janmani
Tathaiva viralo loke Śrī Vidyācāra vedinaḥ

There are so many delicate feelings expressed in Sanskrit words, but we cannot express them in English, because English has no equivalents for these words.

So children, just have a little love for Mother, that is enough. That is enough for your life. Do not think about your *karma* load. Pray to Mother. Immediately you will feel so much relief inside, so much relaxation. You will feel light as a feather, like a bird released from its cage! This is a cage—this body is a cage, always at a low level. And the mind is an even lower cage, always full of negative thinking, full of jealousy and other undesirable qualities, which cause bondage. The mind is a very bad cage. Mother will open these cages and give liberation to our soul, and we will be like a free bird, always singing beautiful songs joyously, like the nightingale, and eating fruits of our own choice.

We will always be in peace without any bondages. This is what happens when you chant Mother Divine's name with pure love, just a tiny atom of love in your heart. That is enough for Mother.

Udyad bhanu sahasrabha: Do you have pomegranates here? Have you seen pomegranate flowers? They are a radiant scarlet red. The pomegranate flower is a very special flower with an indescribable color which is neither red nor scarlet. It is the color of the rays of the rising sun.

Most of you are always inside your rooms here at sunrise. In India they do the *surya namaskara,* the salutations to the Sun God, early in the morning. When the sun rises, they stand facing the sun and do a series of *yogic* exercises known as the *surya namaskara,* and offer water, *arghya,* to the sun. This is very good for the health, for energy in the body, for the red blood corpuscles, for the eyes, and for the entire nervous system. It is very good to be in the sunshine, to take a sunbath, early in the morning. We can get energy directly from the sun. The early morning rays of the sun are very good for the health. So we should see the sun for a few minutes at least early in the morning when the sun rises, but not after eight-thirty. Before eight-thirty is the right time.

In the name *Udyad bhanu sahasrabha,* Divine Mother is praised like this: The morning sunrise is very beautiful with a glowing orange hue, a luminous mixture of red and gold. From where did the sun get this color? From the Divine Mother's feet, which radiate the same shining orange, red and golden light. The effulgence emanates from Divine Mother's feet and the sun gets its brilliant orange glow from them. It is not the natural color of the sun; it is from the self-luminous radiance of Divine Mother's feet.

The Divine Mother is with and without form. For our welfare She has descended to this Earth, and to please us She has taken the form of the Mother, the Divine Mother. But She is the source of all energy; She is an expansion of effulgent light, the divine light which has no form at all. And small sparks from that light became all the planets, including the sun, when this cosmos was created. So the whole solar system was born from that source of energy, and that is why the sun has the beautiful color of Divine Mother's feet. Amma is explaining this to you in a scientific way.

(Amma chants the next shlokas from *Sri Lalita Sahasranama* and the devotees repeat them after Her.)

Udyad bhānu sahasrābhā Catur bāhu samanvitā
Rāga svarūpa pāśādhyā Krodhākārānkuśojjvalā

Amma: Beautiful! Very nice.

Swamiji: It is a great boon to learn the *Lalita Sahasranama.* Amma mentions Sir John Woodroffe, who was a great *shakta,* that is, a devotee of Divine Mother. Some of you may have heard of him. He has written many books about *Shakti,* about the *Sri Chakra* and *Sri Vidya Upasana,* the worship of Devi. He was the first person to explain to the western world who Divine Mother is.

When Sir John Woodroffe came to India and wanted to learn *Sri Vidya*, he went to many *gurus* and Sanskrit scholars to learn the subject. He studied for forty long years. When he went to a *pundit*—a *pundit* is only a scholar, not a *guru*—in order to learn the *Lalita Sahasranama,* the *pundit* was reluctant to teach him. He told John Woodroffe that while you are in worldly life, wearing ordinary clothes, I cannot teach you the *Lalita Sahasranama*. You have to give up everything, wear a *dhoti,* and put on *vibhuti*, then only I can teach you this sacred *stotra.* John Woodroffe was so keen to learn this *shastra* of Devi that he gave up his job and all his possessions, wore a *dhoti* in the Indian style, applied *vibhuti,* and came to the Sanskrit scholar like a *brahmin pundit.* And then sitting near him he learned this sacred *shastra,* the *Lalita Sahasranama*.

But Amma says that you are all wearing ordinary dresses, yet you are learning the *Lalita Sahasranama.* So you can see for yourselves the difference between a *guru* and a *pundit. Pundits* still say that you must renounce everything and join an *ashram* before learning the *Lalita Sahasranama.* No one will teach the *Lalita Sahasranama* or explain its meaning. When Amma was speaking about the *Lalita Sahasranama* in India, many of the *pundits*, who are at a different level, came and asked Amma why She was giving this greatest of treasures to ordinary people.

Amma: Is it possible for you to renounce everything like John Woodroffe? No!

Swamiji: But Amma is Amma! And She is the Mother. And that is why, whatever the secret may be….

Amma: *Nanna*, *Lalita Devi* is your Mother, and today is Mother's Day. It is Divine Mother's wish that you chant Her names. This is Her wish, nothing else. This is Her only wish, my babies. *Sri Lalita Sahasranama* is very sacred, so the learned *brahmins* and *vedic pundits* do not allow ordinary people to learn it. They do not use microphones when they chant. (Laughter) They sing the *Lalita Sahasranama* in their natural voice because they have loud voices. Do you know V? Have you heard her voice? She can very easily sing for several hours in a loud voice without getting tired. She has so much practice, she can sing the whole book from memory. She can sing from morning to evening without any rest. She never even drinks any water.

Devotee: Who?

Amma: One of my daughters, Dr. V.

Swamiji: She sings in the Bangalore Ashram in India. She has such a wonderful memory, we say she is an encyclopedia of *stotras!*

Amma: Yes.

Swamiji: Whenever Amma asks her to sing a *stotra,* she sings it immediately—like a computer, without even looking at a book.

Amma: She remembers so many *Devi stotras*, *Sharada Devi stotras*, *Saraswati stotras,* so many *stotras* and *namavalis.* She never refers to books, everything is recorded in her brain! Imagine the concentration.

(Amma once again chants the first lines of the *Lalita Sahasranama*, the devotees repeating them after Her.)

Swamiji: Whenever you chant anything, the *Vedas*, *Sri Lalita Sahasranama,* or any *shlokas* or *stotras,* it must be from the depth of your heart, and it must be very strong and forceful. There is energy in words, so this energy must be felt and heard in your chant.

Amma: Not only *bhava—bhava* is devotional feeling, energy is different. *Shraddha?* No, no, no, no, no. *Shraddha* is faith. The sound must come from the bottom of your heart with a hundred percent energy. Not soft sound, the sound must be strong, strong and full of energy.

(Amma repeats the first two *shlokas* of *Sri Lalita Sahasranama,* followed by the devotees.)

Mano rūpekṣu kodaṇḍā Panca tanmātra sāyakā

(After several repetitions...)

Amma: Beautiful, *nanna*, beautiful!

If you learn even one line, you must learn to chant it in the correct way, with energy. We need to go a little faster, with a higher pitch.

(The chanting continues as before, a little faster now.)

Amma: *Sri Lalita Sahasranama* is *Veda,* so it must be chanted in the *vedic* style, energetically.
(Amma chants all the lines again, followed by the devotees.)
Is it hard? Okay?

Swamiji: In the third *shloka*, the *mantra* that we just sang, *Manorupekshu kodanda*, is one word, *Pancha tanmatra sayaka* is also one word.

Amma: *Nanna*, the sound of the names in the *Lalita Sahasranama* erases all thoughts. Just like a tape recorder, it has the ability to erase everything. That is the power of the seed letters. It is very difficult to remove thoughts in meditation, because thoughts come all the time, but it is very easy to repeat Divine Mother's names. The chanting of this sacred *stotra*, *Sri Lalita Sahasranama,* erases all the thoughts from the mind from their very roots.

Swamiji: For your convenience, the names have been broken into parts in the English printout. But in Sanskrit there is *sandhi,* a joining up of words, and you must not break the word at all. So in Sanskrit, the following three neames have to be said as one long word each:

> *Manorūpekṣukodaṇḍa Pancatanmātrasāyaka* and
> *Nijāruṇaprabhāpūramajjadbrahmanḍmanḍalā*

And when Amma was teaching this word, everyone….

Amma: Difficult? Babies, my babies!

Swamiji: When Amma was teaching

> *Campakāśokapunnāgasaugandhikalastkacā,*

many of you were looking at Amma's face in wonder! That is also one word!

Amma: My babies, such small babies!

Swamiji: In English this word has been broken into five words:

Champaka āśoka punnāga saugandhika lasatkacā.

But it is one single word:

Campakāśokapunnāgasaugandhikalastkacā,

It is one word. So when you practice....

Amma: Is Amma bothering her babies? Babies, if you learn *Sri Lalita Sahasranama,* the entire essence of the *Vedas* is in your lap; there is no need to learn the *Vedas*. When you chant this sacred *stotra*, you have a direct connection with the cosmos. Your chant rings like a bell everywhere—in all the temples, in all holy places in the entire cosmos, in Manidwipa, where divine energy resides. It resounds everywhere.

Swamiji: These are energy *mantras*. *Sri Lalita Sahasranama* is also called the *Rahasya Sahasranama,* because when we chant it the spiritual energy, the *kundalini*, is awakened. The chanting of this *stotra* is meditation.

Amma: There are sixteen divisions in the *Lalita Sahasranama.* The first division describes the Divine Mother from Her feet to Her *kirita,* crown. This is the description of Mother physically and also spiritually. The inner, deeper meaning, the spiritual meaning is different. It describes the inner beauty of Mother Divine.
(Amma sings several lines continuously.)

Śrī Mātā Śrī Mahārājnī Śrimat simhāsaneśwarī
Cidagni kuṇḍa sambhūtā Deva kārya samudyatā
Udyad bhānu sahasrābhā Catur bāhu samanvitā
Rāga svarūpa paśāḍhyā Krodhākārānkuśojjvalā
Mano rūpekṣu kodaṇḍā Panca tanmātra sāyakā
Nijāruṇa prabhāpūra majjad brahmāṇḍa maṇḍalā

Campkāśoka punnāga saugandhika lasat kacā
Kuruvinda maṇi śreṇī kanat kotīra manḍitā
Aṣtamī candra vibhrāja dalika sthala śobhitā

One whole division is sung like this spontaneously. At the end of the first division they take a little breath. So this is *yoga*, *yoga*, *yoga*. Inside, feel the energy inside, and chant these *mantras* from that energy. One day we will complete learning *Sri Lalita Sahasranama*. It is no problem. Whenever I come to you, I will teach you how to chant the *Lalita Sahasranama*. This is a boon for you.

Hari Om Tat Sat!

West Coast Meditation Retreat, *Seattle 10 May 1997*

ॐ

KNOW DIVINE MOTHER THROUGH MEDITATION

Amma's Dearest Beloved Souls,

Unrighteousness will not endure. Live in eternal *dharma* or righteousness. Feel Mother's divine presence. Feel Divine Mother's presence everywhere. Dwell always in the Divine. Know thy essential nature.

Be not anxious. We have anxiety about so many things in the world. So whenever you have any anxiety whatsoever, immediately remember: "Be not anxious." Have a balanced state of mind. Do not worry about anything in this world, for you do not belong to this world. You belong always to eternal *dharma*. So why this anxiety about all these unnecessary things—"What is this?" "What is that?" and "What did he say?" Don't be concerned with all these questions. Be like a stranger to this world. Be like a witness in this world always. Do not be anxious under any circumstances. Know Divine Mother through deep meditation.

These are just little points. Keep them all as notes in your pocket. Whenever you have free time, or while travelling, open them and remember this meditation retreat. Remember this discourse and imagine yourself sitting in the woods under the big trees in Amma's presence with your brothers and sisters as part of a little family. We feel this is a universal family because it is so said in *Sanatana Dharma,* the eternal path of righteousness. Amma is not saying anything new.

Love, affection and harmony are much more important than devotion. Only when we cultivate these good qualities will we acquire devotion, and through our devotion we attain knowledge. When we attain divine knowledge, we understand the sweetness of divine love within. Develop this cosmic love more and more. When you really have cosmic love in your heart, you will never quarrel with any other being in the world, because you will see everyone as your own self. Quarreling and arguing keep you at the lowest level of existence.

So, be not anxious, for Amma is with you. This is an order from the highest peak of the Himalayas—a very smooth order. All these orders are extremely powerful. When we follow these orders, we are calm but very forceful. A strong and powerful energy lies behind these words. Be not anxious, because when we do not argue with anyone, when we never expect anything from anyone, we are free of anxiety. When we are without expectation there is no anxiety at all. Whatever happens, happens. What can you do about it? Nothing is in your hands. You are like a puppet in Mother's hands. So what can you do? Only surrender. Surrender, surrender, surrender to Mother Divine. Feel Divine Mother's presence everywhere, and dwell always in Mother's divine love. Know your essential nature. Be not anxious. Know Divine Mother through deep meditation.

At this retreat we have been doing a little meditation, not much deep meditation. In Bangalore, during the last Sunday program, before we left for the U.SA., people meditated for eleven hours. (To a devotee:) Tell these babies. These are silly babies! They have no seriousness at all. Tell them what it was like in Bangalore. How was their discipline? Tell them, tell them. Mum never criticizes, but tell them how serious the meditation is in Bangalore.

Devotee: People who had never meditated before could meditate in complete silence hour after hour after hour, even if there was noise in the street. Everyone in the room was very focused. Even when the hall was crowded they were focused. It was the most beautiful thing to see. Some of the people who came to the last retreat in Bangalore were afraid to meditate for long hours, but sitting in front of Amma, they said, a miracle occurred due to Amma's blessing. It became easy for them to meditate for ten hours in Amma's presence. They had never before done that, or anything like it! They came and sat and meditated and were very quiet. Many remained in complete silence—no talking, no distractions at all.

Amma: We need this. We need this here also. Okay? This is the important point: know Divine Mother through deep meditation, not surface meditation. So many children open their eyes and just observe outside things. They have no seriousness at all. Some children wander here and there. But this is your country—what can I say? Do not wander—sit in meditation.

There is a beautiful Telugu song:

Ānati niyyave Devī sannuti cheyyagā
Sannidi cheragā ānati niyyave Devī
Ni āna lenide jagāna sāguṇā
Vedāla vāṇito Virinci viśva nāṭakam

"O my Mother, bless me. O bless me so that I am able to sit in meditation. If You bless me, only then will I have deep meditation—for hours together, days together, months together, years together. If You do not bless me, I will forever wander like a mad person, opening my eyes and observing unnecessary, useless things. All Your other children are in meditation. I am mad because I do not have Your blessing, O Mother!"

If Mother wishes it, immediately you will have deep concentration. You will close your eyes and penetrate the three layers—physical, mental and intellectual—and attain the highest peace of the Eternal.

Here, you have no seriousness—this is only surface meditation. Really, I am not satisfied. You think you have done six hours of deep meditation. No! When you meditate in absolute silence without a single thought, then you will understand. You will immediately go deep within. The *mantra* medicine works inside. All sins are completely burned in an instant, and you have eternal intoxication within. This is true meditation.

Hear this one point and remember it: Know Divine Mother through deep meditation. Know Divine Mother through deep meditation. Only those who meditate seriously with motivated concentration have the ability to sit for ten or twelve hours in meditation. When we conduct meditation retreats all over India, we never invite people who are not deeply interested in meditation, because if we did, the entire atmosphere would be spoiled. We also send people away from the retreats. I sent away one son who had come from England because he spoiled the atmosphere by his negative vibrations. I just asked him to please go away. So, children, Amma plays with you. You are all here, but meditation is really a *yoga*. It is *Ishwara prasada,* the Lord's blessing. It is not a human activity, it is divine. It is beyond everything. You understand?

Meditation is extremely valuable—gems are not valuable, gold is not valuable. Even the most valuable property in this world is \simply dust compared to spirituality—sheer dust, simply nothing. Spirituality is so much more valuable. When we truly understand its value, only then do we attain the highest *dharma* through meditation.

That is why Amma mentioned here: "Be not anxious." Why experience anxiety? What is there in these worldly things? Nothing. Be not anxious. Always dwell in peace. Always meditate mentally. Even if your eyes are open, if you are travelling or in a big crowd, your thoughts must always be of Divine Mother. We need this quality of intensity and devotion to uplift our spiritual level. Then only will we be able to sit for at least one or two hours of deep meditation. Just closing the eyes is not meditation.

So in this beautiful song:

Ānati niyyave Devī sannuti cheyyagā
Sannidi cheragā ānati niyyave Devī
Ni āna lenide jagāna sāguṇā
Vedāla vāṇito Virinci viśva nāṭakam

"When Amma says something without words, without eye movement, even Brahma the creator is helpless and cannot do anything. Only if Amma blesses Brahma can anything happen. So Amma, even Saraswati and Brahma create this entire universe only by Your grace, at Your command."

Only by Mother's command are we able to sit in meditation. Intense motivation is needed, because the meaning of meditation is to go within. From the physical level to the mental, from the mental to the intellectual, and from these three cages to the eternal level—that is meditation. When we always open our eyes and look outward, watching people, how can we have deep meditation or attain our eternal goal?

Inner concentration is needed. In group meditation, if anyone finishes before the end of the session and wants to go out, or even if Amma wants to leave, if she goes, all of you are disturbed because she may touch someone's head, or her sari may touch some of you. It creates a distraction, which is very bad because in an instant, everyone's concentration is disturbed. So if one person finishes meditation and leaves the hall to go outside, immediately the current of energy in the group is cut. We are all part of one circle. What happens? The disturbance spreads from one person to another, and then to yet another, and everyone is disturbed.

This is a science. In *yoga shastra,* scriptures dealing with the science of *yoga,* it is said that in group meditation, all are of one heart, one devotion, one purity, one meditation—only oneness—and all souls rest in one eternal Soul. This is the meaning of group meditation.

Group meditation develops the quality of your meditation. When we prepare some ornaments, sometimes the quality is not good, because we do not have enough knowledge. Some people are real experts, so they prepare ornaments of high quality. In group meditation particularly, the quality of meditation can be aided by everyone's stillness and sincere motivation. If you wish to sit for eleven, twelve or even twenty hours, we will never disturb you. But you must control your mind.

Children come from far away, from Kanya Kumari, Kashmir, from *Veda Pathshalas* or *vedic* colleges, from Benares colleges, and so on. They wish to sit in meditation hours together and learn Sanskrit and *dharma* and all these things. Whenever anyone truly wants and needs these things, we never keep them a secret. If anyone in this entire universe ants to receive knowledge from Amma, if Amma knows, she never keeps it a secret. She gives freely. So learn freely. Learn all these things. Be knowledgeable children in this world.

We know the people who meditate deeply. We select them and send them letters. Amma brings them here at her own expense and gives them training, because they have so much devotion. They do not have to pay a single penny for the meditation retreats. We arrange everything for them—transport, accommodation and good food.

This universe is beautified by your presence. If all people lived in ignorance and in innocence, what kind of world would this be? A very dark world without knowledge. Knowledgeable people are the gems and lighthouses for this world. They give so much light to the universe. So children, understand that these are little points, but very powerful words. "Be not anxious." Anxiety leads to argument, and argument leads to anger. Many unfortunate things happen because of anxiety. So do not be anxious under any circumstances. Keep thy essential nature and know Mother Divine by deep, deep, and still more deep meditation.

Be knowledgeable, children. Be a light in this universe. I expect you to be only in the highest divine Consciousness. So meditate more and more. When you taste true meditation and realize its value, you will want to meditate for longer and longer periods—for ten hours, eleven hours, and one day, for twenty-four hours, then for two days continuously without any interruption! We need it. Ramana Maharshi and Ramakrishna Paramahamsa sat in meditation several days in a row. Even Amma sits steadily in meditation for days, because meditation is our natural state. This is not natural—spending all our time walking, talking and eating. These are unnatural things. Meditation is our natural state, our highest Consciousness. So children, know Mother by deep, deep meditation, one hundred percent meditation.

Experience Mother through intuition. *Dharma* is righteousness. Living in *dharma* supports your life. So strictly adhere to *dharma*. Without discipline there is no spirituality. People practice meditation and other allied disciplines very strictly in the Ramakrishna Ashrams, Satya Sai organizations, Aurobindo Ashram, and in many other spiritual communities throughout India. Without steady discipline there is no spirituality. Because of their wholehearted discipline on the path of *dharma,* devotees attain Self-Realization.

Invoke the grace of Divine Mother. Doubt always misleads you, babies. Faith leads you to the right path.

Selflessness is right, selfishness is wrong. Always live a *yogic* life mentally. Have a rich inner spiritual life. The essence of life is selflessness. Understand this very beautiful law of life. Understand all the beautiful laws of life. When we understand the inherent laws of living, our life becomes so sweet inside. Live by spiritual laws. Lead a regulated life.

Perfection is real joy. Attain spiritual perfection. These simple words carry very powerful feelings. Attain spiritual perfection. Have a definite aim. Be always free. Do not be bound mentally. Do not be bound to anything in this world. Develop mental detachment. Love everyone. Love your family members, your wife, children, neighbors, friends, everyone. Love strangers also. Give your love and service to all, but have a detached heart.

Do not kill any living being—even insects. Do not blame anyone. Do not hate anyone. Do not worry about anything because Amma is here. (Laughs) When Amma is here, why do you worry? Practice cosmic love, equal and unconditional love for all beings—that is beautiful. Divine love is the goal. Divine cosmic love is your treasure. Do not speak negative words. Do not take bribes. Do not make promises. That is also one sort of bondage.

This human life is the result of the prayers of innumerable births. Live it well. Embrace the true spiritual life. Instead, we embrace the people in this world. Embrace the real spirituality in your life.

Spiritual power is real power. See the divine grace of Mother. The true meaning of life is expansion. Have simple living and high thinking as your motto. Pray to Mother for right understanding, a wise heart, a balanced mind and *samata,* equal vision. If you have a balanced mind, your life is also in balance. If you have steadiness in life, your heart and your spiritual life are in unison. If you do not have balance of mind, there is no tranquility in life and no true spirituality either. So aim to have a balanced mind with faith, devotion, wisdom, equal vision and mental equanimity.

Always pray, "O Mother, free us from egoism, lust, greed, anger, jealousy and hatred." Then Mother will fill you with all the divine virtues. Let Mother's name be ever in your heart and on your lips. May you ever remember Mother Divine! May you ever sing Mother's glory! Destroy bad *karmas* through *Atma jnana* or Self-Realization. *Atma jnana* is possible only by meditation. Be always in divine Consciousness. Let divine Consciousness rule your life. Burn away all impurities by selfless service, and radiate the light of true knowledge. Divine love alone can cure all the ills of life.

Spirit gives eternal life. Divine love is the healing stream in your life. *Samadhi,* merging in God-Consciousness, is the key to open the gates of eternal bliss. *Samadhi* is the fourth and last stage of meditation. If we never sit in meditation, how can we attain *samadhi?* Without *samadhi* we can never expect eternal bliss. We need serious motivation and an intense desire for meditation, for only through deep meditation can you understand the spirit inside, taste bliss and attain *samadhi.* The experience of *samadhi* is the main key to open the gateway to eternal bliss.

If you have humility in your heart you will attain immortality and eternal peace. You are not this body; you are the soul. Your soul is the light of lights. The key to spiritual realization is meditation. Amma gives great value to meditation. We have numerous notebooks of spiritual teachings—hundreds of notebooks in so many cupboards. Whenever we have a spiritual thought for the benefit of children, we write it down, and so many books emerge. Make use of them.

The people who come to Amma's public programs, are all working people. They have so many problems, so much restlessness and stress. Though children are waiting at home for them, they still come all the way to see Amma. They only take some coffee and drive long distances, tired from a hard day's work, and without any food. How can the human body bear this incessant activity, stress and strain? Because of their devotion only they come all the way to see Amma, sit in the programs to hear her message, and wait in line to have her put the dot of *vibhuti* on their forehead. Overcome with tension and tiredness, it is difficult for them to understand these spiritual points.

Only when we meditate does it become possible for us to understand the value of spirituality. When we sit silently and meditate for several hours, we gain peace of mind, and a kind of spiritual silence within. Then we can relate to spiritual teachings very easily. If I talk about these points at general meetings, many people do not understand. When people rush and hurry all the time, how can they comprehend what is being said? So Amma only says, " I love you, children. Meditate, meditate." They do not know what Amma is talking about, for they never have time to sit in meditation. But they love spirituality, particularly here in the U.S.A.

When people come to the healing sessions, they forget everything as soon as they come in front of Amma! Afterwards they say, "Oh, I never told Amma about my problems," and they want another interview with Amma. We do not have the time for this, as we are in each city for three days only. So I tell them, "Write down your problems. No one will see your letters, they will be absolutely confidential, and they will be returned to you."

When they do this, they are very relieved, for they feel that Amma knows their problems, and will take care of them. This releases them from tension, and makes their hearts lighter. Amma does not need your letters—Amma knows your problems. I ask them to write them down for their own peace of mind.

At the beginning of our public programs we meditate for five minutes for universal peace, not for ourselves. We meditate on the *Saraswati Mantra* for universal peace. And again, after our program, children meditate on the *Maha Mrityunjaya Mantra* for universal welfare. Not for our own welfare, but for everyone's welfare.

Here, at the retreat, you meditate for yourself because you want to understand Truth, you want to experience realization of your Self, and *samadhi* is the key. Without *samadhi* we can never expect peace in our life. Now you are beginning to understand how much seriousness we need in meditation. Even in Amma's presence, it does not always happen that you are able to meditate. Amma can see through the walls. From her room she sees you all, babies! From across the oceans also she is able to see you wherever you may be. That is not a problem for Mother Divine.

My children, the key for spiritual realization is meditation. The beautiful gate to Self-Realization is good practice—not ordinary practice—one hundred percent high quality practice. Serious intensity, truthfulness, honesty, devotion, inner purity, inner elevation—all these things are necessary for meditation.

The pathway to Self-Realization is thy heart. Inquire: What is life? What is your destiny? Mental purity is the entrance gate to the land of bliss, *ananda bhumi*. *Brahman* is the Absolute. *Brahman* is absolute Truth. When all worldly desires of the heart die, then the mortal becomes immortal.

Without prayer there is no purity. Without purity there is no meditation. When we have purification in our heart, automatically our eyes are closed. We go inward very naturally. Without meditation there is no illumination.

Without illumination there is no salvation. So see the connection, babies.

Whoever knows God or *Omkara* knows the world. *Omkara* means eternal bliss. He who has experienced *Omkara* understands the entire world. The world of multiplicity is reduced to one single unit when one attains wisdom. In the purified heart is reflected the light of *Omkara, Om.* When this inner light shines, the mortal becomes immortal. When that inner light shines, then only do we become immortal.

Here are some more points: Gold and silver are the wealth of ordinary people; peace is the wealth of real spiritual people. So earn this wealth. Our true wealth is always only peace, never material things.

Question: Who is greater than a soldier in a battle? (Answers from participants: One who has peace of mind; one who lives in righteousness; one who is non-violent; one who is in *dharma;* he who conquers his senses and is free from desire; he who knows his Self, Truth; one who sacrifices everything.)

Amma: Beautiful responses, because you are in knowledge. You meditate on the *Saraswati Mantra.*

He who has control over his tongue is greater than a soldier in battle. We have committed millions of mistakes with our tongue—impure words, words of hatred and jealousy, thoughtless and reckless words. All sins are simply from the mouth. Whenever a person has silence—verbal and mental—his words are very pure, like pearls, gems or nectar. All his feelings are sweet because he has won the battle against egoism. Inside everyone there is a big battle going on. In that battle we are unable to conquer the mind because of our egoism. Whatever is in our mind comes through in our words. Impurity emerges through our feelings.

If our heart is pure—in peace, joy and devotion—we never speak ill of anyone, we never hurt others, and we never feel jealous. We win the battle with the mind. This is the beautiful meaning of, "He who has control over his tongue is the greatest warrior." He is greater than a soldier on the battlefield. External war is only for ten, fifteen, or twenty days. This war in the mind is being waged not only in this birth—for billions of births we have been on the battlefield trying to conquer our mind. Now, finally, in this birth we are struggling to conquer egoism through our devotion, our inner purity, our humility, our knowledge and our wisdom. When finally we succeed in vanquishing the mind, silence reigns, and sweet words emerge from the feelings in our heart.

It is not just the tongue—what the tongue speaks comes from the mind. The worst pollution is not noise pollution but feeling and mind pollution—thought pollution—which is more lethal than atomic pollution. If a person meditates and purifies his entire life, it becomes harmonious and balanced. When we meditate on Mother Divine, immediately She blesses Her children and removes *maya* from their life. The key is in Amma's hands. For *maya* is Amma only. When you conquer your mind—*maya*—immediately you have purity, devotion, truth and equal vision. All the divine attributes enter your life. Such a beautiful meaning!

Just reading books is not enough, babies. Sit in front of holy people, listen to their words, print them in your heart. We have imprinted so many things from the world—bad, good, ordinary and unnecessary things. Whatever you see is automatically printed in your brain. If you listen to good things, the positivity and spirituality remain forever in your mind. When you sit in meditation for six hours, the *karma* load of innumerable births is lessened because of meditation. Now we have so much purity and peace from our meditation that when we listen to anything it is directly recorded in our heart.

So children, watch the tongue. Chant the *Saraswati Mantra*. When we sing the *Saraswati Mantra,* Saraswati Devi purifies our voice, the *vishuddhi chakra* or throat *chakra,* and the heart *chakra.* Then we have pure words, pure and positive thoughts, and a positive mind, and these lead to good deeds. We never hurt people. We never injure the feelings of others. We have so much peace within, it is reflected in our words. So chant the *Saraswati Mantra* mentally, and meditate on the *Saraswati Mantra* for soft, loving words.

Meditate with the *Mrityunjaya Mantra* to dispel negative energies. There are so many negative forces in this world. Whenever you chant the *Maha Mrityunjaya Mantra* aloud, the power of this *mantra* prevents the negative forces from entering your life, and you have around you a beautiful, protective shield, a powerful energy field, that never attracts negative energies. So he who has control over his tongue is greater than a soldier on the battlefield. Learn this, babies. Have a hundred percent control over your tongue. If you want to speak, say only good things. If you have any anger, do not utter a single word. Be silent. Walk away from that place, and pray to Mother Divine: "Mother, give me peace. If they hurt me, give me the strength not to return the hurt. O Mother, grant me perfect wisdom."

Wisdom dawns in a pure mind. Wisdom is the only goal of a seeker. Even in a worldly sense, we have very little wisdom. Sometimes you earn some money. You do not make use of it wisely because of stinginess or some other reason. And some people have no wisdom in family relationships. They do not allow others to speak. They do not listen to others. People with these traits always try to control others. This is very bad, very bad. So have wisdom always in your life. When anyone attains wisdom he is always in bliss.

Wisdom is the only goal of the true seeker. Equal vision is wisdom. Dispassion gives wisdom. Dispassion is strength; dispassion is your real strength. So develop dispassion. Experience oneness. *Samsara* means the world, and this world is always changing. *Samsara* is always changing. *Brahman*, Divine Mother, alone is changeless. Abide in *brahmic* awareness. Search for divine knowledge. Destroy your ignorance by meditation. Amma emphasizes the value of meditation again and again. Destroy this curtain of ignorance through meditation. Renunciation is a dynamic virtue. Mental renunciation is a truly dynamic virtue. Detachment is greatness. Detachment alone can bring peace, so develop great detachment.

Let Truth alone rule your life. Without *Atman* all is void. Seek the immortal *Atman,* children. The immortal *Atman* is thy Self. When you experience *samadhi,* all is *Brahman* for you. Cities and caves, gold and mud are the same for you because you never expect anything from anyone. Righteousness is your wealth. We have so much inherent, natural wealth—compassion, detachment, forgiveness, righteousness, truth, contentment. These are the real treasures. Because of the dust of worldliness, we lose all of our treasures. Through your meditation, Amma will return these real treasures to you, which are your natural birthright. Do not be concerned about that, for righteousness is your essential treasure and your real strength.

Mere theoretical knowledge of medicine does not make you a doctor. Likewise, intellectual knowledge of the Self does not make you a realized soul. When we attain *samadhi* in meditation, then only do we understand the Spirit in our life and our oneness with God. We gain a beautiful connection always with Mother Divine. From this moment onwards it is always smooth going. You are permanently in peace. There is fragrance inside. You are the light of lights in this world because you understand the Truth through meditation. So *dharma*, spirituality, is your treasure. Righteousness is your treasure. Your strength is righteousness only, not physical strength, nor money nor power. Real power always comes from our faith in God.

The temple of righteousness is supported by four pillars: compassion, cosmic love, hundred percent purity and spiritual wisdom. These four divine attributes support human life and make the heart a beautiful temple for your Divine Mother. The door of the temple is selflessness. "*Nishkama*" means "selfless, without desire." In this state, we never expect anything—even from God. Such inner beauty! We're so peaceful in this life, without any bondage—like a dove flying free in the sky, we are mentally free. Whatever problems arise, if anyone hurts us, we know the hurt is to the body only, not to the soul. We live our life in this feeling.

An ordinary man is a slave to his thoughts. He immediately wants to implement whatever thought comes into his mind, so he orders others to carry out his wishes. No doubt he will become a dominating force for others. But a sage, a meditator, is master of his thoughts. All thoughts are under his control. A wise man does not impose his thoughts on others.

So be like a sage, children. Do not become a dominating force. There are already so many forces in the world. You are good children, spiritual children. The thoughts that come into your minds often arise because of others, they are not your own. Other people bother us with their thoughts: "Do this, do that, go there." Sometimes we try to impose our will on others. This upsets everyone. Why do we allow others to influence us, and in turn try to influence them?

While an ordinary person is a slave to his thoughts, a spiritual sage, a meditator, a *yogi* never expects anything from the world. He blesses and enjoys whatever comes his way. He does not care whether he gets food or not. He never expects anything. Hate and praise are the same to him. He is always in spiritual consciousness, established in wisdom, with no expectation, bondage or mental attachment. He ever abides in pure Consciousness, the land of bliss.

Thoughts travel through three levels: From *tamas* to *rajas,* from *rajas* to *sattva,* and from *sattva* to *vishuddha sattva.* Now we are in *vishuddha sattva,* without thoughts. We are in silence, with no thoughts or words.

Normally, we are imprisoned in the three cages of thought levels. But in complete silence, we are in *vishuddha sattva.* We are no longer the slaves of our thoughts. Now do you understand the value of silence? That is why Amma asks you again and again to be in silence during meditation retreats. Do not talk to Amma also. Once you taste the sweetness of silence, you will practice it in the world, too.

When you are in a big gathering, sit in a corner in silence. Do not say anything; it is not necessary. Be in silence; it is so sweet. Meditate mentally on the *Saraswati Mantra, Mrityunjaya Mantra, Om Mantra, Rama Mantra,* or any other *mantra.* Because of the vibrations of your *mantra* meditation, the impurities and problems of others will be removed. This is mentioned in the *Vedas.* While travelling by bus, train or on a plane, if a person meditates on *Omkara* and an accident occurs, the meditator can save all the people travelling with him simply through the power of his chanting. See the wonderful power of chanting!

Chanting is great, but silence is greater than chanting, and meditation is the greatest of all.

We chant verbally because we have no concentration inside. When we have silence within, the external drops away and we are in total peace. This is the beauty of silence. Now do you understand the value of silence? Meditate more and more, even after our meditation retreats. Do not waste your vacations. Try to spend your vacations at one of Amma's retreats. Come and sit for long meditation sessions. Keep up your meditation practice at home also. Meditate daily. Never give up devotion, never give up meditation, never give up your spiritual activities.

Wake up early in the morning, say your prayers, continue in your own belief. Amma is not partial to any belief. Mother is wisdom. Follow your own belief and attain Self-Realization. This is Amma's wish.

You need not be concerned about anything. Meditate with your own *mantra*. Pray to your own *Guru*. Keep your *Guru's* feet always in the lotus of your heart. And keep Divine Mother in the *sahasrara,* for that is the Mother's abode. So open the universal lotus by meditation and be always in that self-illumination. The *Guru* shows you the path: "This is the path." This initiation is your new birth. Meditate with your *mantra* and attain God-Realization. Be always in wisdom. If you want to speak, speak only the truth with wisdom.

Do not be afraid to speak about Truth. If you feel shy or afraid to speak about Truth, it is a real shame. We talk about so many unnecessary things in this world. When you have the opportunity to talk about Truth, if you miss that, it is a real shame. So speak bravely, have courage, have more and more strength. Truth and spirituality are your true strength. Be like a soldier on the battlefield.

Do not fear anything. If you have any problems, call your Mother. Dial her personal code number: *"Sri Mata."* It is a free call, a collect call! (Much laughter) Amma responds immediately! Your problem is Amma's problem, your pain is Her pain and your pleasure and peace are Mother's pleasure and peace. So why are you concerned about problems? Keep all your difficulties in Mother's lap and be free in this world.

We are like strangers in this world—here for one day, two days, or ten days. In other words, we are here only for a short time, maybe a few years. Why bother yourself about things that are not important? Many children injure themselves so much because of their sensitivity and tender hearts. Do not hurt yourself like that. Have courage.

There are so many names, children: Soul, Spirit, Self, *Svarupa, Atman, Brahman, Om, Chaitanya, Purusha, Maha Purusha,* but all are one and the same. If you call Jesus, Jesus means *Maha Purusha.* If you call Siva, Rama, Vishnu, Buddha, that is *Purusha.* If you say in meditation: *Atman, Brahman, Sarvajna, Omkara, Chaitanya*—it means the Absolute only. All these are the same; all are one. Whether you call it bliss or Spirit or *Omkara* or Amma, everything is one. You must have this true understanding about these words. If you call any name, every name belongs to the One only. It is *Atman,* Spirit, *Chaitanya, Ananda, Brahman, Maha Purusha.* Do not focus on differences in faith, in religion, in countries—that is the lowest level. Do not bond even to Amma's love. We are discussing philosophy here. Differences are small and superficial. Spirit is beyond everything. Do not be bound by Amma's words, even to Amma's love. Go beyond everything in this world. That is what Amma expects from her babies.

The Absolute is pure existence. There are many points, and you are getting little lessons.

(Question from audience: "How many lifetimes does this take?")

Amma: No more lifetimes. You can achieve this in this birth, in one or two years only, when you meditate properly.

One hour of meditation daily is enough, because you are householders. You have so many problems, you earn money, you live in society, and you need so many things. Amma understands all these things because she has a big family, a universal family. she understands the problems in her family, babies. Your family has only two or three members. My family consists of billions and billions of children! (Laughs softly)

Amma always emphasizes mental detachment. Some people want to renounce everything immediately and become *sannyasis,* renunciates. No, no, no! Do not do that. Be with your family; be not attached to the family. Mental renunciation is much more important than physical renunciation. Amma can understand all of her babies' problems. So have devotion, pure devotion and humility. Meditate for some time whenever you have time—not for six hours out of twenty-four as at this retreat.

Start the day with prayer early in the morning. Prayer purifies our life, our heart and our words, and helps us gain control over our mind and tongue. Then we never bother people with our thoughts. We are in wisdom, and have inner beauty, purity and devotion. Gradually, as you continue your meditation practice, all the impurities and veils of ignorance are burned to ashes. Then you have wisdom and mental detachment in your life.

Do not hurry. Do not hurry at any moment. Lead a *dharmic* and pure life of righteousness. Mentally, always be in spiritual consciousness. Do not reveal your devotion through your dress, hairstyle or anything external. Why? Because if ten thousand of you children also wear the same saffron dress as Amma, how would anyone be able to recognize Amma? They would ask, "Where is Amma, where is Amma?" If she alone is in saffron, they will easily recognize her. For this reason, only holy people wear saffron.

So dress and external symbols are not important. Mental cleanliness, mental purity, inner beauty, these are important. So be like a worldly person externally, but mentally be a *yogi,* a *hamsa,* a swan. And God will know what you are. He will know you are pure inside. When you have knowledge within, Mother is reflected in the mirror of your heart. So always keep your *hridaya,* your heart, perfectly clean and pure.

(A devotee asks a question regarding bondage to spiritual teachers.)

Amma: There is no bondage. So many things bind us. Do not say, " I only love Amma. I never go to anyone else." Do not talk like that. If you want to go to other holy people, go and take their blessings. Whether he is a small *sadhu*, a big *sadhu,* or a great *sadhu*, go and receive his blessings. Do not try to measure holy people with your limited understanding.

Practice meditation daily for one year. Never give up your regular morning meditation. The amount of time you spend depends on your interest and sincerity. When you sit in meditation, do not open your eyes in between, because as soon as you do so, your mind becomes external. When you go inside, inside, inside, you have deep concentration. Begin the meditation with *Omkara* nine times. Why nine times? There are nine *chakras* in the body. The *Sri Chakra* with its nine enclosures is also in our body. All the nine *chakras* are purified and blooming whenever we chant the *Om Mantra.* It is like having a mental bath, which is more purifying than a bath in the Ganga.

Pranayama is the key to meditation. Without *pranayama* there is no meditation at all. Do *pranayama* five times. Then chant the *mantra* given by your *Guru.* Never begin meditation without offering *pranamas* to your *Guru.* Pray to your *Guru* for salvation and pray with your *mantra.* Concentrate on the heart *chakra* or *ajna chakra.*

Gayatri Mantra meditation is completely different. One has to concentrate on all the *chakras* in various ways with powerful seed letters. But in general, you should concentrate on the heart *chakra* because all good and bad thoughts are always in the heart. When we focus on the heart, our thoughts and deeds are purified, and the dust of impurities covering the heart *chakra* is dispelled. When all the *chakras* are purified, divine Consciousness very easily travels through them for there are no more blockages.

Sometimes you may feel sudden pain at a certain spot. That is due to stress. The *karma* load is sometimes here, sometimes there, sometimes in the back or in the joints. The energy gets blocked at particular places. If you practice *yogasanas,* the energy is raised from these particular junction points. Practicing the simple six *yogasanas* which Swamiji has taught you is very helpful for meditation.

There are so many *yogasanas,* more than 1,008. The *rishis* learned them all from nature: from the snake, *sarpasana;* the locust, *shalabhasana;* the lotus, *padmasana.* All the postures come from nature only. We cannot do all those *asanas*. But at least try to relax and practice six. *Shavasana,* the dead body pose, is very difficult. Do you know why? In *shavasana* you must have no thoughts at all. There can be no thoughts in a dead body. So it is very difficult to practice *shavasana.* We think *shavasana* is relaxation. No. (Laughs) It is very difficult to practice *shavasana*.

Hari Om Tat Sat!

West Coast Retreat Seattle *11 May 1997*

ॐ

LALITA DEVI IS MOST TENDER

Om śuklāmbara dharam Viṣṇum
Śaśi varṇam catur bhujam
Prasanna vadanam dhyāyet
Sarva vighnopa śāntaye

When you practice meditation, sit in *padmasana*. If this is not possible, sit in a comfortable position. In the olden days the sages sat under the big, wise trees, and chanted the *Veda*, such as *Sri Lalita Sahasranama*. That is why the *Vedas* are called *aranyaka*. *"Aranyaka"* means "of the forest, woods;" so *aranyaka* means chanting under the trees in woods. When you wish anyone, "Good Morning," or say "Hello," or greet them by the gesture of folding your hands in *namaskara*, you show your love. In the same way we show our respect to God by sitting in a good posture in *yoga*. Sitting in *padmasana* or *ardha padmasana* is a *namaskara* to God.

Om śaraṇāgata dīnārta paritrāṇa parāyaṇe
Sarvasyārti hare Devī Nārāyaṇī namostute

Om Śrī Cakra vāsinyai namaḥ
Om Śrī Lalitāmbikāyai namaḥ

Imagine the *Sri Chakra* on your head, in the *sahasrara chakra*. Imagine Mother's divine feet in the *bindu sthana,* the innermost triangle in the *Sri Chakra.*
(Amma now teaches the opening lines of *Sri Lalita Sahasranama* to the devotees at the retreat. She says each divine name, and the devotees repeat it after Her:)

Śrī Mātā Śrī Mahārājnī Śrimat simhāsaneśwarī
Cidagni kuṇḍa sambhūtā Deva kārya samudyatā
Udyad bhānu sahasrābhā Catur bāhu samanvitā
Rāga svarūpa paśāḍhyā Krodhākārānkuśojjvalā
Mano rūpekṣu kodanḍā Panca tanmātra sāyakā
Nijāruṇa prabhāpūra majjad brahmānḍa manḍalā
Campkāśoka punnāga saugandhika lasat kacā
Kuruvinda maṇi śreṇī kanat koṭīra manḍitā

When we chant Sanskrit *vedic shlokas* we need more energy in the sound.

Udyad bhanu sahasrabha: "Udyad bhanu" means the "morning sunrise." *Bhanu* is a Sanskrit word meaning the sun, millions of rays of sunlight. The tender morning sunlight is the color of Mother Divine. We cannot see Mother, only the millions of rays of tender sunshine, in a beautiful shade of orange. *Catur bahu samanvita:* Mother has four delicate arms like graceful lotus stems. In one of Her hands She hold a *pasha*, a noose; in another an *ikshu kodanda*, a sugar-cane bow and five flower arrows. Her two other hands hold the *krodhakara ankusha,* a goad to control anger, and a lotus. Look at *Lalita Devi's* picture. Mother's eyes have so much tenderness. *Lalita Devi* is not *Kali, Bhadra Kali*, but Saraswati, Lakshmi. Mother's face is so soft and tender. So *Udyad bhanu sahasrabha* means that millions and millions and millions of glowing rays of morning sunlight are emanating from Divine Mother's feet. This divine effulgence, with the radiance of the rising sun, pervades the entire universe.

Make a note of this: After *Sri Mata,* put a line. After *Sri Maharajni,* put another line. *Srimat simhasaneshwari* has two words. The next few are each one long word:

Cidagnikuṇḍasambhūtā
Devakāryasamudyatā
Udyabhānusahasrabhā
Caturbahusamanvitā
Rāgasvarūpapāśādhyā
Krodhākārāṅkuśojjvalā

The next two are names with separate words:

Mano rūpekśu kodaṇḍa
Panca tanmātra sāyakā

The following are all one word each:

Nijāruṇaprabhāpūramajjadbrahmāṇḍamaṇḍalā
Campakāśokapunnāgasaugandhikalasatkacā
Kuruvindamaṇiśreṇīkanatkoṭīramaṇḍitā

You can chant *Sri Lalita Sahasranama* only in your last birth.

Nāma sahasra pāṭhaśca yathā carama janmani
Tathaiva viralo loke Śrī Vidyācāra vedinaḥ

It is the last birth on Earth for whoever chants this *Lalita Sahasranama.* So this is really the last birth for you, children, because you chant the *Lalita Sahasranama* with pure devotion. If you meditate and chant *Sri Lalita Sahasranama* for these two days, all the *chakras* inside will start getting purified. So whenever you chant the *Lalita Sahasranama,* always imagine Mother''s divine feet on the universal lotus in the *sahasrara chakra.* Pray *"Gurur Brahma Gurur Vishnu"* before starting the *Lalita Sahasranama.*

Mother Divine once appeared before a great sage and asked, "What boon can I give you? Ask!" The sage saw

Amma's tenderness, Her divine love and Her indescribable beauty and answered,

> *Na mokṣākānkṣā bhavati vijnānicchāpi na punaḥ*
> *Śruti mukhī sukhecchā na punaḥ*
> *Vijnānicchāpi na punaḥ*

"I do not want anything, O Mother, not even divine knowledge. I do not desire happiness here or in any other *loka.* I do not ask even for divine *vedic* knowledge." So what does he expect from Amma? Perhaps he expects *Brahmatvam*, the position of Brahma, the Creator? "*Na hi Brahmatvam*, I have no wish for that position either. I do not want *Vishnutvam* or *Ishwaratvam.* I want only your divine love, Mother!"

This is so beautiful! When the sage chanted the *Lalita Sahasranama,* Mother Divine appeared before him. He had renounced everything, and thus was full of humility. The universe was like dust to him. This is the effect of chanting *Sri Lalita Sahasranama.* When you chant it, this becomes your last birth.

If you learn a few *shlokas* of *Sri Lalita Sahasranama* every day, you can complete learning it in one or two months. If you sit in meditation like this for forty or sixty days, you will have absolute silence in meditation. Chant some devotional hymns, sing some *bhajans* and meditate daily. Always stay in divine Consciousness with no thoughts of the family, the world, the office, phone calls, money, nothing. Be always in divine Consciousness.

If you do this for forty to eighty days, you will attain God-Realization. There is no doubt about it. In the beginning we have no inwardness. For one or two days we are outward only. When we listen to discourses, chant and meditate all day, we become inward from the third or fourth day onwards. But on the third day our meditation retreat is over! When you finally begin to get inwardness, the meditation retreat is over. (Amma laughs.)

This is *maya*. When you really want to sit in meditation in silence the retreat is over. We should really have a fifteen day course. After practicing spiritual activities continuously for a few days, on the fourth day you really get inward. In ten days you have a real course. If the retreat is just for two or three days, you remain restless. You want to talk on the phone with your family, or to write them letters. All these are disturbances, and even four or five day meditation retreats are not enough. However, in ten days, you enjoy real meditation. You are near beautiful waterfalls, in fresh air and silence. There is no sound at all, no communication with the world. We have such beautiful places. Maharshi Vasishtha meditated there—Vasishtha, the *Guru* of Sri Rama. Even Vishvamitra meditated there. Gautama, Bharadwaja, Kanva—all the seven great sages meditated there.

A *brahmachari* throughout out his life, Kanva was a Mother-loving devotee. He prayed to Mother, "Please become a small infant baby and sit in my lap." That was his only desire. Immediately the Divine Mother, the cosmic Mother, becomes a small infant baby and She is in his lap! The entire *brahmanda*, all the planets in the universe are shaking. The *devatas* are praying, "Leave Amma. Leave Amma!"

"No, I will never leave Amma. Amma is my baby. I want to play with Her," he replies. He plays with Mother Divine.

So whatever your wish may be, Amma fulfills it. If you wish for something, She *must* give whatever you wish. If you wish for material enjoyments, She will fulfill your desire. If you wish for Her, She will fulfill that desire too. If you wish for the status of Brahma, *Ishwara* or Siva, She will give it to you. There are countless planets in the universe. For each and every planet there is a Brahma, a Vishnu, and an *Ishwara;* there is *srishti, sthiti* and *laya*—creation, maintenance and re-absorption. So She can easily make you the Brahma of a planet.

Dīkṣaṇa sṛṣṭyāṇḍa koṭyaiḥ namaḥ

Do you know the meaning of this *mantra*? "A single ray from Amma's eye creates innumerable planets." From only one ray, millions of planets are born. You cannot imagine Mother Divine with your limited mind. You simply cannot! When you love Mother Divine, *Lalita Devi,* everything else in this world appears to be tasteless. If you eat a sweet—a soft, tasty sweet—and then someone gives you raw food, you would not eat it, because you have already eaten very tasty food. You reject every food because you have tasted truly delicious food. So you want only that food.

If you chant the *Lalita Sahasranama* regularly, you get so much tender intimacy with Mother. You do not need to know *yoga*, the *Vedas*, *pranayama, dhyana, chakra dhyana* or anything else, for Mother is always in your heart.

The *rishis* in ancient days were in meditation for many years at a time. They were surrounded by anthills and became like skeletons. All their flesh and blood dried up due to the heat of meditation, so that only their skeletons remained. They were in deep *samadhi.* In deep *samadhi,* with pure love and affection, devotees enjoy Mother's presence and say "O Mother, you are always in this temple—this body is your temple. I am an insignificant creature in front of You. I think of You O Mother Divine, as cosmic energy, the beauty of nature, pervading everything. I feel You everywhere. I feel your presence inside and outside, everywhere! So Mother, You cannot leave me. Do not leave me under any circumstances. Forgive all my mistakes, forgive me and never leave me. If you leave me, I will have no one. I am alone in this world, like a stranger. There is no one in this world for me."

So in the entire world, the entire universe, everyone may leave, but Mother never lets go of your hand.

(Amma and devotees repeat the opening lines of *Sri Lalita Sahasranama* several times.)

Beautiful! Excellent! Wonderful! There are one hundred eighty-two *shlokas* in *Sri Lalita Sahasranama*. If we have eight days of meditation, then we can finish learning the whole *Lalita Sahasranama!* You need eighty days. Do you have that much time for Amma? Yes, babies. For eighty days we would be like this: Morning meditation in the *Brahmi muhurta*. One hour of *Brahmi muhurta* meditation is equal to many years of meditation.

The rays of all the planets, including Rahu and Ketu have an influence on our body. Sunlight and moonlight affect our body. In the same way, the negative energy of the bad planets affects us, depending on our birth star. Sometimes we are tired and unhappy for no reason due to the effect of planetary rays. The *Brahmi muhurta*, between 3:30 and 4:30 a.m., is cosmic time—a very good time for meditation. The rays of the planets cannot influence the body during this period. *Brahmi* is one of the names of Saraswati Devi. *Brahmi* means divine knowledge, the pure knowledge of supreme Consciousness. So keep that *muhurta* for meditation out of the twenty-four hours of your day. When a spiritual aspirant meditates at that time, he becomes a swan, a *paramahamsa*, okay? So become swans, babies.

Amma always expects all her children to go beyond Divine Mother. Sit in *brahmic Consciousness* in *Brahmi muhurta*. Always sit there, not in the six weeds. Amma expects all of her children to touch the cosmos. That is Amma's wish, my babies: Always sit on the highest peak of spirituality without any anger or jealousy, in perfect purity.

When you meditate regularly, you have so much purity inside. All the *chakras* are immediately cleaned by meditation and the *kundalini* energy awakens and rises up from the *muladhara chakra.* In the *Lalita Sahasranama* it is said:

Mūlādhāraika nilayā Brahma granthi vibhedinī
Maṇipūrāntaruditā Viṣṇu granthi vibhedinī
Ājnā cakrāntarālasthā Rudra granthi vibhedinī
Sahasrārāmbujārūḍhā sudhāsārābhi varśiṇī
Taḍillatā samarucih śaṭcakropari samsthitā
Mahā śaktiḥ kuṇḍalinī bisatantu tanīyasī
Bhavānī Bhāvanāgamyā Bhavāraṇya kuṭhārikā
Bhadra priyā Bhadra mūrtir
Bhakta saubhāgya dāyinī
Bhakti priyā Bhakti gamyā
Bhakti vaśyā Bhayāpahā
Śāmbhavī Śāradhārādhyā Śarvāṇī Śarmadāyinī

Generally in life we have some ego problems. Whenever we meditate on Mother Divine, *Sharma dayini,* the bestower of happiness and peace, immediately crushes all our ego problems. When we pray to Mother just once, She smashes and crushes the ego into dust and sends it from our life permanently. She is *Sharmada.* There are eight evils inside. In Sanskrit they are called the *ashta madas.* Mother destroys all those eight problems in our life and gives liberation from the body, mind and intellect.

There are three beautiful entrance gates to Self-Realization: The first is the *Brahma granthi. Brahma granthi* means all nature, the five elements in the body. When we meditate, tremendous energy is produced in the body. If we sit in meditation for only five or ten minutes, we have no energy at all. When we sit in meditation for hours together, all the *chakras* inside are opened. The *kundalini* first opens the root *chakra.* With your divine eye you see the *chakra* blooming inside—the colors, the petals, everything. This gate is for creation.

Mūlādharaika nilayā Brahma granthi vibhedinī
Maṇipūrāntaruḍitā Viṣṇu granthi vibhedinī

The second gate is the *Vishnu granthi*. This is the place of the Sun God, in the *manipura chakra*. The third gate, the *Rudra granthi* is in the *ajna chakra*. When anyone meditates, these three knots, the main knots in our body, open.

Ajnā cakrāntarālasthā Rudra granthi vibhedinī
Sahasrārāmbujārūḍhā sudhāsārābhi varṣiṇī

When the *kundalini* travels through all the *chakras* and attains the highest *chakra*, the universal lotus, the *sahasrara chakra*, then you come back to your Mother's sweet home. That is your Mother's home. Your Mother is there. I am there. So you attain Mother's place, and enjoy Mother's home, the land of joy, of infinite, indescribable bliss! You can only *experience* that.

We need many hours of continuous meditation to reach the land of bliss. We need eighty days, one hundred twenty days, three to four months of absolute silence. That is why in the olden days the sages never even took food or water. This is not possible for us, for we are living in *Kali yuga*. We have to eat, drink and take rest between meditation sessions. When we meditate in silence during the *Brahmi muhurta,* that meditation is equal to several years of meditation. We take a little break, have a little coffee or something, and meditate again from five to six-thirty. Then we offer water and red flowers to the Sun God while chanting the *Gayatri Mantra*. This is followed by some chanting of *vedic shlokas* and *stotras*, such as *Sri Lalita Sahasranama*.

After breakfast, we have *yogasanas*. The *yogasanas* are very important for meditation, because if there is a blockage anywhere in the nervous system it is released by *yogasanas*. That is why *yogasanas* are very important for meditation. When energy is released from the important junction points, we attain deep concentration in meditation.

Our next session of meditation is from eight to nine-thirty, one and a half hours. After this there is a little break for coffee, water or juice. Then there is another hour and a half of meditation. We have one more meditation session at twelve o'clock, then we take *prasada*—the *salagrama* water is the *prasada* of God. One handful of *prasada* is really enough. We need not eat much. One handful of Mother's *prasada* brings so much contentment because the water we have used for the *abhisheka* of the *salagrama* is God's *prasada* blessed by God.

After lunch there is rest for one hour, followed by more meditation. So when we sit like this continuously in group meditation, for the first three or four days it is difficult to concentrate. After the fourth day we begin to have concentration. Even those whose minds are constantly wandering here and there are able to go inward and gradually they stay inside. If we continue to meditate like this for sixty, ninety or one hundred twenty days, the results are amazing! We attain God-Realization!

Discipline is very important. And we also need *yogasanas*, because we sit continuously for long periods in meditation. The *yogasanas* relax the body. Some people think that *yogasanas* strain the body. They do not know the value of *yogasanas*. *Yogasanas* give great relaxation to the body. Every *yogasana* makes the backbone stronger and straighter. When the backbone is straight we have a hundred percent concentration in meditation.

Swamiji: Take the example of a thermometer. When our temperature is high, the mercury rises in the column in the thermometer. In the same way, after many hours of meditation, heat is generated in the body, and the *kundalini* rises to the *sahasrara.* Otherwise it will stay at the *muladhara* only. It will not go upward if the heat is not enough. Also, when the backbone is bent or curved, it is difficult for the energy to travel to the *sahasrara.*

Amma: So sit straight up in meditation without any movement in the body. This body is only a cage. Leave this cage. The second cage is the mind. Leave the mind cage also, for there are three more cages in the mind—*sattva, rajas* and *tamas*. Leave the mind cage and the intellect cage also: "I learned this, I learned that," is the ego cage of the intellect. Leave that cage also. And surrender, surrender, surrender. Meditate with devotion and you will attain bliss. You will get direct messages from Mother Divine. Meditate and get a permanent connection with Divinity!

Hari Om Tat Sat!

West Coast Retreat, Seattle *12 May 1997*

ॐ

YOU ARE THE SOUL, YOU ARE PURE!

Śaraṇāgata dīnārtā paritrāṇa parāyaṇe
Sarvasyārti hare Devī Nārāyaṇi namostute

Embodiments of Divine Souls, Amma's Most Beloved Children,

Just now I sang some Sanskrit *shlokas* for universal peace. One of the *shlokas* talks about *artha vishanna:* There is so much pain, and unhappiness in life. When anything happens, if anyone chants the divine names mentally, or prays to God, immediately their stress and mental pain is removed by the power of these divine prayers. All prayers have this effect.

God is only one. Innumerable rays are there in the sun, but the sun is only one. There are so many names of Gods and Goddesses. We sing all the different names of God so beautifully, but God is always only one. God is omnipresent, omnipotent, and omniscient. God is oneness, only one, there is no duality. This is clearly stated in *Sanatana Dharma*:

Ekamevadvitīyam Brahma nānyad asti akincanaḥ

God is only one. God has descended in so many forms for the comfort of His children, giving them a choice of paths to follow. If you need God, He comes according to your wish. God always fulfills all of your wishes.

You children who are on the spiritual path understand that our life is like a long play, lasting seventy, eighty, ninety or a hundred years at most. Those who have a true, intense desire for spirituality in their hearts understand the value of this life. They pray to God with pure devotion and they want only God-Realization.

This morning, so many children came to Amma for healing. In every letter they asked only for Self-Realization. Everyone mentioned in his or her letter, "I only want to realize God. I want to be one with God. I want to become more and more pure. I want to attain divine wisdom. I want to attain God-Realization." This is really beautiful, I cannot explain in words—there is really so much beauty.

Only those who have this inner vision will understand the Reality in this world. There are so many things we know about, but we cannot understand the Reality because of our ignorance and innocence. But when God gives real wisdom in your heart, your heart will be opened by the power of your prayers, and you will see Divinity in each and every cell of the universe. So many children particularly mention this point: "I want to realize God in my life, I want to see that Divinity inside and everywhere in the universe—everywhere." That is so beautiful!

So children, Amma wants all of her children to attain purity and God-Realization in this birth. Offer your entire life to the Divine. My children, embodiments of Divinity and *dharma*, in every religion, in every faith, we have compassion, service, wisdom, purity and prayers. Every religion has the same goals. The paths are different, but the destination is the same. The ultimate goal is only one. So have wisdom in your devotion. It is very important. Wisdom is very important in spiritual life. Without wisdom, we cannot attain the beautiful Self-Realization in our life. So have wisdom.

There are four paths which you may follow, which are all the same. If you want to follow the spiritual path of *karma yoga*—selfless service—give your selfless service to this universe. Selfless service offered to all beings is the greatest *yoga* to merge with the Eternal. Your destiny is only eternal bliss. So children, give your selfless service without ego, without self, without any expectation from others, without expecting even a word of thanks. Always give—give, give, give, give whatever you have in your heart: Your love, your service, whatever you have, give it. If needed, give your life also for mankind. That is so beautiful! Sacrifice everything for God—that is selfless service. In many of the *shlokas* in *Sanatana Dharma* we learn so many things about selfless service. However, we are not able to understand the sweetness in *karma yoga*. The *Bhagavad Gita*, written several thousand years ago, summarizes the points about *karma yoga*. Expecting anything from others causes so much unhappiness inside us. If we never expect anything but just give our service to others, we feel real *samadhi*—the feeling is so sweet. So children, if you like selfless service, that is also a *yoga*, a great *yoga* like meditation.

The path of devotion is so sweet—singing *bhajans,* worshipping deities, praying, chanting, or any good activities. Devotion is nectar! But do not show the devotion outside. Keep the real devotion inside and elevate and expand yourself to the highest destiny of merging with the Absolute.

The third path is *dhyana,* the path of meditation. Meditation is complete silence—so we cannot see the depths of devotion inside. A person who appears to be worldly on the outside might have a heart pure as crystal, and great inner beauty. When the heart is like a crystal, Divinity reflects there. So when all the clouds of selfishness and ignorance are gone from our heart, we have so much wisdom and liberation from all of the limited, immoral tendencies. We enjoy the purity inside. The sweetness of silence, inner beauty, equal vision, purity, true devotion, a balanced mind, forgiveness, detachment—all of these divine attributes bloom like fragrant flowers in our heart.

So offer all these fragrant flowers to the Divine, children. And then elevate more and more in your heart. Meditate! Truth is only one. Always remember this. Truth is one. Truth is one. God is one. Love is one. Cosmic love is only one.

Children when you attain deep *samadhi* in meditation, you will experience *brahmic* awareness. You will feel that your Self is everywhere in the universe. Your Self is in an ant, in mud, in a particle of ash, in soil particles, in sand, in rivers, in oceans, in birds and animals, in grass blades, in flowers, in planets—everywhere! We often sing the song, *Sri Mata, Jai Mata*. In that song:

Pavana gagana me Srī Mātā

Pavana means "air." Air is the vital breath, vital energy. So Divine Mother is there in air. You yourself are Divine Mother! Divine Mother is there in fire in the form of energy. We use so much energy from fire. She is there in water also in the form of energy and power. We use so much energy from water. Energy is everywhere. We cannot imagine this universe without energy. So Mother Earth and all of nature—water, fire, ether, air, earth and each and every cell of this universe—are filled with the energy of Mother Divine.

When you attain *samadhi* in meditation, you feel this energy in yourself and everywhere in the universe. That is beautiful! Then you cannot bind yourself to any particular path: "This is my faith or religion," "I belong only to this land," "He is the only *Guru*, I never go other *gurus*." These are very limited feelings. Go beyond all these feelings. All faiths belong to your Self only: Your Self is wisdom; Your Self is Truth; Your Self is time: past, present and future; Your Self is *dharma*, righteousness; Your Self is *Omkara;* Your Self is the *Bible*, the *Ramayana*, the *Upanishads*, Jesus, Buddha—everything is your Self only! All faiths, all religions, all humankind, all planets, all the galaxies belong to your Self only. That is realization, Self-Realization. So in meditation you attain the highest peak. Everyone belongs to your Self only and you belong to everyone. There is no difference between the two. So you are not the little "me." Now your idea of "me" is very limited. In *samadhi* you attain so much liberation, wisdom, purity and inner beauty in your life. You have forgiveness and a soft, sweet heart. You love all of nature as your Self. So babies, attain that highest peak like a great swan, a *paramahamsa.* (Amma laughs.) A beautiful *paramahamsa. "Paramahamsa"* means "divine swan." So attain the highest peak through meditation.

Dhyana, meditation, leads to *jnana. Jnana* is the path of self-inquiry. Every path is the same, children. It leads you to the Ultimate.

Righteousness is the main base for spirituality. So sit on the base of righteousness. Righteousness only rules the entire universe. Where there is righteousness in life, we have wisdom, inner beauty, liberation from all of the limited, immoral natures, and we have so much inner purity and silence. We understand the value of our life. Life is a boon, the greatest boon.

Babies, do not waste any more time. Learn Mother's language. Mother's language is silence. Learn that language. Love Mother Nature. When you love Mother Nature you will become so wise.

Have *satsang* with wise people. You will get so much purity in your life. Go for the *darshan* of any holy person, saint or *swami*—even a small *swami* who has come to your city or town. If you know about it but you do not go there, that is a sin. This is said in *Sanatana Dharma.* We have *karma.* Because of our *karma* we are not able to go and see holy people. Go for their *darshan* and take their blessings. Even if you don't know their language, it does not matter;

just have their *darshan* and take their blessings. If you have ten blessings, you are so blessed! (Amma laughs.) If you give respect to Amma—one person—give a million times more respect to others. That is beautiful! Amma is yours. She never thinks about herself. Whether you give her respect or not, she never bothers about it. But give your respect to all saints and wise people.

If there are people leading an ordinary family life who give you good messages about good matters, and good spiritual messages, go and listen to them too. If you have spiritual friends, do not spend time with them in unnecessary talk. If your friend is a spiritual person, listen to what he says about good subjects. See only good things and listen only to good things. Do not find faults in people. That is bad, very bad.

In the *vedic* path, there are two visions—the vision of knowledge and the vision of love. If we have knowledge, we automatically have love. If we are always finding faults in others, our vision will be negative. So do not speak negatively about anyone under any circumstances. Even if they have wronged you, forgive them and love them—give them more and more love like Jesus. See how wise Jesus was. At the time of crucifixion, Jesus prayed for the welfare of the robbers. See the beauty of that. That is Divinity. So be like Jesus in compassion and forgiveness. Be like Buddha: Buddha wanted to sacrifice his life for a small lamb. So be like Buddha, okay? That is so beautiful. So much beauty! When we attain purity in our life, we never care about our physical body and physical life. So children, for innumerable births, billions and billions into billions of births we have been doing the same meaningless things—eating, walking and talking. We have done nothing new. Realize your Self at least in this birth. Divine Mother is in your heart.

There is a beautiful song:

Madhura madhura Meenākṣī
Madhurāpurī nilaye
Ambā Ambā Jagadambā (2x)
Madhura madhura Meenākṣī
Vāgvilāsinī madhura madhura Meenākṣī
Mātangī marakatāngī
Madhura madhura Meenākshī

This is a beautiful spiritual song. So many of my children sing this song to classical music in India. One day I asked one of my babies: "What does this song mean?" She answered: "The meaning of the song is that the Meenakshi Temple is in the city of Madurai. It is a beautiful city, and Mother speaks very sweetly." There are so many sweet cities. There is so much spiritual energy in India. We can hear the sound of the *Vedas* from the land. This is really true. We can hear the sound of the *Vedas* from the land. Even the rivers in India sing the beauty and glory of Divine Mother. *Om* is in the sound of the oceans—we can listen to the sound of the *Vedas* everywhere including the sound of the cosmic dance of *Nataraja*. We feel the spiritual energy in India everywhere. I am not speaking about the physical India, but about the spiritual India. It is so beautiful—we cannot express that beauty in words. India belongs to everyone in this world because of spirituality. Millions and millions of years ago, the greatest and highest values of honesty, nobility, purity, good character, sympathy, liberation, wisdom and Mother Nature were taught so beautifully in India. I cannot express all this in words.

So the literal meaning of this song is: "Think about the beautiful city of Madurai, where there is a beautiful temple, the Madhura Meenakshi Temple, in which Mother resides." "Meenakshi" means "one whose eyes are shaped like fish." That is Meenakshi. However, when we interpret this song in a spiritual light, *Madhurapuri,* or "the city of Madhurai" signifies our entire human body. *Madhura* means "sweetness, nectar."

When you chant the names of Mother Divine, your body becomes *Madhurapuri,* full of nectar. Nectar is in your body, and whatever you speak is more than nectar. Your feelings are more than nectar. Your acts are more than nectar. Your entire life is more than nectar. Mother sits in your heart lotus, and She always speaks with you as *"madhura vachani,"* "one who talks sweetly," with a soft, hissing sound like "ssss...ssss." You can always hear Mother's voice in your heart. You have a permanent connection with Divine Mother, and you feel Her presence in every moment of your life. This is the real meaning of this beautiful song.

This body does not belong to you, it belongs to Mother Divine. It is Her temple. In this temple, compassion is one pillar, truth the second pillar, wisdom the third pillar and beautiful divine cosmic love the fourth pillar. Selfless service is the main entrance gate of this temple. Imagine Mother as always present in this temple. Then you will always have silence, inner beauty and divine knowledge. There will be no ignorance at all. Then your words are not your words, they are Mother's words. And all your actions—whatever you do in this world—belong to Mother only, not to you.

If we have the ego, the limited "I, me, my," then everything is ours; all this ignorance and innocence is ours only. If you really feel Mother in meditation in the heart temple, all your actions belong only to Divine Mother. So children, this is the spiritual meaning of this song. Whenever we sing or hear this song, we feel, "Oh, it is so beautiful!" The *raga* itself is so beautiful. But the literal meaning of these songs is on a very low level, not on the highest level. When you elevate yourself spiritually, everything changes in your view, and you understand the Truth inside. You have an inner vision. We need that vision, children.

We have been chanting the *Saraswati Mantra.* There are three seed letters in the *Saraswati Mantra*: One is *Ayim*—that is for Saraswati Devi; the second one is *Srim*—for lighting, Maha Lakshmi; and the third seed letter, *Hrimkara*, denotes energy, Divine Mother. We have *svara*, the sound of *nada,* sound, inside—and lighting. Lighting means we have so much wisdom and liberation from all these limited things, and we feel divine energy inside. So much energy!

When you sit in meditation, imagine your energy moving through the *chakras.* If you just sit in meditation without any concentration, the energy is wasted in many ways. So *chakra* meditation is very important for enlightenment. When people sit and meditate on the *Gayatri Mantra* or the *Saraswati Mantra* with the help of *chakras,* they immediately have so much liberation.

Children, Saraswati means divine knowledge—not worldly knowledge. You get so much inspiration from the knowledge of Saraswati Devi—so much inner beauty and purity from Divine Mother. All that you think and say—each and every word—comes from the inspiration of Mother Divine only. You have a permanent connection with Mother in your heart. You feel as though Mother is always in your heart, and each and every cell of your body is filled with Divine Mother's love only.

Try to sit in meditation on auspicious days between 3:30 and 4:30 in the morning—particularly on your birthday and other special days. The nine planets—not counting Earth there are eight planets—do not influence our body between 3:30 and 4:30 a.m. It is during these hours only that cosmic lighting comes to the entire universe, recharging all the planets. If anyone sits in meditation at this time, it is equal to ten long years of meditation at other times. So try to sit in meditation during these hours. It is very good for concentration and for much self-illumination in your life.

So be noble. Try to speak only the truth. Speak gently. Think before you speak—think over and over again and speak truthfully, gently and sweetly. Do not use bad words in any circumstances.

We will now chant the *Saraswati Mantra*. The sacred *Saraswati Mantra* removes all pollution from our tongue. We have committed millions of mistakes with the tongue only. It is really bad. Children, be in wisdom and understand the difference between good and bad, the Real and the unreal. Be always in righteousness. Let righteousness rule your entire life. You have great support in righteousness.

Children, your Self is the support of the entire universe; your Self is Divine. You are an embodiment of the Divine. Amma always calls you "Embodiments of Divine Souls." You are not a sinner. This body committed sins—you are not the sinner. You are the soul; you are pure. You have so much nobility in your soul. Children, you are so pure. When you meditate, leave the body behind along with its limited mind and intellect, and be in your Self in meditation.

The *mantra* is a ladder to lead you to the highest peak of peace. So attain God-Realization and practice more and more devotion. Ask Mother, "Grant me a right understanding mind and devotion—at the right time, not when I am on my death-bed." In India people follow a practice. There might be a patient who is too sick to think about God. Because of his attachment to the world he has never thought about God throughout his life. At the last moment on the deathbed, his people bother him saying, "Say, Rama! Say, Rama! Say Narayana, Narayana!" He has so much pain at the last moment and he might be in an unconscious state—sometimes the mouth is not working. This body has been over-used like an old garment:

Vasānsi jirṇāni yathā vihāya

"Like an old cloth, not like a new one." (*Bhagavad Gita,* Chap.2, shl. 21) In his last moments he cannot recognize or remember the name of Rama, so what does he say? He says, "Ra... Ra..." He cannot even say the full word, "Rama."

One of my sons asked me: "Amma, is it at all useful for him to say "Rama'?" Yes, it is really useful for him even if he never spoke of God throughout his life. It *is* useful if at the time of death we say even once—Jesus, Rama, Krishna, Buddha, *Omkara*, or any name of Divine Mother. It is useful if we say any divine name—or even half a name—in our last moment. This is true even if you do it without devotion, without respect, without faith, without fear or without knowledge. Also:

Ananta koṭi godāna phalitamanta

"It has a lot of merit—equal to the merit of donating an infinite number of cows." When we give millions of cows to anyone in charity, we get so much relief. In India, if people are sick, they immediately give something in charity to orphanages or homes of senior citizens or other needy people. Sometimes they give some cows or an acre of land to some poor person. The moment they give anything in charity, they feel great relief from pain on their sick-bed.

At the last moment, when a person says *Rama nama* or *Siva nama* once, if he repeats just half a *mantra*—even without knowledge, without any devotion or without faith—it will give him great liberation from all the sins committed in innumerable births. So children, you are always chanting divine names, and always singing divine *bhajans*, and meditating—you have no sin at all! You are the embodiments of purity, the embodiments of *dharma*.

Meditate! Meditate, and attain Self-Realization, babies. If we can meditate in our last moments, it is good. But if we meditate throughout life, we enjoy the fragrance of peace in our entire life. This is so beautiful. So babies, be wise, be wise and be always in righteousness, in righteousness! Righteousness is the greatest virtue; it is a dynamic virtue! Cultivate righteousness in your life. See Divine Mother everywhere in the universe, that is Amma's wish.

Srī Mātā Jai Mātā Srī Mātā (2x)
Tana mana prāṇa me Srī Mātā (2x)

"Tana" means "body," *"mana"* means "mind," and *"prana"* means "life." All three are Sri Mata only.

Tana mana prāna me Srī Māta
Srī Mātā Jai Mātā Srī Mātā (2x)
Pavana gagana mé Srī Mātā (2x)
Nayana nayana mé Srī Mātā (2x)
Aṇuva aṇuva mé Srī Mātā (2x)
Janana maraṇa mé Srī Mātā (2x)

Here in the last line, *"janana marana"* means "in birth, and in death also, your real mother is Divine Mother." You have no death—you just leave the body after some years. But you have salvation and you merge with your eternal Mother. There is really no death. Death is salvation. Both birth and death are Mother Divine only. There is only *Sri Mata*. Beautiful!

Swamiji: *Jai Karunamayi!* Just now Amma was saying that this morning when you came for the *homa,* the fire ceremony, many of you asked this question: "If we have been following a particular *Guru,* and we have a particular belief, is it okay to go to any other *guru,* or is it wrong to follow them, or even just go to see them?" Others have asked this question in other places also. To this question Amma has answered many times that we must have wisdom; and wisdom can be acquired only in spirituality. If we do not have wisdom in spirituality also, then it is not spirituality.

Wherever you go, see your *Guru* in the other *gurus* also, because you have accepted him as your *Guru*. The *Guru* is the one who dispels the darkness of our ignorance and the *Guru* is held to be as high as Brahma, the creator, Vishnu, the preserver, and Siva, the destroyer. But the *Guru* is said to be above them also. You have been instructed by your *Guru* and put on the right path, and therefore, if you are confident in yourself, you will not ask this question at all. This is because wherever you go, you will see your *Guru* in all he holy ones. Even now Amma has said: "You may go, you may get the blessings which you seek." And what is wrong about getting ten blessings at a time? There is nothing wrong in it.

But the *Guru* is the one who will be exact in directing you according to your nature, according to your spiritual level and according to your mind. He will instruct you regarding the path and practices you should follow. Some people have the habit of going and asking other *gurus* what kind of meditation they should do. If your *Guru* has instructed you in the right way you must not ask other *gurus* the same question. It is not right. Follow the instructions of your *Guru*.

Be universal. Let me tell you about an incident regarding Ramakrishna Paramahamsa. When Swami Vivekananda asked the great master, the great *paramahamsa*: "Can I go to the Brahmo Samaja and listen to the lectures?" Ramakrishna Paramahamsa replied, "Why not? You can go and listen to them." A little later, when another disciple came and asked Ramakrishna Paramahamsa: "Can

I go to the Brahmo Samaja?" He said, "No." Another devotee who was listening to all this got confused and asked, "Why, Swami? You told Vivekananda that he could go and you told this person not to go."

Then Sri Ramakrishna laughed and answered, "Vivekananda has attained the highest knowledge and therefore, wherever he goes he sees only the One. He doesn't change. I am very sure about that. But this disciple is somewhat weak in mind. So if he goes there, he might become doubtful and start thinking, 'Which is the right path?' That is why I have told this devotee to stick to his *sadhana.* And after he finishes his *sadhana* and attains realization, wherever he goes, he will recognize the One."

That is what Amma always says—you have to see the oneness. The oneness is very important, and this can be attained by the great spiritual practice of meditation. And Amma says many times, meditation is nothing but purification of mind.

One of you just asked Amma whether She is the incarnation of Saraswati Devi. Actually we must not ask Amma such questions. Amma has never said that She is the incarnation of Saraswati or any other deity. But we, the disciples, have said here that Amma is the incarnation of Saraswati Devi. And many people say that Amma is the incarnation of *Lalita Parameshwari.* Some say She is the incarnation of Lakshmi, and some love Her just as their compassionate mother. It is due to our own views and feelings that we give these names to holy people, divine souls. Amma has never said "I am God."

Whenever Amma speaks She says "I have come to you only as your near and dear mother." However, we think and feel according to our understanding that She has all these qualities and therefore say She is so and so. But Amma says frankly that She is above name and form also. The great souls descend to this Earth to make us understand the great truths in spite of our limited understanding. They elevate us from this lowest level of consciousness and take us to the highest levels. During the three days of our meditation retreat it was wonderful to meditate with Mother and have the direct experience of Her energy.

Today we had the *Maha Mrityunjaya homa,* the *Maha Saraswati homa,* and the *Maha Gayatri homa.* They were very powerful. The *homas* were performed in nature directly under the sky. It was really wonderful to do it here, in this far-off country, the United States of America. I felt, as if I were back in India, it was wonderful. We receive the greatest energy in taking the blessings, and being in the presence of the fire ceremony, the *homa*. A lot of you felt the vibrations. Many of you wanted to spend more and more time in meditation. Amma was saying that She felt very happy when people gave Her letters during the healing session saying that they wanted only salvation. People did not come for physical healing, they wanted mental healing. They said that they wanted realization of the Self, and they wanted to be elevated spiritually. That was their only desire and only aim. It is to fulfill this need that Amma has come to us.

Jai Karunamayi!

Seattle *13 May 1997*

ॐ

SRI MATA IS ALWAYS IN FRONT OF YOU

Swamiji: *Jai Karunamayi!*

Just now Amma was speaking in Her own language, Telugu, that is, Her physical language—I'm sorry! Actually this year's tour started in Dallas. There Amma was giving discourses completely in Telugu because most of the people were Telugu-speaking, most of them being from India. However, over here you have the rare opportunity to listen to Amma's discourse directly in English. But as many of the Telugu-speaking people here have expressed a desire to hear Amma's voice in Telugu, Amma has blessed them today and spoken in Telugu. The rest of you want to know and understand Her speech. To translate the language is hard, and to translate the feelings of Amma is even harder because in translation the feeling and the meaning sometimes changes as we are always in a lower level of consciousness.

Telugu is one of the four languages of South India. The others are: Tamil, Kannada and Malayalam. The Telugu language is thought to be a very sweet language and as Amma was saying now, it is a musical language, more musical than Sanskrit. It is the elder sister of Sanskrit, so most of the words used in Telugu are common to Sanskrit. The sound of Telugu words is soothing and it gives rest to our mind also. Some of you have experienced this here. Even though you do not understand the language, you must have understood the vibrations of the sounds of this language.

Amma: Mother is not partial to any language. Mother is Saraswati. There is only one language, the language of the heart. Your pet knows your love. Your pet's language is the heart's language. There is no other language between you and your pet. Language is very powerful, but silence is the most powerful language. Be silent daily for at least one or two hours. When it comes to love, there are no language differences. Speaking is different.

Swamiji: *Jai Karunamayi!* Many devotees who have come have brought notebooks to be blessed by Amma so that they can begin to write the *likhita japa* of Divine Mother's name, "Om Sri Lalitambika." Amma will be blessing each book by writing the first name, after which you can start the *likhita japa*. Before that, I would like to tell you the difference between *japa* and *dhyana*. In *japa* we have the consciousness of what we are doing.

Dhyānam nirviṣayam manaḥ

"*Dhyana* is freeing the mind from all thoughts." You must not have consciousness at all. For this we need a lot of practice. To write this *japa* properly, you must not just take the book and go on writing till the pages are finished. Each *mantra* must be written with full concentration. That is very important. And the vibration will be high when you do this. This is because, according to Amma's wishes, these books will be installed in the great temple which is being built in Amma's *ashram* in Penusila in Andhra Pradesh, in Southern India. A big *stupa,* a pillar as big as the temple, is being built in the meditation hall, where already thousands and thousands of books have been installed. The deity will be installed on the foundation of all these *likhita japa* books. So all these books will be in the meditation hall where a thousand people can sit and do meditation. And Amma's view is that each and everyone's vibration of *dhyana* on this *mantra* has to be in that *stupa*. Therefore you have to write this *japa* with full concentration. *Likhita japa* means "written *japa*."

You might ask one more question, "What should we do with the books after we finish them?" You can just mail the books to the Indian address on the card we have given you. Mail it to the address for the Bangalore *ashram.*

(Amma requests Swamiji to relate the experience of a devotee who had undertaken a pilgrimage to Mt. Kailasa. Amma mentions that many people have spiritual experiences there. They can hear the sound of Mother's divine bangles and the sound of Her anklets when they lie down near the Manasarovara lake. The lake is golden, has pure water with no pollution at all. Manasarovara is no doubt Parvati, She says. From Mt. Kailasa, we can hear the sound of *Omkara.* So people never touch the sacred Kailasa mountain. They just have its *darshan* and do the fifty three miles *parikrama.*)

Swamiji (describing the journey to Mt. Kailasa)**:** One has to walk for 800 miles—not on a plain road but on a mountainous path—going up and down….

Amma: Without food…

Swamiji: …until one reaches an altitude of 25,000 feet above sea level. So on one day pilgrims will climb one thousand feet, rest there and then go on. As the oxygen becomes thinner, after a week or so they will be on multivitamin tablets only, with no food at all. They cannot carry anything. They cannot carry their clothes or belongings because they become heavy as they reach higher altitudes. Some of Amma's devotees have gone there, but first the government has to give permission after they approve their physical fitness. Amma says if Lord Siva wills, He gives us the permission. If Lord Siva thinks that you can come, only then you can go. People go in batches of thirty and there are nearly fifteen batches every year.

One of Amma's devotees went three years ago. This was before he became a devotee of Amma's. He is a very pious man, does regular meditation and is always inward.

Amma: He does the *Gayatri mantra* meditation.

Swamiji: One day as they were climbing, after journeying for a week or so, they had to cross different ridges of mountains and in one place there was a ridge of only one foot to cross. If one were to slip there, one would fall nearly a thousand feet to the lower level. As the devotee was crossing that point—remember, at that time he had not yet come to Mother—he slipped and was about to fall. At that time, he said, a small girl about eleven or twelve years old appeared, caught hold of his hand and prevented him from falling down. He was not able to thank the girl. He just watched her as she led the way in front of him. He was about to ask her something but she kept walking in front of him and he followed. After some time she disappeared, and he was left wondering who that girl might have been. He thought that perhaps she belonged to the mountain area, as some mountain people lived there and she may have spotted him and come to help him.

After the journey to Manasarovara and Kailasa, the devotee returned to India. One day while in Bangalore, he saw an article about Mother in a magazine and he came to Mother to get his child initiated with the *Saraswati bijakshara mantra*. There were thousands and thousands of people waiting eagerly for the *Saraswati bijakshara*. This was during Navaratri, when Amma was inscribing the *bijakshara* on everyone's tongue. The devotee came to the doorstep of the main hall, and as he saw Mother, he was shocked. He was completely taken aback and was unable to speak. He was in a sort of unconscious state and he sat down. Many people thought he had fainted and they gave him some water. Afterwards they asked him, "What happened to you? You are not feeling well?" He replied, "I had been to Kailasa and Manasarovara, and on the way I had slipped. A small girl suddenly appeared and she took my hand and helped me. And the same face which I saw that day is the face of Amma here. It was none other than Amma only who came and helped me and saved me. And that was the greatest experience!" And he said that he had not seen Amma before. But he said, "I still remember and it is imprinted on my mind that it is none other than the same Mother in the form of a young girl of eleven or twelve years."

In the *shastras* it is said that Devi appears in different forms, and one of them is the *Kaumari rupa*, that is, a young girl of ten to twelve years. That is the form in which the devotee saw Amma before coming to Her. That is why Amma always says that even if you don't come to me, my blessings will always be there with you. And that was the greatest blessing and experience of the devotee, which I shared with you all today. *Jai Karunamayi!*

Amma: So come back to Mother's sweet home, the real Kailasa. Texas is not our place. We have a separate home. Kailasa is our home.

Swamiji: We have a video film about Manasarovara and Kailasa which we will bring next time. The devotees who have gone there have filmed it, but not professionally, as one cannot carry big cameras. The film was taken with a small camera, and although the quality is not good, you can still have a glimpse of Kailasa and Manasarovara.

Amma: Amma is always at the front door,

Mokṣa dvārā kavāṭa pāṭanakarī

She is always waiting for Her children. O my babies, come, come, come!

Swamiji: Amma gives us an example here. Suppose you are coming from a different country, you will need a passport to enter this country. You have to pass customs and immigration and you have to show your passport wherever needed. And even when you come out and are walking alone on the road, the police may stop you and ask for your identification; then also you have to show your passport and establish that you belong to a different country. (Amma laughs) And when you come to your home, even there you may be watched. There may be guards there to whom you will have to show your identity. To every person you have to prove your identity. (Amma laughs and exclaims, "Pathetic!") But when you come to your real home, your Mother will be there ready to open the door. She never asks for your passport. She knows you.

Devotee: Last year at the East Coast meditation retreat in upstate New York there were about fifty of us. We meditated for about three days with Amma, for about five hours a day—not all at one time. We meditated for an hour at a time with breaks in between. On the last day we had meditated for about five-and-a-half hours. Amma had us sit in two concentric circles for our last meditation. She had already told us that She was very pleased with our meditation. We meditated for about two hours. Some of the devotees attending had never meditated for more than ten minutes before the retreat, but they had the desire to come and through the grace of Amma they were able to sit and meditate for that period of time.

When we finished the final meditation. I looked up and Swamiji was there doing *pranam* to Amma and he was staying for a little longer than usual. So I got my glasses and looked to see what was happening and there was a mound of *vibhuti* covering Amma's feet. This is the sacred ash that Amma puts on our forehead. The *vibhuti* had materialized while we were doing our meditation. Of course, all of a sudden people began to realize what had happened and they converged and began to take a bit for themselves. Afterwards Amma told us that Lord Siva had been very pleased with our meditation and that the *vibhuti* was the blessing of Lord Siva. *Jai Karunamayi!*

Amma's Discourse:

Om śaraṇāgata dīnārta paritrāṇa parāyane
Sarvasyārti hare Devī Nārāyanī namostute

Embodiment of Divine Souls, Amma's Most Beloved Children,

I have not come to you as a spiritual master. I have not come to you as a *guru* or Divine Mother. I have come to you all the way as your own near and dear mother. My children, you are already on the beautiful, divine spiritual path. This is the right path. Where there is *dharma,* righteousness, there only is divinity. Where there is divinity, there only is peace. So we need peace. It is not available in the external world. Peace is only found within.

Seeing God in beautiful idols in temples is one stage. It is a very good stage because in this *Kali yuga* we forget all these spiritual things. We are afraid and we have a lot of negativity. So, seeing God in temples and having faith in God is one stage. Seeing God in holy people and in good things is another stage. Seeing divinity in oneself and in others—that is a beautiful state. That is spiritual consciousness—seeing divinity everywhere; not only in the good, but also in the bad—that is the highest stage. That is the real essence of spirituality.

Children, you are already in your path. There are innumerable paths in this world, innumerable religions. But Truth is only one. If our path is devotional, *bhakti yoga*, or if it is the path of knowledge, *jnana yoga,* or *dhyana yoga* or *nishkama karma yoga*, the goal is the same. When our little self is one hundred percent less, then only *yoga* starts. In selfless service, if our self disappears one hundred percent, our service is wonderful to this universe. That is the *karma yoga* mentioned in the *Bhagavad Gita*. So we are already on the path.

But why this anger in our heart? Why again do we have lust, greed, and these little, little things in our heart? For so many years—twenty, thirty, or fifty years, we have been chanting the *Vishnu Sahasranama*, the *Lalita Sahasranama*, the *Bhagavad Gita*, and performing spiritual activities. Yet we have some curtains—anger, lust, greed, hatred and jealousy. These are little, little weeds. There is a beautiful divine plant in our heart. That is the cosmic consciousness. When we elevate ourselves to the highest peak of purity, to desirelessness, this consciousness touches the cosmos. We belong to each and every religion in this world. We belong to this universe. The animal kingdom, bird kingdom, and everything else is ours only. But we get stuck in some little, little points: "Oh, this is my religion. Only my religion is good. Only my feeling is good." Really, your feeling is very good and sweet, but it is our responsibility to give respect to other religions also.

The sun is only one but its rays are innumerable. There are billions upon billions of rays. God and Truth are only one. The paths are many. So why do we quarrel, particularly in spirituality? Why do we argue, "Do not go there, do not see her, do not enter the temple, do not enter this mosque." By doing so we bind ourselves to a mortal frame and to our mind, because we are in this limited frame.

So children, only in this spiritual path we have that wisdom. Wisdom is so beautiful. It beautifies our entire life so that we may attain God-Realization. You know, the main aim of human life is Self-Realization. Seeing divinity in one's heart and in everything good and bad is the highest *turiya* state in spirituality.

India has given the beautiful *Sanatana Dharma* to the entire universe. In *Sanatana Dharma* there is a beautiful saying,

Vasudhaika kuṭumba

Just now we chanted a beautiful *mantra*,

Lokāḥ samastāḥ sukhino bhavantu

"May the entire universe always be in peace and prosperity." We wish all this for the entire universe. That is liberation. So we need that liberation—liberation from our anger. Anger is a little weed. It controls the cosmic tree in our heart. Lust, greed, hatred, jealousy, and pride are also little, little weeds. These six weeds we must immediately remove from our heart, which is a beautiful garden. We must elevate ourselves to the highest peak of *samadhi*. That is Realization. That is the essence of spirituality.

Since innumerable births we have been searching for this reality. Reality is not outside; it is always inside. Peace is always inside. So we need liberation from these lowly natures and elevation to the highest peak of *dharma*. Where there is *dharma*, there only is real wisdom. If we do not have wisdom in our life, and if any desire remains in this birth, then again we take one more birth. This is like a *chakra—janana marana chakra*. Mother resides in the *Sri Chakra*; children reside in the *janana marana chakra*. Mother is wearing the *trishul*; the children are wearing the *trigunas*, not the *trishul*. We should have liberation from these negativities such as anger. Anger is not sweet, it is bitter. In the *Bhagavad Gita*, there is a *shloka*,

Krodhāt bhavati sammohaḥ

"If there is anger, that is the main entrance for *naraka*, hell." Where there is peace, that is the entrance for liberation, the main gateway for wisdom.

So children, meditate and pray to God with tears. The prayer must not come from the lips. It must always come from the bottom of our heart. From the bottom of our heart. Wake up early in the morning and pray to God with a pure heart, without any desire. Desire is the impurity of the mind, the force of motion of our mind. Desire creates so many problems. Desirelessness is the highest peak of purity. Purity is the gateway for wisdom So where purity and inner beauty, *anta sveccha,* exist, we have wisdom in our life. We have limited ourselves to a small part. When this energy spreads (*vyapaka*), as the nature of our *atma* is *vyapaka*, it spreads through the entire universe. Now it is like a small atom in our heart, enclosed by the little, little, little weeds. Just vacuum all those weeds from the heart and have liberation—liberation from anger, liberation from lust, liberation from greed, liberation from jealously. Jealousy is like jaundice to our mind—it is not sweet. We are the soul; we are not this body. This body is like a dress, a dress for our soul.

So only those who have spiritual elevation in their lives are able to open their third eye and see divinity everywhere. They are always in that Supreme Consciousness, that is, bliss and peace. They have this experience, "O, I myself am wisdom, I myself am Truth, I myself am past, present and future." You yourself are time and you yourself are attributeless. And you yourself are the entire cosmos. The whole cosmos belongs to you only, to your soul. You are bliss! The *Vedas* and all religions belong to you. Why are we stuck like a little cassette and are so limited here, thinking, "O, only this is my path, I never go and visit any *guru,* I don't like to go to the temple." We limit ourselves.

Spirituality leads you from this mortal frame to immortality, to the permanent peace, the permanent bliss that is like a hidden treasure in our hearts. So open the heart and invite divinity. Kill the ego and pray to God for purification. You know that meditations and all those things are just for remodeling our life, remodeling our life to divinity, for our upliftment towards divinity. Meditation gives purification and a lot of inner beauty to our life. Where there is inner beauty, there we have all the divine attributes, such as compassion, kindness, equal vision, wisdom, truth, peace, and bliss. We have all these divine attributes, *sugunas,* just like gems and jewels in our heart. Wear these jewels. For a spiritual aspirant these jewels such as kindness, compassion and real devotion, are very much needed—not the show of devotion.

Have one hundred percent faith. Achieve your destiny in this birth itself. Achieve that destiny and realize what is good and what is bad. Search the inner reality inside first. Seeing divinity inside is good, that is a divine virtue. Honesty is the greatest wisdom. If we have real truth and we pray to God with true devotion, we will have all these divine attributes in our heart and gradually be elevated to the attributeless state because divinity is only oneness. There is no second.

Ekamevadvitīyam Brahma
Nanyad asti akincanaḥ
Satyam jnānam anantam

You know all that. So we will just summarize the little points. One is faith—have one hundred percent faith, discriminating faith. Without faith, even if we pray for hundreds and hundreds of years there is no meaning in our spirituality. Faith is the main basis. Where there is faith there is everything—more and more real devotion in our heart. Where there is no faith, any religion, country, or personality is gradually ruined because faith is the main power. Faith develops will power, faith gives immense strength and real knowledge. So have faith, discriminating faith.

Develop your dispassion more and more, and meditate and pray to God. If you like *bhakti yoga*, proceed on that path. If you like meditation, you proceed on that path. If you like singing, sing some *bhajans* or songs. In music there is nectar, but silence is the language of God. There are innumerable languages. Mother Saraswati is not partial to only Sanskrit. If it is the language of the birds or animals, or the language of the ocean or wind—She likes every language in this universe. But because Her language is absolute silence, we must learn that language too. In silence only we learn so many things. If we are restless, walking here and there and wandering in this world, we will not learn anything.

So children, silence is the beautiful language of the Divine. Learn that language. Wake up early in the morning, at least by five o'clock. Pray for fifteen to twenty minutes. Meditate. Meditate on the Self—Truth. Truth develops inner beauty so that we have spiritual consciousness and we enjoy peace and bliss in our Self. Then we are able to see divinity everywhere in the universe. So peace is not available by just going and sitting in Himalayan caves. It is not possible. We must conquer the enemies. Who is the enemy of peace? Our desire. Our desire is the first enemy of our peace. So reduce the unnecessary desires and have a good desire, that is, Realization. Realization of the Self is to see divinity in bad also. Then we have forgiveness and the beautiful flowers will bloom in our heart.

It is mentioned in the *Lalita Sahasranama*:

Caitanya kusuma ārādhyā
Caitanya kusuma priyā

"Mother is like the beautiful ever-blooming flower—the flower of spiritual consciousness." That is the tenth gate in our body in the *brahmakupa*, the universal lotus. So open all these *chakras*. All the inner flowers are blooming because of cosmic love and cosmic consciousness. We have *Brahmic* awareness. We enjoy the silence and bliss in our life. Our life becomes so sweet. There are no words in any language to describe that state. That is only by our experience.

So, children, send this ego problem away permanently. The main problem is innumerable births of "I," "me," and "mine." This is our only problem. So immediately send this problem from your heart and open the gate. Ask Mother to grant a divine grand life. A divine grand life means only peace. Where there is peace, there only is divinity. Where there is divinity there only is *Sanatana Dharma*. Be seated in that seat of *dharma*. Do not walk in those little, little paths of anger, lust, greed and jealously. Those are slippery paths, not good paths. No good fragrance at all. For births together, since billions and billions and billions of births, we have been on these slippery paths. The path that is so beautiful, indescribable—that is only the absolute truth, benediction, wisdom. So oneness is important. That is the essence of spirituality.

What is the essence of human life, children? What is the essence of our human life? The essence of our human life is selfless service. We must give our service to this universe, but we should never display it. We must always be behind the curtain and give our service one hundred percent to mankind. That is our responsibility, because you take so much from nature. You never repay anything to Mother Nature.

If you love Mother Nature, you will become wise. It is also one of our responsibilities to love this entire nature—the animal kingdom, the bird kingdom and the entire universe. You are everything. Everything belongs to your soul only. If we have that *Brahmic* awareness, we can never hate anyone in this world. We will have a lot of cosmic love in our hearts. That is the highest state of spirituality. So Mother wishes that Her children will earn that highest state. Give your selfless service. Be humble. Humility is a jewel for a seeker. Humility is the enemy of egoism. Develop humility and send egoism away. Permanently send away egoism in this birth.

We have three stages of the mind. In the stage of *tamas*—*tamasic* food, *tamasic* words, *tamasic* thinking—we never listen to anyone else's words, even if it is good for us. Because of our *tamasic* nature we have many faults. So *tamasic* food and habits and excessive sleep are not good. The spiritual consciousness is also working in *tamas,* but only a quarter percent.

Rajas also can be very, very dangerous to society. Commanding and forcing others, imposing our will on others, and expecting people to do things according to our wishes, this is *rajas*. We tell people, "You must be like this or like that." We cannot give wisdom to others. How pathetic it is! So a *rajasic* nature is more dangerous than a *tamasic* one.

In *sattva* we have spirituality, humility, inner beauty, devotion, knowledge, all these good qualities. And we can develop our spirituality more and more if we meditate, pray, sing, worship, and have *darshan* of holy people. Just one dust particle of theirs is enough to give us elevation. Even thousands and thousands of sittings of meditation are not equal to one particle of dust from a holy person. So in *sattva* we have humility, spirituality, real devotion, and we have faith, discriminative knowledge, and all these good qualities. Gradually we elevate ourselves from *sattva* to *vishuddha sattva*.

Vishuddha sattva is the place of the *vishuddha chakra*. In the heart *chakra* we have all these good natures—we are pure, we never tell lies, we never cheat others, we never injure others' feelings, including their religious feelings, and we have a lot of respect towards everyone in the world. So gradually when you are elevated to the *vishuddha chakra,* you are in pure consciousness, you are in silence, you have peace, you have bliss, and you have awareness. You are in the consciousness of *Brahman*. And your third eye, your eye of wisdom, is open here in the *ajna chakra*.

(Amma points to the forehead.) The entire cosmos is in between your two eyebrows. You feel that little Mother Earth is a very tiny particle compared to the cosmos, and where am I? Oh, that is a very beautiful state! So stage by stage, stage by stage, you are elevated. It does not happen in one day but by gradual practice.

To practice spirituality, intense desire is needed and all the divine attributes, the jewels, are very important. Children, you already have all those. Elevate yourself more and more and more and more and be always in wisdom, be always in Truth, be always in *Omkara*, be always in oneness, nonduality. There is no secondness, duality, in this universe. Only oneness. So remove these curtains, these black curtains between your eyes and your heart. Your entire life is covered with these curtains of illusion. So remove these curtains immediately. Send away egoism permanently from your life. Egoism is the main problem. Birth is a long play. This is a play of forty years, fifty years, seventy years, or ninety years. In this play we are always assuming a role. Be a spectator in this play. A spectator enjoys the play more than an actor. So enjoy this play, this cosmic play. Stop your part and balance your mind.

Meditation and spirituality control our emotions. Sometimes we have so much emotion for unnecessary little, little things. We do not have a balanced state of mind because there is no meditation and no purity. So if we meditate we can enjoy the balanced state. We will have equal vision. We will love every religion, everyone, even if they have committed sins. We will have that understanding, the right understanding. We will have knowledge. We will love this entire nature. We will go beyond the body, mind and intellect, and we will see divinity in everything in this universe. That is spirituality. That is *Sanatana Dharma*.

Sanatana Dharma is not for Indians only. Mother is not partial to anyone. Divine Mother Parashakti is:

Sanātanī Ārya Ārādhya Devī
Akhaṇḍa Caitanya Brahma svarūpiṇī
Koṭi koṭi yoginī gaṇa sevitā
Akhilāṇḍa koṭi brahmaṇḍa nāyakī
Ādī madhyānta rahitā
Kānti dhuta japāvalī

Sṛṣti kartrī Brahma rūpā
Goptrī Govinda rūpiṇī
Samhāriṇī Rudra rūpā
Tirodhāna karīśwarī

All these forms are only Mother's form. Mother is *Omkara*. She is the Absolute. Our main aim is to attain Realization at least in this birth. So many billions of births we have failed, failed, failed. We are stuck in little, little points—in anger, in lust, in greed, in hatred—little points. Really these are not big points.

There is a great reason for this life. What is that reason? If we have real knowledge, if we have awareness in our heart, immediately we will start our eternal journey with a definite aim—to attain bliss. So, children, be like an infant baby in Mother's arms. The one- or two-day-old infant baby always closes her eyes and smiles in her sleep. When her mother touches her she is so happy. When anyone else touches her, she immediately senses the other's presence and she cries. She doesn't like others' vibrations. She only likes her mother's vibration. So always be in that bliss, children. Do not invite the little things any more—send them away permanently from your heart, and beautify your heart with all these divine attributes.

Forgiveness is the greatest penance.

Kṣamā tapas kṣamā yogam
Kṣamā jnānam kṣamā sarvam

Where there is forgiveness there is everything. When we have cruelty in our hearts we are not beautiful. Along with physical beauty, inner beauty, *anta saundaryam* is also important. Children, you already have all those good qualities, so elevate yourself more and more and attain God-Realization in this birth at least. Stop this *janana marana chakra*—the cycle of birth and death and again rebirth. This is a cycle. Stop this birth and death cycle. Achieve the destiny of the *bindusthana* in the *Sri Chakra*. That is your abode. Come back to your Mother's sweet home. Enjoy divinity always—in yourself and everywhere in this universe. God is not only in one particular place, He is everywhere. So have that experience and enjoy bliss, peace, and oneness in this birth.

Meditation purifies our life; it purifies each and every cell of our body. It gives us self-confidence, self respect, willpower, balance of mind, and gradually, attributelessness. First we need all these. So, children, whatever your religion may be—that is not the question. All religions lead to one goal only—that goal is only bliss, peace. The question is not about which religion is good and which religion is bad. Every religion emphasizes Truth and wisdom. Have wisdom at least in spirituality. We do not have wisdom in our life—in our office, our family, our country, the universe. We have rules and regulations everywhere. For a little happiness we work so much, suffer so much and we lose everything. Only spirituality, only Truth supports your entire life. You will develop strong willpower in your life. Develop that more and more, and if any problem comes to you, it will not touch your heart. You will be stable and forgiving and always in that spiritual consciousness. This is so beautiful.

So Truth is our main aim. To attain this Truth we must have purity. Purity is the gateway for wisdom. Where there is purity, there only is honesty. Where there is honesty, there we have all these beautiful divine flowers blooming in our heart: the root *chakra,* the *svadhisthana chakra,* the *manipura chakra,* the *anahata chakra,* the *vishuddhi chakra,* the *ajna chakra*, and finally the tenth gate, the universal lotus, the *sahasrara kamala*. That is your seat. Come back to your Mother's sweet home—*Omkara*. You are in a hostel, a temporary hostel. We are searching for happiness here, but really there is no happiness in these limited things. For a tiny bit of happiness we are working and working and working and our entire life is just wasted. Happiness is always inside. It is in the form of bliss. So search for that bliss, have willpower, be always in wisdom. Try to understand reality and attain God-Realization in this birth. This is Amma's only wish for Her children.

Children, never injure the religious feelings of others. If your friends have a particular faith, give respect. That is our responsibility. Go to all holy people, have their *darshan* and get their blessings. If they are really enlightened, you will have a good blessing. If they are not enlightened, also you get blessings. Your salutations go to the Absolute only. So there is no problem.

Do not criticize anyone. Criticism, hurting, and using bad words—that is the pollution of our tongue. After taking the holy *tirtha* and repeating *mantras*, we criticize people. Is it good? It is not good. And with angry words, we hurt only our own people, our own family members. Is it good? So control the anger, gradually control this weed and then remove this weed. Whenever you have anger go to another room. Do not talk to them. If people have hurt you ten times, forgive them. Love them. Because you are on the spiritual path, you have devotion and such qualities in your life. If you continue hurting people hundreds of times, what is the meaning of your spirituality? Never come down from that highest peak to the lower level. That is a different level. Because people do not understand, they have anger.

Anger is one nature. That is a weed, just a little weed which covers the cosmic tree. So immediately burn all these weeds with a laser beam, which is the *mantra*. Chant the *Narayana mantra,* the *Om mantra,* the *Siva mantra,* or whatever *mantra* you have.

The power of the seed letters in the *mantra* cannot be described. They remove the ignorance, illusion, and dark forces in our life and give enlightenment to the seeker. This also depends upon your *sadhana*. Your *sadhana* is your best friend in this world. Listen to your friend's words. If your *sadhana* is without any interruption, you will always have good feelings, and you will have some message from your pure heart telling you what to do and where to go. You will always get messages from your heart, from your soul. So listen to your heart. Always listen to your heart. Be always in pure consciousness. Be always in wisdom. Be always in divinity. Divinize your thoughts.

In the *Rig Veda* many years ago, our thoughts have been mentioned. Now we have so many polluted thoughts—negative thoughts, very poisonous thoughts. Because of our poisonous thoughts we have polluted this Earth more than atomic pollution and all other kinds of pollutions. Those pollutions are only one percent. Our negative thinking is millions of times greater than this atomic pollution. "Let noble thoughts come to us from every side," is a beautiful saying in the *Rig Veda*. Always have noble thoughts—they beautify our entire life. We should divinize our thoughts, which will then beautify our lives with peace, forgiveness, equal vision, discriminative knowledge, discriminating faith, true devotion, and humility. Decorate your life with all these beautiful ornaments and be attributeless. In meditation only it is possible. So you know all those things.

Once more Amma is just summarizing those points with Her children on this beautiful evening. It is so beautiful here, it seems to be like Tirumala with the *murtis*—here in this special, temple atmosphere with pure vibrations. So, children, take a vow that from now on we will never invite these negative qualities into our hearts. Send them away permanently. Have peace, more peace and experience the real bliss in this birth. That is Amma's wish towards Her children. *Hari Om Tat Sat.*

Once again we will meditate for universal peace for five minutes. Daily try to repeat the *mantra* twenty-four times. (Amma recites the *Mrityunjaya mantra* and then the *Saraswati mantra* with devotees.)

This *Saraswati mantra* is for pure thoughts, good words, pure feelings, immense knowledge, spiritual inspiration, and good education. So this *mantra* gives a lot of inspiration in our life. The *Saraswati mantra* purifies our words, our life and gives a lot of inner beauty.

Om Ayīm Śrīm Hrīm Saraswatī Devyai namaḥ
Om śānti, śānti śāntiḥ

16 May 1997

Chicago

ॐ

OFFER THE FRAGRANT INNER FLOWERS TO AMMA

Amma's Beloved Divine Souls,

Self-Realization can be attained by deep meditation alone. When we chant the *Om Mantra* nine times before we start our meditation, the *kundalini shakti* that lies asleep in the *muladhara kunda*, the hollow at the *muladhara chakra,* awakens and begins to travel upwards. She moves through all the six *chakras*—the root *chakra,* the *svadhishthana chakra,* the *manipura chakra,* the *anahata maha chakra,* the *vishuddhi chakra,* the *ajna chakra* and finally reaches the *sahasrara chakra*, or universal lotus at the crown of the head. Mother, as the spiritual energy *kundalini,* travels in a fraction of a second through all the *chakras.* If there is a lack of regular meditation, Mother does not stabilize at the *sahasrara chakra,* but returns to the root *chakra.* .

When we practice regular meditation and pray for deep meditation, we attain *samadhi*, and the *kundalini shakti* stabilizes at the *sahasrara,* resting in pure Consciousness. Then we attain God-Realization. We experience supreme energy, Mother Divine, in every cell of this universe, in every cell of the cosmos! We see Mother everywhere, in everything—in air, fire and grass blades, in mountains and oceans, in the whole cosmos, everywhere! Mother is omnipresent, omnipotent and omniscient. Mother is absolute silence. Mother is beyond divinity, beyond truth, beyond time. She is beyond the *Vedas,* beyond motherly love, beyond imagination, beyond everything.

So children, meditate on Mother Divine with pure devotion from the bottom of your heart. *Devi puja madhuram*—worship of Mother is sweeter than nectar!

Generally we think *puja* means external worship. In *Sri Lalita Sahasranama, Devi puja* is different. It is not external worship. We worship Mother Divine with seed letters, the powerful *bijaksharas* of Her divine names. When we meditate on Mother, all the inner flowers of the *chakras* begin to bloom. Our inner garden is full of innumerable, fragrant flowers. What is that fragrance, children? It is boundless peace and wisdom. So meditate and enjoy that infinite peace inside.

Even in our worldly life, we sometimes experience peace for fifteen minutes, twenty minutes, one hour, ten days or fifteen days because of our meditation. We are peaceful in the presence of holy people. When we practice any spiritual activity, we are in peace for a little while. But we soon get drawn once again into the world-intoxication of *maya* and face innumerable problems. *Maya* is very subtle. You understand these things more than Amma. So children, go beyond *maya*. *Maya* is nothing but the bondage of ego.

Do not kill animals or insects, kill the ego immediately. Cultivate humility. You must cultivate humility because humility is the greatest enemy of egoism. So when we cultivate humility there is no egoism in our life. When Mother is seated in the lotus of our heart, we have no egoism at all. We are free from lust, anger, jealousy, greed, and everything negative. We are completely liberated from all these little burdens. And we are filled with great peace, wisdom and tranquility. We enjoy divinity in each and every cell of our body. We feel that our body is a sacred temple, and Mother Divine dwells inside. So children, always feel Mother's divine presence within.

Meditation is actually the beautiful fine art that remodels our entire life into divinity. All the change takes place inside—it is not external. Then we have no ego problem, no anger, no lust, greed, jealousy or hatred—no problems at all. All the clouds of ignorance disappear in the light of divine wisdom. So children, open the gates to wisdom—be always in *dharma*.

When we meditate on Mother Divine, innumerable cosmic flowers bloom inside. Offer those flowers to Mother, but not with your hands. There are so many kinds of *anjalis,* offerings. One is *pushpanjali,* when we offer flowers to God with cupped hands. Just now you offered flowers to Amma as *pushpanjali*. In meditation we offer the inner flowers to Mother Divine. We offer the purity of the inner divine qualities to Mother. Offer those flowers to Amma—Amma wants those flowers only.

Caitanya kusumārādhyā caitanya kusuma priyā

Innumerable flowers are there in our sweet, inner garden. It is a very beautiful garden, but it is now full of weeds, so we cannot find any flowers inside. Children, give Amma the opportunity to vacuum all the weeds and water your inner garden with the nectar of love. Then the tree of knowledge inside will grow to touch the cosmos and you will have spiritual elevation. That is the beauty of inner worship and meditation.

So children, when will you learn that meditation? When will you offer the inner cosmic flowers to Amma? Always you offer her only roses and other flowers. Those flowers have all been created by Amma. Amma now wants you to offer her the inner cosmic flowers. So bloom all the flowers of divine qualities and offer them to Amma—the flowers that blossom in meditation. When you meditate, automatically, without your consciousness, all the fragrant flowers of divine attributes come to Amma and they themselves worship Amma! This happens in deep meditation only—not in surface meditation—in deep, deep meditation. So learn the art of remodeling your entire life into divinity. That is real meditation.

People sometimes say, "What is there in meditation?" So many people have this kind of opinion about meditation. Look at Lord Siva—He is always in meditation. Anjaneya, Hanumana, meditates on Lord Rama, and Sri Rama meditates on Lord Siva! All the innumerable Gods and Goddesses are always in meditation. Look at the mountains. Amma feels all the mountains are in silent meditation. All the planets are in meditation. The oceans are in meditation—all nature is in meditation except for us—we cannot meditate because of our mind. The mind is always in the lowest level of *tamas, rajas* and *sattva.* Mother is beyond *sattva,* She is even beyond *vishuddha sattva,* the highest, purest *sattva.* She is beyond everything. Mother is indestructible power. She is the source of energy, *mula shakti,* the origin and root of all energy. Without Mother there is no consciousness at all in the universe. Even an ant cannot move without Her command.

So babies, attain God-Realization by pure devotion, pure *bhakti*. Devotion is more important than anything else. Devotion is the main foundation of spirituality. Devotion teaches us selfless service, service without any trace of ego. Service is not sweet while the feelings of "I, my, me" are still in us. True service must be totally without ego.

The world is full of so many pains and problems. People bear mountains of pains, and when they get an opportunity to talk to Amma personally, they burst. They want only God-Realization!

Yesterday and today Amma met so many children individually. I love you so much, children; I love you all so much! All of these children asked Amma only for spirituality and divinity. They never asked Amma for material benefits. People think that all those who come to the healing sessions come to get relief from physical suffering. No! Most of them do not ask for anything material. They are wise babies; they have so much wisdom.

They have the right to ask Mother for anything. You are my children. You have the right to come to Amma and ask for anything. But all of my children ask Amma for spirituality and wisdom only. I love it! I cannot express my joy in words, children.

Oh my babies! Embodiments of divine souls, Amma's most beloved children, elevate and expand yourselves! Give up all your problems to Amma. I will burn them immediately. Give all of your *karma* load to Amma. She will burn it all with her pure cosmic love. Elevate yourself to the cosmos! Elevate yourself to the pure Consciousness of bliss! Attain transcendental peace.

So my children, Amma expects to see her babies always on the highest peak of divine Consciousness—in *samadhi.* This is possible only through meditation. It has been said beautifully in a song, *Devi dhyanam madhuram.* When we meditate, we immediately feel that all the flowers are beginning to bloom in our inner garden. *Sarvam Devi madhuram:* we feel the presence of divine Consciousness in each and every cell of the cosmos.

Once I was in Tirumala, which is a center of *Sanatana Dharma.* They have preserved the *Vedas* by computerizing them. There are thousands of very learned *vedic pundits* in the Tirumala Temple.

When I was in Tirumala, one of my sons asked me, "Amma, write something about Lord Venkateshwara."

"Why son?"

"Because you like Sri Venkateshwara."

"I like everything. I like every form of God, my son. I have no time to write. If I have five minutes, I want to wipe the tears of my babies. You write something about Lord Venkateshwara; write something about Lord Jesus."

"So you love....?"

"I love everything. I have the same feelings wherever I go. Whether it is a church, a mosque or a temple, or whether I am in a forest, in a car or on a road, I feel the same vibrations everywhere. I have the same feeling. I feel no difference at all."

This is pure Consciousness. So babies, feel divinity everywhere—in churches, mosques and temples; on the roads, in your homes, in your hearts; in cities, caves and mountains—feel divinity in all life, in the good and the bad. To a true *yogi,* mud and gold are equal. Be a real *yogi* and see oneness everywhere. Elevate yourself to that level of divine beauty!

Amma again and again asks all her children to cultivate *dharma.* Righteousness, though close in meaning, is not the correct word for *dharma. Dharma* is the main pillar of our life. Without *dharma,* life is meaningless, a billion times meaningless! So children, let *dharma* rule and support your entire life. *Dharma* supports this universe; *dharma* supports the cosmos. When we cultivate *dharma* in our life, we can stand alone in the universe without support from anyone. That is the beauty of divine *dharma.* So my dear children, practice and cultivate *dharma.* Be always in *dharma.* Never give up *dharma.* Never give up *dharma!* Be always steadfast in *dharma.* Use the word *dharma,* not righteousness.

When we live in *dharma* we have wisdom, inner beauty, equal vision, forgiveness, kindness, compassion, detachment, discriminative knowledge, everything. We have so many divine attributes in our life. But you must go beyond these attributes also, because Mother is attributeless. Attain Mother Divine. Go beyond all divine attributes, children, and merge with Divine Mother. Enjoy infinite joy inside through meditation.

It has been said in a beautiful song, *"Devi puja madhuram, Atma nivasam madhuram."* "Worship of Devi is sweet as nectar, for She dwells eternally in your soul." She is always here, in your heart. Feel Mother inside—always, always and always, Mother is within you!

Open your third eye and see Mother's divinity everywhere. Mother is endless and boundless—enjoy Her supreme tranquility inside. Only true *bhakti* blesses us with divine virtues, that is why devotion is so important. *Bhakti* is nectar. I love *bhakti* so much. We can offer selfless service to the world only when we have a firm foundation of devotion. *Bhakti* bestows knowledge on us and makes us inward very naturally. Only a seeker who has inwardness is able to understand divinity, not everyone. If we are always involved in external things, we can never attain divine, infinite joy in our life.

So my dear children, once again Amma summarizes the same points with you. Again and again She wants to imprint these words into your minds and hearts. I am not just giving a discourse; my words come from the bottom of my heart. I speak to you not with my mind, but with my heart. So children, understand the Reality in your life. Cultivate divine *dharma*. Be always in *dharma*. Where there is *dharma,* there only is wisdom. Where there is wisdom, there only is dispassion. Where there is liberation from all limited immoral qualities, we have peace. We enjoy everlasting peace inside. This is the real fragrance, the real essence of our life.

There are four pillars that support this body temple: The first is *dharma*, righteousness; the second is wisdom—liberation from all immoral natures; the third is cosmic love. When we have cosmic love, we love the entire universe as our own self. The fourth pillar is the beauty of divine Consciousness—being always in supreme Consciousness. The main entrance gate to this beautiful temple is selfless service. Selfless service is the greatest *yoga* to merge with the Eternal. So children, give your selfless service to the universe. Love Mother Nature. Then only will you attain wisdom.

Sit alone in your room and meditate with tears. Pray to Mother from the bottom of your heart, "O Mother, grant me pure devotion and right understanding. Destroy my thoughts, and all the impurities and negativities inside me. Where can I go, and who can I ask, but You?"

The auspicious divine fire of knowledge burns to ashes billions of thoughts in a fraction of a second. So children, meditate. My babies, meditate.

Intense desire for God is very important for a seeker. Without a deep longing for the Divine we cannot sit in meditation. Surface prayer and meditation for five minutes are of no use. Without faith, prayer is powerless. When your prayer comes from the bottom of your heart it reaches Amma immediately, for She is always in your heart. She is always here—She is not outside. She is also *sarva vyapaka*—She is everywhere! Oneness is Mother—there is no secondness at all.

Ekamevadvitīyam Brahma nānyad asti akincanaḥ

The entire *Veda* stands on this one *mantra,* which contains very powerful seed letters.

Yesterday Amma spoke about the *Lalita Sahasranama,* the thousand names of Mother Divine. We cannot describe only the physical beauty of Mother. Her true loveliness lies in Her inner beauty—Her unconditional love, boundless kindness and infinite compassion. Mother is beyond compassion; She is beyond motherly love; She is beyond everything. We cannot see Mother Divine but She has descended to this world in so many forms. When Her children pray to Her, She comes in beautiful forms to comfort them. That is Mother's responsibility towards Her children. So in *Sri Lalita Sahasranama*, we find that the essence of every name of Devi is oneness with Mother. Oneness, oneness, oneness! It is very beautiful—beyond beautiful!

So children, try to learn the *Lalita Sahasranama.* Learn just one name a day. The seed letters in every name are extremely powerful. This sacred *stotra* has come to us from the cosmos, so learn to chant it. Praise Mother, sing Her glory! Be a real devotee. Meditate on Mother. Offer your entire life to Mother Divine as *prasada.* Tell Her, "Mother, I have nothing to offer You but the impurities in my heart. Please burn all these weeds from my heart. I want to offer my entire life to You. O Mother, please come into the temple of my heart and make me Your instrument." Our body is a car, and Mother is the driver. Without Mother this car cannot move.

Babies, understand the Reality. Truth is bitter; it is not sweet. But when we attain Self-Realization, we taste the Truth, and the experience is very powerful. Truth is very powerful. Truth is indestructible. Truth is one. Truth is everywhere. Truth is divine. Truth is Mother. So practice truth. Be always truthful. Be always noble inside. Have only noble thoughts, not low or negative thoughts.

Children, go beyond this mortal frame and attain immortality! Meditation is the ladder that leads you from this mortal frame to immortality. So meditate. Elevate yourself, expand yourself. The nature of our soul is elevation and expansion. We are unhappy because we have confined our self to this mortal frame, and to the cages of mind and intellect. We have ego because we think we are the body. The ego makes us selfish. If we go beyond the body, mind and intellect we attain wisdom. We taste supreme tranquility and bliss in *samadhi.* So children, elevate to that level. Attain the priceless diamond of eternal, divine bliss. Experience Mother Divine in all the stages of waking, dreaming and deep sleep.

(Amma speaks in Telugu.)

Translator: *Jai Karunamayi!*

I am going to translate, or try to translate, what Amma has said. It is impossible to translate what Amma says. And pardon me, if there are any mistakes in it, they are mine.

Swamiji asked me to summarize Amma's teachings and messages also.

Today Amma spoke about the *Lalita Sahasranama.* *"Sahasra"* means "one thousand," *"nama,"* means "names," and *Lalita* is Divinity, Divine Mother Herself. She is *shakti*, divine energy. She is *chaitanya,* supreme Consciousness, super Spirit.

Amma started by asking, "Who is *Lalita*?" *Lalita* in Sanskrit is one who is the embodiment of *lalitya*. It is really impossible to translate *lalitya* into English, but I'll try to give you some words with a close meaning. *"Lalitya"* means "very soft and tender." One who has these qualities and is self-effulgent and serene is *Lalita*.

In Dallas, Amma talked about three of the thousand names of Devi in one day, and believe me, it was very beautiful, because the inner meanings Amma gives for each of these divine names are so wonderful.

Amma also told us about the *Navaratri* celebrations. These are the nine nights sacred to Devi that usually fall in the month of October, culminating in *Vijaya Dashami.* *"Dasha"* is "ten." It was on the tenth day that that Divine Mother, *Lalita Devi*, manifested in Her real *svarupa*, Her real form.

For the *Navaratris,* the nine days, She was *Mahishasura Mardini*. She killed an *asura,* a demon, called Mahisha. I think that many of you who have read Amma's Biography know that Sri Karunamayi in Her human form was born on the auspicious *Vijaya Dashami* day. Then Amma said something magnificent—only Amma can say such things! She said that Mother Divine is *Brahmatita*—She is beyond *Brahman.* She is *Jnanatita,* beyond knowledge. The word *"atita"* means "above and beyond." She is *Chaitanyatita,* beyond supreme *Consciousness*. And She is *Atmatita,* beyond the Spirit, the Soul!

The beautiful part about it is that the four *Vedas*[1] have four great sentences or aphorisms called *maha vakyas*. Amma said that Divine Mother is *Brahmatita*. The *maha vakya* from the *Yajur Veda* is *"Aham Brahmasmi,"* "I am *Brahman*."

Then Amma said that Divine Mother is *Jnanatita*. The second *maha vakya* from the *Rig Veda* is *"Prajnanam Brahma." Prajnanam* is the highest cosmic spiritual knowledge. That is what Amma talks about all the time—we must have cosmic vision, not human vision or divine vision. Amma always tells us that we should not limit ourselves to this mortal frame: "Go beyond this mortal frame and attain immortality."

The third name of Divine Mother Amma gave was *Chaitanyatita*. The *maha vakya* from the *Sama Veda* is *"Tat tvam asi,"* "You yourself are divine Consciousness."

The last name Amma gave for Mother Divine was *Atmatita*. The fourth *maha vakya* from the *Atharva Veda* is, *"Ayam atma Brahma,"* "This *atman* is *Brahma."*

So Amma is telling us that Divine Mother is above and beyond the four *maha vakyas* of the *Vedas—Aham Brahmasmi, Prajnanam Brahma, Tat tvam asi* and *Ayam atma Brahma.*

Amma also said that Divine Mother gives you everything you want, you just have to ask Her. She is Maha Lakshmi. She has eight different forms, known as *Ashta Lakshmi*. She comes as *Dhana Lakshmi*, Goddess of material wealth. *Dhanya Lakshmi* is the Goddess of food grains. *Santana Lakshmi* is the Goddess of progeny. One of Her beautiful forms is *Jnana Lakshmi*, Goddess of spiritual

---

[1] The names of the four *Vedas* corresponding to the four *maha vākyas* associated with them have been inserted from *Self-Knowledge, Atma Bodha,* by Adi Shankaracharya, text and commentary translated by Swami Nikhilananda, published by Ramakrishna-Vivekananda Center, N.Y.

knowledge. Amma said another wonderful thing—once Lakshmi Devi comes to us as *Jnana Lakshmi*, She never leaves us. All the other Lakshmis come and go. It is so beautifully said! Once you get knowledge, ignorance is removed for ever.

Divine Mother holds the whole universe, the whole cosmos in Her hands. She sees everything that happens in the cosmos. So you don't have to tell Mother anything, She knows everything. And She has such a wonderfully compassionate heart, She tells Her children, "Lay all your *karma* load on my lap. Open your heart and let the wisdom come in and let the light shine."

Amma also said that Devi is:

Antara mukha samārādhyā bahir mukha sudurlabhā

She is attained by turning within through meditation and mental worship. Why? Because it is very difficult to see Her in the external world. So when you want to see this Divine Mother, you have to be perfectly pure. When you become pure, you see Her in your own heart. This is the absolute truth. Mother is the *atman,* the soul of everything. So pray to Divine Mother all the time, all the time. And when you ask for fire, Mother gives you water. Why? Because She knows what is good for you. If Her ignorant child unwittingly asks for fire, the compassionate Mother will *not* give her fire.

Amma also said that Mother is the sovereign of *srishti, sthiti* and *laya,* creation, preservation and destruction. But *laya* is really not destruction, it is re-absorption into Mother. The *atman* never dies. There is no *marana,* death, for the *atman*. It simply becomes one with the Divine Mother Herself. That is *laya.* Devi is the mother of all creation—She is the mother of Brahma, Vishnu and *Ishwara.*

Amma advises all of us to recite a *mantra* of our choice at least for a few minutes every day. If you want to recite the *Gayatri Mantra*, please do it. If you want to recite the *Aditya Hridayam,* that is okay. If you want to recite the *Bible*, that is also fine. Recite whatever you like, but you must do it every day.

Amma quoted a beautiful *shloka* from the *Bhagavad Gita:*

Vāsānsi jīrṇāni yathā vihāya navāni
gṛhṇāti naro parāṇī
Tathā śarīraṇi vihāya jīrṇān anyāni
sanyāti navāni dehī

"Just as a person discards old, worn out clothes and puts on new ones, the *atman* leaves the old and worn out body and takes a new body."

Why are you crying about this body? The body is mortal, the immortal *atman* must move on. So Mother said, "Wake up! You are in this body. This is a wonderful opportunity for you. Wake up! Remove all your selfishness and ego. Pray to Mother Divine, go beyond the body and attain enlightenment. Then you will become *Brahmatma svarupa*—you will yourself become *Brahman,* you will achieve the ultimate goal of human life! Once you have that realization, you become everything. You have no limitations at all."

So we must turn inward, purify ourselves and fill our hearts with divine light. In this world we need both *adhyatmic* nourishment, spiritual food for the soul, and *bhautic* nourishment, food for the body. But even more important than the literal knowledge of the great holy texts—be they the *Torah*, the *Bible, Koran* or the four *Vedas*—is *vishuddha bhakti.* "*Vishuddha*" means "the purest of the pure," and" "*bhakti* is "true devotion." So we need the purest of pure devotion and *antaranga prema.*

Prema is love—not human love but divine love, cosmic love. *Antaranga* means that it must come from the very bottom of your heart.

And here Amma said that when you pray to the Lord, no matter what form of God you pray to, do not put the flowers mechanically on the altar with your hand. Offer the inner flowers with deep love. Untie all the knots of negativity inside and bloom the lotuses of the *shad chakras*, the six *chakras*. These are the fully-blossomed flowers you must offer to Mother Divine with all the love in your heart. When you worship Her in this way, Mother will bless you with enlightenment! The *atman*, the soul, has no *marana,* it has no death. It eventually goes back to Mother and merges in Her.

And Amma said that the people of America are very fortunate, materially speaking. They do not have to worry about the daily necessities of life like many people in India. When you are free of such worries, you have a better chance to meditate. It doesn't matter where you live. All you need for meditation is a pure heart full of devotion. This whole world is one—it is *Vasudhaika kutumbam,* just one family. Children, do not see any distinctions whatsoever, such as the color of the skin, physical differences, or divergences in caste or creed.

At the end of Her beautiful discourse, Amma returned once again to *lalitya*, supreme tenderness and purity, with a an interesting story. There is a very holy place in Andhra Pradesh, South India, called Sri Sailam. There is a group of holy places there—Tirupati, Kala Hasti and Sri Sailam. There are some beautiful stories about Sri Sailam and Kala Hasti.

There is a poor boy who lives in a village near Sri Sailam. He goes to his mother—many Indian boys go to their mothers when they want something, not to their fathers—and says, "The summer holidays are here. All my friends are going away somewhere. Where do I go?"

The poor mother does not have much money. She looks at her son and replies, "You have an elder sister called *Bhramaramba*. She is the Goddess of Sri Sailam. Her husband Mallikarjuna is your brother-in-law. He is *Ishwara*, Lord Siva. Why don't you go to see them and bring them home? You will have a very nice summer holiday."

The poor boy believes what his mother says. So he sets out for Sri Sailam and finally reaches the town. He goes inside the temple and tells the priests, "I would like to talk to my sister and my brother-in-law." So they ask him, "Who are your sister and brother-in-law?" He innocently answers, "*Bhramarambika* and *Mallikarjuna*, *Ishwara* and Parvati Devi."

The priests don't know what to think. They point at the stone images of the deities in the temple and say, "That is your sister and that is your brother-in-law. Why don't you go and talk to them?"

And what Amma said here is wonderful! She said that when you pray—it doesn't matter whether you pray to a picture or a stone image or something in your mind—it is the feeling in your heart that matters. So this boy first goes to his brother-in-law, Sri Mallikarjuna and prays to Him, "Please show me Your form and come home with me." Nothing happens. He prays to his sister. Nothing happens. So he begins to beat his head at the feet of the image of *Bhramarambika Devi.* A few drops of blood stain the feet of *Bhramarambika Devi's* image.

And Amma said, "But you know, She is *Lalita*, the one who is soft and tender, serene and self-effulgent, the Divine Mother who gives everything Her children desire." She appears at once and embraces the boy. "Don't worry. My husband and I will both come with you."

There is deep meaning in this story. We pray to Devi in a woman's form because a mother's heart is infinitely tender. Amma ended Her discourse by saying that in this polluted *yuga* in which we live, *Kali yuga*, when we pray to Mother with a completely pure heart, She blesses us with salvation. There is no question about it, absolutely none at all. So pray with a beautiful, open heart, free of negativity, and salvation will be yours. *Jai Karunamayi*!

Amma: The conclusion of the story is very beautiful, beyond beautiful! Now let us all meditate for five minutes for universal peace.

Swamiji: Tomorrow Amma will be giving individual *darshan* and blessings to people.

One of the devotees who came for Amma's *darshan* and healing today was a doctor. I asked her, "You are a physician and you have been healing a lot of patients yourself—why have you come here?" She answered, "Amma is divine. We doctors can heal only physical ailments. But what about mental healing? So many of us need mental healing, which only Amma can give."

A little while ago Amma was saying that many people make the mistake of thinking that everyone who comes to the healing sessions comes for physical healing—relief from problems such as leg pains, back pains, or head pains, etc. But Amma found that most of the people who came to Her asked only for enlightenment and spiritual realization. Amma liked that very much. Throughout Her travels in this country, 99.9% of the people who came to see Her asked for spiritual richness and salvation only. That is what Amma likes, that is what Amma wants. That is what Amma's main message is about: We must know what to ask for. We have only to ask Divine Mother with a true heart, and whatever we ask for will be given to us!

Jai Karunamayi!

Chicago *17 May 1997*

ॐ

MEDITATE - MEDITATE ON MOTHER DIVINE

Dhyāyet padmāsanasthām vikasita vadanām
padma patrāyatākṣīm
Hemābhām pītavastrām karakalita lasad
hema padmām varāngīm
Sarvālankāra yuktām satatam abhayadām
bhaktanamrām Bhavānīm
Śrī Vidyām śānta mūrtīm sakala sura nutām
sarva sampad pradātrīm

Om praṇatānām prasīdasya
Devī viśvārti hāriṇī
Trailokya vāsinām iti
lokānām varadā bhavām

Embodiments of Divine Souls, Amma's Most Beloved Children,

In this beautiful *dhyana shloka,* it is said:

Dhyāyet Parāmambikām

The inner meaning of these words is, "Meditate on Mother Divine." *"Dhyayet,"* means "meditate." If we always live at the physical, external level, we can never attain Divinity and infinite joy in our life.

You know that Jesus is God, Rama is God and Krishna is God. During the lifetime of these divine ones, many had their *darshan,* but not all of them saw their divinity. When Sri Rama manifested on Earth, only a few people understood Him to be God. *"Jivan muktas"* means "enlightened souls." Rama's mother, *Kaushalya*, was an enlightened soul, and so were *Mantri Sumantra*, the prime minister, *Sumitra*, Sri Rama's stepmother, Shabari, Vasishtha and a few others. These people were always inward because of their inner beauty, silence and gentle behavior. They had great love for God and they believed the entire universe to be God only. They not only believed that Rama was God, but that Rama was everywhere, Rama was everything. So they understood the beauty of Divinity, and had attained true realization in their life. They were *jivan muktas*.

This happened not only in the lives of Jesus, Rama and Krishna, it happens in the lives of all holy people. Many of us have been blessed with the divine *darshan* of holy persons, but we also have so many black curtains of ignorance covering our hearts. We cannot understand the divinity in the Divine because of the curtains of the dark forces of selfishness, ignorance and innocence. Our ignorance is a kind of blindness, but when we meditate we gain purity and true vision.

Dhyāyet padmāsanasthām vikasita vadanām

At the surface level, these words mean: "Divine Mother is so beautiful, just like a fresh blooming lotus flower, and She is seated on the lotus." That is the literal meaning. But the inner meaning of *"dhyayet padmasanastham"* is: "Sit in the lotus posture and meditate." What happens when we meditate on Mother Divine like this? After some years of this meditation, we feel that the inner flowers are blooming. The cosmic flowers of the *chakras* bloom inside and we experience infinite joy within. This inner bliss is reflected in our smile, and our face also begins to bloom—that is the true meaning of *"vikasita vadanam"*—we are happy and we are always in peace. This smile is not an ordinary one—our inner peace is most naturally revealed in this smile.

Sometimes, in this world drama, we put on a mask and smile even when we are unhappy. That is a pretense, that is not *vikasita vadanam. Vikasita vadanam* means the blooming face that reveals infinite inner joy—the bliss of inner silence. That is the beauty of *vikasita vadanam.*

Padma patrāyatākṣīm

Here Divine Mother's eyes are described as lotus petals. In the middle of our forehead we have an eye, which is the third eye or the eye of knowledge. These words refer to that eye. When we open our third eye, the entire universe is seen as divine. Each and every cell of the universe is divine. That is the true experience of Divinity! We feel that each and every cell of this universe is nothing but Mother Divine. Mother Divine is truth, Mother Divine is wisdom, Mother Divine is attributeless. We *feel* this, and the experience fills us with joy—infinite joy that cannot be described in words.

Hemābhām

Mother Divine is effulgence. What is Her light like? It is self-luminous and beyond description. We can only enjoy that divine golden effulgence inside, and experience our soul as the light of billions and billions of suns. That is the true nature of our soul.

Hemābhām pītavastrām karakalita lasad
hema padmām varāngīm
Sarvālankāra yuktām satatam abhayadām
bhaktanamrām Bhavānīm

When a seeker attains divinity inside, he has so much humility and wisdom in his life. Humility is the greatest enemy of egoism. So when we meditate, the ego-curtains are burned by our devotion and purity, and we have wisdom. Then, like the *gopikas,* the milk-maids of Vrindavana, we are in peace in all the four stages of waking, dreaming, deep sleep and *samadhi.* We are naturally very peaceful. That is the stage of *jivan mukti.* A *"jivan mukta"* means "a liberated soul."

Some people say, "This one is not a *jivan mukta*, that one is not a *jivan mukta."* Let us understand the behavior of a true *jivan mukta.* His silence and love towards the world reflect his liberated state. There is no *karma* or bondage for a *jivan mukta.*

Śrī Vidyām śānta mūrtīm

So children, *"Shanta murtim"* means "embodiment of peace." Mother is *Shanta murtim.* She is the very embodiment of peace. You feel Her peace inside, outside, everywhere, all the time. If anyone scolds you, you never retaliate or behave in the same way. Because you understand that your body is only a cage—it is only flesh, blood and bones. This body is only a very limited mortal frame, it is not you. Your Self is divine; your Self is pure; your Self is ; your Self is transcendental bliss! You are pure , so you cannot respond in the same manner when someone shouts at you or insults you. Instead you love him and bless him. That is the beauty of spirituality. We have so much elevation and wisdom only in spirituality.

The opening *dhyana shlokas* of *Sri Lalita Sahasranama* begin with the words:

Dhyāyet padmāsanasthām....

"Meditate, meditate on Mother Divine"—these are the opening words of *Sri Lalita Sahasranama.* Only if it is our last birth will we be able to meditate on the Absolute. Pray to Mother, "Amma! Cut down all my unwanted bondages."

We bind ourselves to unnecessary things in this world. Mother loves Her creation; She feels great responsibility towards Her children. So Mother, with Her unseen hands, removes all our mental bondages—the dark forces of selfishness, ignorance and innocence. These are the qualities that cause bondage. Our first bondage is to our body; our second bondage is to our mind. We have billions of bondages because of the mind. So when we pray to Mother Divine, She cuts all the bondages with Her *khadga,* Her invincible scimitar. The unseen hands of Divine Mother remove all the bondages from your heart, and Mother gives you so much elevation in devotion. You have purity and humility in devotion only. So cultivate devotion. Pray to Mother and seek pure devotion. If you have *bhakti,* you have everything in your life. Devotion is the most important thing for a seeker. The *mantra, "Bhakti vashya, Bhayapaha,"* indicates that Mother can be won only by love, for She loves *bhakti* so much. *Bhakti* means pure devotion, not show devotion. When we attain true *bhakti*, Mother blesses us with many boons. The first boon is liberation from anger, which is a very bad quality.

Trividham narakasyedam dvāram nāśanamātmanaḥ

"There are three doors to hell." The first door is anger. We get angry about unnecessary things. Do not go to that door, babies—do not go through that door. The second door is lust, and the third door is greed and attachment—bondage. These are the three doors to hell. And there is only one door to salvation—selflessness. The little egoistic self should be less, less and less! Where there is self, everything is self-boosting only—everything is "I, me, my." There is no salvation at all. When we leave this egoistic self behind, we have so much peace, humility and wisdom in our life.

Mother is wisdom; Mother is divine; Mother is pure and Mother is supreme bliss. So how can we attain the highest purity of that blissful state? By going within—deeper and deeper inward in meditation.

Dhyāyet padmāsanasthām....

"When you meditate, sit in lotus posture." When we sit in meditation in the lotus posture like Lord Siva, all the *chakras* immediately begin to bloom. When we meditate on the *Gayatri Mantra, Saraswati Mantra, Om Mantra, Namah Sivaya Mantra, Narayana Mantra* or any other *mantra*, the powerful *bijaksharas* of these *mantras* make the *chakras* bloom inside.

Everything happens by Mother's wish alone. Only if Mother wishes, can you sit in meditation. If She wishes Her son to become a *yogi*, then immediately it happens. If She does not wish it, Her son becomes a worldly person, and remains entangled in worldly intoxication.

Mother's wish is supreme. So pray to Mother for wisdom. "Mother, grant me a grand inner life. I am suffering with so much poverty—poverty in devotion, wisdom, knowledge and peace. Give me pure love, pure wisdom and liberation. There is no peace of mind in this world. Peace of mind is to be found only in Your lotus feet. O Mother, bless me with health, wealth and everything auspicious."

Rogān aśeṣān apahamsi tuṣṭā
Ruṣṭā tu kāmān sakalān abhīṣṭān

If Mother wishes, immediately—within a fraction of a second—even the most dreadful disease can be cured. So pray to Her, "O Mother Divine, to whom can I go in this world? Grant me the great boon of peace. Grant me whatever You wish. You know more about me than I do. You know what I truly need."

So children, pray to Mother for pure devotion, inner purification and inner richness. That is very important. Yesterday we sang a song, a beautiful song, asking Mother for only one boon:

Brahmānandā Maṇidvipa vāsinī
Brahma jnāna sukhkam dehī

"I want only bliss, transcendental bliss. So my dear Mother, grant me the greatest boon of transcendental bliss."

There is a beautiful story about Vishvamitra. Have you heard about Vishvamitra, children? He was the *Guru* of Sri Rama. *"Vishva"* means "the universe," and *"mitra"* means "friend." So "Vishvamitra" means, "the universal friend."

Vishvamitra was a king. Once he went to Maharshi Vasishtha, a great sage, who was full of humility and inner beauty. He was a *Brahma jnani.* Sri Rama had two *Gurus*—Vishvamitra and Vasishtha. In Vasishtha's *ashram,* there was a cow called *Kamadhenu,* the wish-fulfilling cow. She was like a mother to Vasishtha.

Once, after a war, Vishvamitra went with his whole army to Vasishtha's *ashram.* At that time he thought, "How can this old sage feed all my men?" His thoughts were reckless and low. We also think about others in many negative ways due to the poverty in our hearts. If we had inner beauty we would not think about others in a low way even in a dream.

Vasishtha wanted to feed the whole army. As soon as this wish arose in his mind, countless beautiful golden plates, filled with many varieties of food preparations, suddenly appeared. Vishvamitra was a king, but even he had never tasted such delicious food. There was enough to feed the entire army! It was amazing.

Vishvamitra asked Vasishtha:

"Where did this food come from?"

"It came from my *Kamadhenu.*"

" Oh, I want that *Kamadhenu*."

This is greed. Vasishtha refused to give the *Kamadhenu* to Vishvamitra, and the king, due to his selfishness and ego, became very angry. He wanted to take the *Kamadhenu* from Vasishtha's *ashram* by force.

Immediately, an army larger than Vishvamitra's appeared from one of the hooves of the *Kamadhenu!* Vishvamitra was astonished. He bowed before Vasishtha Maharshi and begged for forgiveness.

"How did you get this power?" he asked.

"This is the power of *Brahma jnana*. I do not work miracles, this is *Brahma jnana shakti*."

"Brahma jnana? What is *Brahma jnana?*

"*Brahma jnana* means oneness with God."

"I want to know more about *Brahma jnana*. Please tell me."

"Go and sit in meditation."

"How should I meditate? With what *mantra?"*

"Just sit in meditation. If Mother wishes, She will come and give you the *mantra*. Why are you worrying about your *mantra*? That is Mother's responsibility, not yours. Go and sit in meditation."

Vishvamitra began to meditate, and he sat in meditation for four thousand years! First he meditated facing south, then facing west, and north and east—one thousand years in each direction. There were countless obstacles, but Vishvamitra remained unshaken, and after four thousand years he attained Self-Realization. Before he attained knowledge of the Self, many Gods and Goddesses appeared before him. Each of them said:

"O Vishvamitra, stop your meditation. What do you want? Do you want wealth? Gems? Gold? Or do you want a long life? I will grant you anything you desire."

But Vishvamitra never opened his eyes. He sat in meditation in absolute silence for thousands of years together. Then one day, Maha Lakshmi Devi appeared before him and said:

"O Vishvamitra, I will give you the entire wealth in the world."

"O Mother, I want nothing from You. I want only *Brahma jnana."*

Then Brahma came and said, "Vishvamitra, stop your meditation. Come with me to *Brahma loka.* I will make you the Creator. You can sit on my throne."

"No. The position of the Creator is very limited. I do not care about it. I want only *Brahma jnana."*

He continued his meditation. Vishnu, Lord Siva, even Mother Gayatri appeared before Vishvamitra. They all said to him, "Stop your meditation."

These were all tests. If a seeker still has body-consciousness, he stops his meditation. He thinks, "Brahma Himself is asking me to stop meditating, so I will stop." But Vishvamitra was a really great sage; he became the *Guru* of Sri Rama. Vishvamitra's steadiness in meditation is a lesson for us. It is a teaching for all mankind. There are many ups and downs in *sadhana,* and many obstacles come up during meditation. If we stop meditating, we can never attain *Brahma jnana.* If we practice meditation like Vishvamitra, no matter what obstacles we have to face, we will attain *Brahma jnana* like Vishvamitra.

In the end, Maha Gayatri Devi manifested before Vishvamitra and said, "Stop meditating. I will give you *Brahma jnana*."

Vishvamitra answered, "O Mother, why have You limited Yourself to this tiny form? I want to go beyond Your physical form. I do not want to merge with Your limited human form; I want to be one with You in the entire cosmos! I want to be in the oneness of *Brahma jnana.* So do not stop me, Mother, let me meditate."

Mother Gayatri disappeared. Vishvamitra meditated and meditated, this time facing the east. After four thousand years of meditation, he attained *Brahma jnana*. People lived for thousands of years in olden days. In this *Kali yuga*, even boys of five and six have body pains. Our bodies are not suited to meditation. We are afflicted by hunger, thirst, anger and many other limitations. The demons of so many bondages are inside. We are unable to sit in meditation. Meditation is the work of Siva, not of human beings.

So children, if it is our last birth, then only will we have the desire and enthusiasm for meditation. When Divine Mother graces you, you go into meditation spontaneously. It is all due to the grace of Mother Divine. So if Mother wishes Her babies to remain limited to this body cage, we are always entangled in worldly things. If Mother wishes us to be in the mind cage, we keep struggling with *tamasic* and *rajasic* thoughts. And if we have one more birth, we again limit ourselves to the very tiny atom of our intellect. We think, "I am very intelligent; I know everything. I have read so many books, I know the *Vedas.*" We are full of ego. Only when Mother wishes, can we go beyond these three cages and attain knowledge of the Spirit—Self-Realization—real purity and eternal inner bliss.

I really wish all of my children to be always in that highest, pure . Meditate, babies, meditate. Pray to God for purification and wisdom. Yesterday, too, Amma made the same point: Meditation is the greatest art—it remodels your entire life and leads you to the attainment of realization. It is a very beautiful art. We go inside in meditation and understand our greed, selfishness and ego. Finding faults in oneself is not sweet, but that is the meaning of self-inquiry. Only when we understand what is inside can we change and become wise. If we just chant *mantras* externally, we keep finding faults in others, "He's like this, she's like that."

When we meditate and go within, we never find faults in others. That is the beauty of spirituality.

So children, go inside. Meditate. And be always in eternal *dharma*. Be always in eternal *dharma*. *Dharma* is Mother Divine.

Ājnā cakrāntarālasthā Rudra granthi vibhedinī
Sahasrārāmbuja ārūḍhā sudhā sārābhivarṣiṇī

Our nervous system is full of nectar. When we meditate for several years, all this nectar goes to the *bindusthana* located in the *sahasrara* at the crown of the head. When the spiritual energy, *kundalini,* stabilizes in the *sahasrara,* we attain *samadhi*, and all the 72,000 *nadis,* subtle nerve channels in our body, are drenched with nectar. How beautiful it is! In all the stages of waking, dreaming and deep sleep, we feel the Divine everywhere, in each and every cell of the entire universe. Seeing God only in a picture, only in a temple, is the A-B-C-D stage, the kindergarten stage, of spirituality. It is not the Ph.D degree. Always seeing God in limited ways and saying, "Only this is God, only Amma is God, only my father is God," is very limited! *Sanatana Dharma* is limitless, boundless. In *Sanatana Dharma*, each and every *Guru* is the same. The sun is one, the moon is one, the Earth is one, air is one, fire is one, the *Veda* is one, Mother is one, mankind is one—everything is one. All divine persons are also one. There is no difference at all. All divine incarnations are one—Jesus, Rama and Buddha are all one—only one. If we see any difference between Rama, Buddha, Krishna and Jesus, it is very pathetic; it is not wisdom.

Some say, "Only Rama is God. Krishna is not. I don't like Krishna, I only love Rama." (Laughter) They have no wisdom. "I like only Devi, I don't like Siva." (More laughter) This kind of attitude is pathetic. Mother Divine is everything, so see Her in all the Gods, see Her in each and every atom of the universe—in the bad also. Due to lack of meditation, you are unable to understand this point. When you meditate regularly and attain *turiya,* the fourth state of *Brahma jnana sthiti*, then only will you understand my point. Only when you attain the highest peak of desirelessness and bliss, will this entire universe be seen like a transparent glass full of water—the universe is the glass and the water, divine. Similarly, this body is a transparent glass, and the water in it is Divinity!

Sanatana Dharma is beautiful, and there is so much wisdom in spirituality. Sometimes we limit ourselves and say, "I will pray only to Rama, I will sing only about Rama. I will never sing Krishna songs." Krishna is also Rama. God comes to us with many names and forms. We see differences because of our limited mind, but this is not wisdom. Amma says again and again, "Be in wisdom, taste wisdom, understand wisdom, feel wisdom—wisdom, wisdom, wisdom!" Where there is *dharma*, there only is wisdom. If we never follow *dharma*, we limit ourselves and we have no wisdom at all. Our mind is always working through the three attributes—*tamas, rajas* and *sattva.* We are caught in the never-ending cycle of birth and death. If even one thought remains in our heart, it becomes the seed for one more birth.

Through all our innumerable births—billions into billions of births—from the fifth to the sixtieth year, twenty-five thousand million thoughts arise in the mind. How can we get rid of all these thoughts? Only by the fires of devotion and meditation. *Yoga* is the greatest fire. When we sit in meditation, tremendous spiritual energy is generated in the body. This energy travels through all the *chakras* and opens them. Only in Indian culture, the ancient *rishis*—completely purified by meditation—actually saw with their inner eye how the *kundalini shakti* passes through all the *chakras* and reaches the *sahasrara.* When this happens, the seeker atttains Self-Realization. This knowledge is not to be found in any other culture in the world. Yes, this is the truth.

So children, you are meditators; you have so much devotion, purity and humility inside. Amma wishes all of her children to elevate more and more, and expand more and more—that is Amma's wish. This is possible through pure devotion and regular meditation only. So be in silence and meditate daily.

Meditate with your *mantra* for five minutes, then sit in silence for five minutes. If the mind begins to wander, repeat your *mantra* again for five minutes. If the mind is in peace and silence, do not chant the *mantra* mentally—remain in silence. If the mind starts thinking about worldly things, silence it with the vibrations of your *mantra.* Meditate with your *mantra*. The power of the *mantra* burns the impurities in our heart; it burns all thoughts. Mind is nothing but a bundle of thoughts. When we sit in meditation, innumerable thoughts arise from the *chid agni kunda* of the mind. Burn all these impurities by the power of the seed letters of your *mantra*. Meditate with your own *mantra*, whatever it may be.

Mantra is really not secret. In India, everyone knows the *Gayatri Mantra*, *Rama Mantra, Siva Mantra*, *Vishnu Mantra*, *Narayana Mantra*—so many *mantras*. Here people think that there are many limitations and that *mantras* are very secret. The *mantra* is not secret—the secret is inside: Awaken the *kundalini*, open the heart—that is the secret. Opening the heart with regular meditation is the secret. *Mantra* is not secret! Yes, this is the truth, one hundred percent the truth. If *mantras* were secret, how could they print the *Gayatri Mantra* in books? We have so many books about the sacred *Gayatri Mantra*. And all the *mantras,* innumerable *mantras* are to be found in the *Vedas*.

The secret of *mantra* is to open our heart, understand the truth, and attain wisdom—that is the secret.

How should we practice? Keep your practice secret, practice in silence. Meditate early in the morning; do not make a show of your meditation. Do not show your devotion to anyone except God. That must be secret. *Sri Lalita Sahasranama* is called the *"rahasya sahasranama,"* the "secret *sahasranama." "Rahasya"* means "secret." The title itself says that it is secret. "Secret" here means "the essence is inside." The essence of each name of Devi is Self-Realization. The main aim of our human life is Self-Realization only. The Self is always in you, within you!

So children, go beyond the three cages of body, mind and limited intellect, attain inner purity and Self-Realization. That is the secret. That is the essence of *Sri Lalita Sahasranama.* Each and every beautiful *mantra,* each divine name, teaches oneness with Mother Divine, only oneness! This body is not your self, it is Mother, Mother, Mother! *Sri Lalita Sahasranama* tells us, "This mind is not your self, this intellect is not your self—everything is Mother, Mother, Mother!"

Jāgrat svapna suṣuptinām sākṣi bhūtyainamo namaḥ

"In all the stages of consciousness there is only *sakshi,* one witness—that witness is the Self." How beautifully it has been said:

Antara mukha jana ānanda phaladāyinyai namo namaḥ

Antara mukha jana, knowledge attained by turning within. When a seeker meditates by going inward, then only does he understand the true aim of life and enjoy infinite bliss. That is the meaning of this beautiful *mantra*. Many different meanings of this *mantra* are given in books—external meanings, only the literal meanings. Because of our mental level, we cannot understand the true inner meanings. The *Vedas* and *Upanishads* are very high. The wisdom contained in these sacred scriptures can be understood only by one who meditates. Only by regular spiritual practices, meditation and devotion are the high truths of the *Vedas* and *Upanishads* revealed and true wisdom attained. When we limit ourselves with ideas such as, "I like Rama only, I like Krishna only," it is very, very pathetic.

So children, think for yourselves and try to summarize all Amma's points. Sit in the court of your heart and be the judge. Give the right judgment. Live in *dharma* and listen to the decision of your heart. Do not listen to my words; do not be influenced by the *Vedas* also. Listen only to your own heart. Live your life according to the decision of your heart—that is beautiful!

Pray to Mother Divine with tears, from the bottom of your heart. Pray for purification. Bother Mother again and again for the boons of humility, equal vision, forgiveness, compassion, detachment, discrimination, knowledge and peace. Pray for inner beauty and oneness with Mother Divine. Bother Her, and pray to Her with tears wherever you go, feeling Her presence everywhere. Whether you pray in your home, in a church or temple, in the presence of holy people—even when you pray while driving—always pray with intense devotion. In Amma's presence you have so much humility, and outside you behave in another way. (Laughter) That is not *dharma*. Feel the Divine everywhere. That is *dharma*, eternal *dharma*.

Dharma is very, very powerful. Without faith, without *dharma*, all of our prayers are powerless, powerless, a thousand times powerless! So babies, pray—pray for *dharma*, stand for *dharma*, live for *dharma*, live in *dharma*, let eternal *dharma* only lead your entire life. That is beautiful. Without *dharma*, life is billions of times meaningless, meaningless, meaningless! We live just for eating, walking, talking and for earning some meaningless paper money. When we pray to God for purification, immediately our ego is burned by the power of five minutes of sincere prayer. If our prayer is real, the sins of innumerable births are burned immediately, because prayer is very, very powerful. Pray in silence, "Mother, grant me true knowledge and understanding about Yourself. I am always caught in this egoistic self, so give me liberation from anger, weakness and jealousy, and give me purity. I surrender to You completely. Please lead me to the eternal *dharma*, Mother!"

So divinize your thoughts, children, divinize your thoughts. Our world is so beautiful; the entire universe is very beautiful. But because of our thoughts we pollute this beautiful universe. The great sages of *vedic* times knew about the pollution of *Kali yuga*. That is why it has been said in the first canto of the *Rig Veda,* "Let noble thoughts come to us from every side"–noble thoughts, always noble thoughts, not negative thoughts.

So if any negativity comes into your mind, burn it immediately with your *mantra*. Chant your *mantra* mentally and pray to Mother Divine, "Mother, please remove this weed immediately from my heart. Help me, for I cannot do it alone. You have thousands and thousands of hands, Mother, I have only two. What can I do?"

Mother is beyond everything. If you really want to see Mother, you must also go beyond the cages of body, mind and intellect. Mother is *Premamayi*—She loves the whole cosmos. So if you want to see Mother, have at least a little cosmic love in your heart. She is full of love, so at least have a tiny atom of love in your heart. Mother is *Vedamayi,* so learn at least one *mantra*—chant only *Om*. *Om* is Mother

Divine. At the beginning of our program, we chanted the *Om Mantra* nine times. The essence of all the *Vedas* is *Om*. When we say *Om* once, it is like reading all the four *Vedas*. And when we pray to Mother Divine by chanting the *Om Mantra* nine times, it is equal to chanting all the *Vedas* nine times!

Children, in the diary of your life, forty-five, sixty, seventy pages are already over—only a few pages are left. Utilize these pages by writing good things only, not unnecessary things. Okay? Amma wishes all of her children to be always in pure—that is Amma's only wish.

Hari Om Tat Sat!

(Amma addresses the Telugu-speaking people in the audience. The gist of Her talk is given below as translated by Swamiji.)

Jai Karunamayi! Many people in India perform *Sri Lalita Sahasranama puja.* The chanting of the *stotra* is different to the *puja*, or worship. The *puja* is called the *namavali,* in which each one of the thousand names of Divine Mother is chanted with *namah*, and with each name, a flower, a little *kumkum* (red powder), or *turmeric* (yellow powder) is offered at the lotus feet of Divine Mother. The *Lalita Sahasranama Namavali puja* is said to be the highest and the most auspicious worship for Mother Divine. It takes nearly one and a half to two hours to complete. External purity is very important for this *puja.* One should take a bath and wear fresh clothes. A red silk sari is auspicious for this worship. Only one with great merit from previous births will be able to perform this *puja* of the divine lotus feet of Divine Mother.

A large *mandir,* temple, is coming up in the Penusila Ashram in India. Penusila is situated in Andhra Pradesh, a southern state in India, which is very close to the temple town of Tirupati. This *ashram* is deep in the forest. The whole area is very beautiful, and a great inspirational center for *Bharata Mata* is also being built there. This temple of Mother India will give spiritual inspiration to the entire world. A *vedic* school will be started there. The building will have two floors, with a large hall where a thousand people can sit at a time and meditate. And that hall will be called *Sampurna Prajna,* complete supreme knowledge.

It will have a temple of *Sri Lalita Parameshwari,* the supreme Goddess. The images of Lakshmi Devi, the Goddess of prosperity, and Maha Saraswati Devi, the Goddess of knowledge, will also be installed in the temple. As of now, fifty percent of the construction has been completed, and the architectural work is proceeding well.

You will be surprised to know that the entire foundation of this massive construction has been filled with *kumkum* and *turmeric,* not sand as is usual in India. Do you know from where all the tons and tons of *kumkum* and *turmeric* came? Innumerable devotees in India who performed *Sri Lalita Sahasranama puja* packed the auspicious powders after the *puja* was over, and sent the bags to the *ashram.* In this way we received tons and tons of *kumkum* and *turmeric,* and all this powder has been poured into the basement. Try to imagine how strong the vibrations of all this auspicious powder from so many *pujas* must be! No other temple has this kind of foundation. It was Amma's idea to utilize in this way all the *kumkum* that thousands of men and women had sanctified by their *pujas* all over India for years together.

So all this sacred powder was poured into the basement, which is nearly fifteen feet deep. The powder was pressed down, and water poured on it to make it settle down firmly. So can you imagine how much *kumkum* was used? The vibrations of *kumkum* from *Sri Lalita Sahasranama puja* are extremely powerful because each and every pinch of the vermilion powder is saturated with the energy of Devi's divine name! Anyone who sits in that hall will feel those pure vibrations and will immediately be filled with peace and bliss.

It has been beautifully said in the *Vedas*, "Where woman is respected, there reside all the Gods and Goddesses." This is a very great saying in India. That is why women are respected so much in India. Without respect for women, there is no world at all.

Yatra nāryantu pūjyante tatra ramante Devatāḥ

" *Naryantu*" means "women." *"Pujyante,"* means, "they are respected." *"Puja"* here means "respect," not worship, not physical worship. Except for your wife, you must respect all women like your sisters or mothers. That is very important.

In India, women are not addressed by their given name—the word "Amma" is added to their name. "Amma" means "mother." For example, if a woman's name is Kamala, she will be addressed as Kamalamma. They add "Amma" as a sign of respect, for they see her as an embodiment of Divine Mother Herself.

Wherever Amma travels, She has been inspiring people to perform the great *Lalita Sahasranama puja.* Now thousands and thousands of people are doing it. Soon, halls will not be large enough to hold all the devotees—people will have to sit in open places, such as school playgrounds or under huge tents. One devotee will chant the thousand names of Mother Divine, and thousands of people will do the *puja.*

Sri Lalita Sahasranama Namavali worship not only purifies the place where the *puja* is performed, but the entire Earth is blessed with prosperity. The whole universe is enriched with peace and prosperity by the powerful vibrations of this divine *stotra.*

As said before, only if one has performed great merits can one recite or perform the worship of *Lalita Parameshwari.* Women have great will power, *sankalpa shakti.* They should utilize it in the right manner for a great cause—the elevation of all.

It is very important to develop inner vision. One should be able to see divinity everywhere. Seeing divinity only in the good is not great at all, we have to see divinity in the bad also. We must have equal vision—we must see goodness not only in the good, but in everything. This can be achieved when we practice meditation.

Divine Mother does not always reside in the *muladhara chakra.* The *muladhara* is the root *chakra* at the base of the spine. Mother, as *kundalini* energy, ascends to the *svadhishthana,* the second *chakra* and then comes to the *manipura chakra* at the navel. When the spiritual energy, *kundalini*, awakens the *manipura chakra*, the seeker begins to glow like a gem glittering with inner radiance. When the *kundalini* reaches the *anahata chakra*, the heart center, the seeker experiences inner silence. He does not speak, he is constantly absorbed in the peace and bliss of silence. Just above the *anahata chakra* is the *vishuddhi chakra* at the throat. When the *sadhaka* reaches that stage, he always speaks the truth. Whatever he says becomes a *Veda vakya,* the word of the *Veda*. That is why, whenever we go to spiritual people, we sit silently for several hours, just listening to their words, because whatever they speak is the *Veda.* It is Truth; it is the absolute Truth, because the holy ones are always immersed in supreme .

Kalidasa was the greatest poet of all time. In his youth, he was known as *Kaliya.* He was a very innocent and ignorant man before he became a great poet. He was married to a queen, who was a devotee of Divine Mother. Due to fate, she had to marry the uneducated and ignorant Kaliya. She was very worried and prayed to Mother for Her grace. Divine Mother, full of radiance, immediately appeared before her. Her jewelled crown was decorated with the glowing crescent moon. From that *chandra kala*, the soft rays of the moon, came forth *Ayim*, *Srim* and *Hrim,* the sacred *bijaksharas* of the *Saraswati Mantra,* and entered into the body of *Kaliya*. In this way Kaliya received the blessing of the greatest knowledge of Maha Saraswati Devi from Divine Mother. He then became the world-famous poet, the *maha kavi,* great poet, who wrote timeless classics like *Abhijnana Shakuntalam*, and *Megha Sandesham* and *Kumara Sambhavam.* These are the greatest works of poetry written by any poet in the world.

There is another incident about Kalidasa. In the city of Ujjaini, the Divine Mother is worshipped in the form of *Kalika Devi*. Kalidasa used to go every morning to worship the Divine Mother in Her temple. One day—it happened to be his birthday—he wanted to compose a *stotra* glorifying Divine Mother. It was *Brahmi muhurta,* 3 a.m. In India, many spiritual seekers get up at 3 a.m. to meditate. *Brahmi muhurta* is from 3:30 to 4:30 a.m., and is the best time for meditation.

Kalidasa went to the temple at 3 a.m. and began to write on his palm leaves. There was only a small oil lamp for light. He got some inspiration about Divine Mother, and visualizing Her inner beauty, he began to write a *shloka*.

Just then, a strong gust of wind blew out the lamp. So he asked his mother, who had accompanied him, to bring another lamp. She brought one and kept it beside him. But the same thing happened—once again the lamp went out because of the strong wind. He became impatient and angry, and ordered his mother in a harsh voice to bring a big lamp. His mother immediately went back and brought a big, wooden torch of light. On her return, she was astonished to see Kalika Devi Herself standing beside Kalidasa, holding a light for him! Kalidasa was totally absorbed in writing his poem, oblivious of the presence of his beloved Deity!

This is how Mother Divine is captured by the deep devotion of Her sincere devotee!

Hari Om Tat Sat!

New York *18 May 1997*

ॐ

LIVE YOUR LIFE IN DHARMA

Embodiments of Divine Souls, Amma's Most Beloved Children,

Be always in *dharma.* Attain wisdom by the practice of *dharma*. Cultivate *dharma* in your life—without *dharma*, life is useless. *"Satyam"* means "Truth," *"sama drishti"* is "equal vision," *"pavitrata"* is "purity" and *"jnana"* is "wisdom." We need all these in our life, and we can get them only through *dharma.*

So children, give *dharma* the opportunity to rule your entire life. When we have *dharma* in our life, we have everything. *Dharma* alone can stand in this world without any support. Yes, *dharma* is Truth, *dharma* is wisdom, *dharma* is beauty, *dharma* is the light of all lights! *Dharma* only rules this entire universe—not only this universe, it rules the entire cosmos! Without *dharma*, there is no existence.

So be always in *dharma*. You are already on the spiritual path. You already have devotion and purity. But you need to cultivate even more devotion and purity to attain wisdom in your life. So meditate—spend at least three or four hours daily in meditation. We have twenty-four hours in a day, so spend two hours in the morning and two in the evening in meditation.

Meditation is the greatest of arts. It removes all the impurity in our life and gives us a wonderful connection to *dharma*. Actually, meditation is nothing but inner purification. In meditation we feel deep and pure devotion, and our heart is filled with divine love—cosmic love. We feel, "O, Mother is always in my heart!" Everything is dust compared to devotion. Money, name, fame—we never expect anything from this world. Our whole heart, our whole life, is filled with joy—infinite joy! We feel bliss and dwell in eternal peace.

So meditate, children. Meditate on the Truth. Keep your own belief and walk your own path, but be in *dharma*—that is important. All the *mantras*—the *Saraswati Mantra,* the *Gayatri Mantra,* the *Jesus*, *Rama*, *Krishna* or *Buddha Mantras*—they are all the same! All true *Gurus* are one. The sun is one, the moon is one, the Earth is one; air, water and fire are one, mankind is one—everything is one—and God is also one!

Ekameva advitīyam Brahma nānyad asti akincanaḥ

When you meditate and go beyond the cages of the body, mind and intellect, you attain *samadhi. "Samadhi"* means "equal vision, wisdom and the experience of oneness—*Ekam eva advityam Brahma."* There is no secondness at all, only oneness, oneness, oneness! The individual personality merges with the universal Personality—that is *dharma.* You can go beyond these three cages only through deep meditation, not surface meditation. If we sit in meditation for just five or ten minutes, the fire of that meditation is not enough to burn all the impurities within. There are so many fires in our life: Anger is one kind of fire, hunger is also one sort of fire, and *yogagni,* the fire of *yoga*, is a very powerful fire.

Pure devotion is a great fire. Purify each and every cell of your body with *yogagni,* the pure fire of devotion. *Yogagni* and *atmagni,* spiritual fire, beautify your inner life. So burn all the impurities in your heart by the pure and tender fire of devotion. *"Lalitambika"* means "the tender Mother." In the *Lalita Sahasranama,* Devi's Thousand Names, the first name is *Sri Mata*, and the last one is *Lalitambika.* Every child knows about his own mother. Every Mother-loving seeker feels that all nature is his mother. Mother is in the stars, Mother is in the earth, Mother is in the air, in fire, in water, in the whole universe, in the entire cosmos! Mother is in all mankind. Mother is Truth. Only in the purest and deepest devotion that wells up from the bottom of our heart can we touch and experience Truth. Compared to that experience of oneness, everything in this world is tasteless. This worldly intoxication is completely tasteless—millions and millions and billions of times meaningless! When we attain Truth, we understand the play of *maya. Maya* is very subtle. So children, you are already on a divine path. Continue on your path, have your own belief, pray to your own God and your own *Guru* and meditate.

There is a beautiful *bhajan:*

Mānasa bhajare Guru caraṇam

"Place your *Guru's* lotus feet in your heart lotus."

Devī caraṇam praṇamāmyaham

Try to imagine Divine Mother's feet in your heart. We have so many beautiful cosmic flowers inside— the *muladhara* lotus, the *svadhishthana* lotus, the *manipura* lotus, the *anahata* lotus, the *vishuddhi* lotus and the beautiful *ajna chakra* lotus. The final lotus is the *sahasrara,* the thousand-petalled universal lotus. So imagine Divine Mother's feet always inside.

Devī caraṇam praṇamāmyaham

The entire cosmos is under Mother's divine feet, so She is beyond everything. Mother is beyond the *Vedas,* beyond imagination, beyond every rule and beyond everything in the world!

Only by pure devotion and deep meditation can you attain Self-Realization. The main aim of human life is realization—realization of the Self. Your Self is oneness, your Self is Truth, your Self is wisdom and purity, your Self is benediction, your Self is infinite, transcendental bliss—your Self is everything! So children, attain that Self. Pray to God for purification. Always pray to God. Sit alone in your room when you pray. And your prayer must not come from your lips—it must come from the bottom of your heart. Then only will Mother accept it immediately, for She is always here—inside the heart.

Avoid lip-prayer, avoid lip-*Vedanta,* avoid lip-service. Be a true *sadhaka,* a seeker who does his *sadhana* regularly. Yes, that is the essence of the *Vedas* and *Upanishads*—regular spiritual practice. The *Vedas* are beautiful, but practice is greater. You must practice meditation with intense desire for liberation. Intensity in *sadhana* is extremely important. Not surface meditation, not surface devotion, we need deep devotion, deep meditation, and an intense desire—from the bottom of our heart—for the attainment of Truth. So sit alone and pray to God with tender devotion. Mother's name is *Lalita,* for She is very tender. In the *muladhara chakra,* the movements of *kundalini* are ever so tender—not noisy or rough, but very soft. When *kundalini* is awake in the root *chakra,* our every feeling, every emotion, every word and every movement becomes tender. So offer Mother all the fragrant inner flowers—all the seven divine lotuses of the seven *chakras.* Bloom the inner flowers with one hundred percent pure devotion and offer your entire life to Mother Divine. Sacrifice everything for Mother Divine!

Stay as you are, wear your normal clothes, keep your own hairstyle, live in your own home, but be not attached to worldly things. Be always in pure devotion and be a real *yogi* inside. Be like a great swan inside—that is important.

Mother is inside; She can see what is in your heart. So children, elevate and expand. The nature of the *atman* is elevation and expansion only. Pure devotion enriches your life. In devotion you understand real bliss and experience the sweet taste of Truth. Experience is not imagination. You must *experience* oneness with Mother Divine—oneness, no secondness at all. That is very beautiful! There is a beautiful song:

Brahmā Viṣṇu Maheśwara jananī Devī Bhavānī

"Bhavani" means "She is both the creator and the destroyer of illusion."

Brahmā Viṣṇu Maheśwara jananī

"Devi is the mother of Brahma, the Creator, Vishnu, the preserver, and also Lord Siva, the destroyer."

She is *Siva Keshavadi Janani.* She is the mother of Siva and Keshava, Lord Krishna, the incarnation of Sri Vishnu. Her address is *Brahmananda Manidwipa*—the blissful Isle of Gems. *"Manidwipa"* means "the *Sri Chakra."* The *bindusthana* is the central point of the *Sri Chakra,* so that point is *Brahmananda*—eternal, supreme bliss. *"Brahmananda"* means "transcendental bliss." The devotee prays to Mother Divine for *Brahma jnana sukham,* the eternal supreme bliss of the knowledge of the Self, the experience of the oneness of the divine Consciousness within. *"Brahmananda sukham"* is "the joy of the supreme bliss of Consciousness." So *Brahmananda sukham* and *Brahma jnana sukham* are the same. Children, make only this *one* beautiful application to Mother Divine:

Brahmā Viṣṇu Maheśwara jananī
Devī Bhavānī
Brahmānandā Maṇidvipa vāsini
Devī Bhavānī
Brahma jnāna sukhkam dehī
Brahmānanda sukham dehī
Devī Bhavānī Lalitā Bhavānī

Divine Mother *Lalitambika* is beyond everything—beyond the *Vedas,* beyond Brahma, beyond Vishnu and Maheshwara. Mother Divine is the mother of everyone in the universe! So when you pray to Mother, your heart is filled with Divine Mother's love. Pray to Mother for desirelessness. Sit on the highest peak of desirelessnesss; then only will you have liberation from all the six inner weeds. Remove these six weeds from the garden of your heart. If you cannot do it, let Amma vacuum all the weeds for you. Amma can vacuum all the weeds from the entire universe!

There is a beautiful tree inside—the cosmic tree of Truth. The six weeds cover this cosmic tree. They are very small weeds but we give them so much importance. Not only in this birth, through innumerable births we have been only in the intoxication of greed, jealousy, money, name and fame—very meaningless things, meaningless as dust. We carry so much dust, so much *karma* load on our shoulders. So let Amma vacuum all the weeds from your heart, and remove all your *karma* load. Elevate yourself to the Truth and touch the cosmos by practicing regular meditation. And with the pure fire of devotion elevate and expand yourself. That is Amma's expectation for all her children.

My children, why are you caught in this *maya?* Oh, it is very sad—again and again, in every birth—being always entangled in *maya.* Go beyond this *maya!*

So children, how can we remove these weeds and be free of *maya?* Pray to Mother Divine from the bottom of your heart with one hundred percent faith and devotion. Pray to Mother for *Brahmananda sukham*—the transcendental bliss of pure Consciousness. And surrender, surrender, surrender completely to Mother! You need one hundred percent discriminative faith and mental detachment. Love *everyone* in the universe. Love them all as much as you love Divine Mother—love them *more* than Divine Mother. But always have mental detachment. Mental detachment alone brings peace inside. Without peace, life has no meaning. We need peace; the fragrance of peace is wisdom.

Children, open the doors of your heart. Kill the egoism inside. If that is not possible for you, try to cultivate humility, for humility is the greatest enemy of egoism. Let *dharma* alone rule your entire life. Where there is *dharma*, there only is detachment. Where there is detachment, there only is peace. Where there is peace, there only is wisdom. You get liberation from all the six weeds. If the six weeds are still inside, you can never attain salvation.

It is said in the *Bhagavad Gita:*

Trividham narakasyedam dvāram nāśanam ātmanaḥ

Desire, anger and greed are the doors to hell. Devotion, dedication, detachment, inner beauty and equal vision are the doors to bliss. So where are you, children? Do not miss your exit! If you miss your exit, you miss everything. You may have to go back and travel several hundred miles to get back on the correct road. So careful, be very careful.

Already for forty, fifty, sixty or seventy years we have been in this worldly intoxication. So children, do not waste any more time. Be a pure devotee, a true seeker, a real aspirant. Be like a pure swan in your inner life. Keep your devotion in your heart—do not show it outside. Show-devotion is not sweet; inner devotion is much sweeter. We feel humble and peaceful in the presence of pure devotees—their presence fills us with cosmic love. When we are with people whose devotion is only external, we feel disturbed and restless. So children, practice humility and cultivate pure devotion. We need pure devotion—pure, pure, pure *bhakti.* Pray to Mother Divine for pure devotion. "Mother, my devotion is not pure, that is why I am full of so many impurities. I still have anger and countless desires. I have meditated thirty or forty years, but I am still full of ego. I am so proud. I think, "I am this, I am that," and because of my pride I have never been able to touch You. Yet You are always in my heart, You are always within me."

Where can Mother go? She is always, always and always within you—always! But you cannot see Her because of all the black curtains of ego inside. So burn all these curtains with the fire of pure devotion. Pray to Mother with pure devotion, one hundred percent devotion. This prayer must not be for the fulfillment of any desires; it should be for liberation and salvation only. See Shabari in the *Ramayana.* She is waiting and waiting and waiting for Sri Rama throughout her life. When Lord Rama finally comes to Shabari, she never asks for any material things. She prays to Sri Rama only for salvation from the body. She is already liberated from the ego and has no desires at all. She just asks for liberation from the body. "Grant me *moksha,* O Lord! This body is a great burden for me. Please give me liberation!" There is so much beauty in her prayer!

Children, you know all these points. Amma is once again summarizing them with her babies. Turn within and meditate. Go *inside*. Only a seeker with inner vision is able to understand the Reality. The world is full of real and unreal things. By our purity and inner beauty, with *viveka,* discrimination, we understand the difference between the real and unreal—what is good for us and what is unnecessary for us. Then we avoid all useless things. Why do we give so much importance to meaningless things in our life? This life is very short, but it is a boon from God! Because of your prayers and the good *samskaras* of innumerable previous births you have been born in this human body. You have been blessed with devotion for God from the beginning of your life. This is not given to everyone. Amma never gives devotion to anyone! You have to earn the devotion in your heart. So elevate yourself, go beyond the body. We are always thinking about this body, so how can we get liberation from the six inner weeds?

The mind is always on three levels: *sattva, rajas* and *tamas.* You must go beyond these three levels and attain Self-Realization in deep meditation. Mother can only be understood in deep meditation, not surface meditation:

Antara mukha samārādhyā bahir mukha sudurlabhā

In the thousand names of Devi in *Sri Lalita Sahasranama,* Divine Mother has been described like this: "O Mother, only one who meditates inside is able to understand Your Self and Your beauty. You are beyond all beauties, even beyond motherly love, so we cannot understand Your divinity by reading books or listening to discourses. When our mind is external, we can never understand Your reality or Your sweetness. When we go deeper and deeper within we can taste a tiny atom of Your sweetness in inner bliss." That is enough for a seeker.

So children, Mother is always with you—always, always, always! Open your heart, invite Divine Mother inside and merge with your Mother. Merge your individual personality in Her universal Personality. Oneness with Mother is the essence of all the thousand names of Mother Divine in *Sri Lalita Sahasranama.* Feel Mother always *inside.* When you experience Mother inside, you have peace, you have wisdom, you have bliss—you have everything. Mother is in the physical body in the form of *kundalini.*

We are influenced by so many dark forces: we like money, we like name and fame, we are always running after worldly things—*meaningless worldly things.* We are caught in *maya,* entangled again and again in *maya.* When Mother opens your third eye and gives you *brahmic* awareness, you have everything. You have wisdom, you have purity and all the divine attributes bloom in your heart without your consciousness. This happens only through pure devotion. That is why Amma reminds you again and again: "Have devotion, devotion, devotion—not show devotion, but pure devotion." Keep your own belief, pray to your own God, pray to your own *Guru,* continue on your own path. But cultivate more and more purity and devotion.

This world is really beautiful, but the soul is much more beautiful, and still more beautiful is divine bliss. So children, taste that bliss, taste that transcendental bliss! So many great sages and pure devotees attained Self-Realization by their pure devotion. The path is long and the goal distant, but do not feel, "Oh, I am alone." Amma is always with you. Unseen, Amma's hands embrace this entire cosmos! Open your third eye and see Her.

Children, embrace true spirituality. Love all beings, not only your friends and relations. Embrace the real spirituality in your life—that is important. Open your heart, open your third eye and see the beauty of Mother Divine in each and every cell of the universe—Mother is everywhere! She is in past, present and future, in wisdom, in Truth, in equal vision, in purity, in good and bad. She is in churches, mosques and temples, in human beings, in all living beings, in oceans and mountains. The entire cosmos is filled with Her divine bliss! Taste that nectar, enjoy it, and attain realization by your pure devotion and detachment.

When you have detachment, you have peace, no doubt about it at all. In peace only you feel divinity inside; so do not go and search for divinity outside. First see divinity in yourself, and then you will be able to see divinity in each and every cell of this universe, filled with the love of Mother Divine only. With cosmic love, conquer this entire universe. Have pure, cosmic love in your heart; cultivate pure devotion by discriminating faith. Daily practice meditation, always be honest and lead a moral life. Go beyond all immoral tendencies. The body is mortal, but when you meditate, you attain immortality.

Remember, children, meditation is only a path, it is not the destination. *Omkara,* the *svasvarupa,* the oneness of *Brahma jnana,* the eternal bliss, pure Consciousness, indestructible Divinity, the Absolute, can only be attained in Self-Realization through meditation. *Dhyana yoga, karma yoga, bhakti yoga,* and *jnana yoga* are only paths—they are not the ultimate goal. So understand the Truth by opening your third eye. Ask Mother, bother Her, sit on Her head and do not ask Her for candies and for limited things. Ask Her only for *Brahma jnana.*

Your mind has been deceiving you for innumerable births. It is your first enemy. So send the mind immediately and permanently from your life. Do not invite it again and again into your life. Renounce all limited thoughts—"I am very intelligent; I am very capable," etc. Such thoughts are sad and pathetic. Give them up completely. Only Divinity is working in the body—this body is a temple for Mother Divine, a sacred temple. It has four pillars—truth, wisdom, *dharma* and love. The entrance gate of this temple is selfless service. In selfless service, we never expect anything from anyone.

We are mad about worthless paper money and meaningless name and fame. But remember, children, you are *soul*, you are great! You are everything—everything is your Self only. Do not think, "I am a *vedic pundit,"*—this is pathetic. You are *not a vedic pundit!* You are Soul, you are *Brahman,* your Self is Truth, your Self is indestructible power, your Self is divinity, your Self is the source of all energy, your Self is *Veda,* your Self is the light of all lights! What is *not* your Self? Your Self is wisdom, your Self is everything in the universe! But we keep limiting ourselves: "I am a professor," "I am a great artist," "I am a wonderful mother." We have these limited feelings because of our ignorance and our identification with this mortal frame. Go beyond this mortal frame, children! You have been in ignorance and illusion for billions of births. This is very sad. Go beyond everything and attain the Ultimate. That is the final goal of meditation, the essence of the *Vedas*, the essence of *Sri Lalita Sahasranama,* the essence of the *Bible,* the essence of all scriptures. God is infinite, so children, experience that infinity.

Suppose we want to visit some beautiful gardens. A map may show us how to get there. It may also indicate that there is a beautiful lotus pond, a lovely rose garden and a great fish aquarium in the gardens. But can we experience the beauty of these things simply by looking at the map? If we really wish to enjoy all the things in the gardens, we have to visit the gardens and see them for ourselves. In the same way, reading books about spirituality is like looking at a map. No book can ever give you the experience of divine bliss.

You limit yourself when you feel, "Only this is my God; only this is my belief. I will never go to any other place." If you limit yourself to one particular way of thinking, you get stuck there. Limitation is not the nature of our soul. The nature of the soul is expansion and elevation. So touch the entire cosmos! Go beyond the cosmos and become Divinity—become one with Mother Divine! This oneness is described beautifully in the *Lalita Sahasranama.* Every meaning of every *mantra* is beyond beautiful, beyond beautiful! This oneness cannot be expressed in words, it can only be experienced inside.

So meditate babies, meditate. Leave everything to Mother. Surrender to Her completely. She can fulfill all of these little, little desires for worldly things. The main thing is to keep bothering Her always: "Mother, grant me pure devotion, bless me with salvation. Give me *moksha,* give me liberation from the six inner weeds. Oh, I have so much anger; kill my anger!"

Children, do not kill insects or animals. Do not kill anything in this world. You have no right to kill any living being. You did not create them. Instead, kill your ego immediately by pure devotion. When the mind wanders here and there, meditate with your *mantra*. Do you have a *mantra?* Initiation is a new birth. After initiation you meditate with your *mantra*. Whenever the mind wanders, repeat your *mantra* mentally and burn all the thoughts by the power of the seed letters of the *mantra.* Every seeker has his own *mantra*—the *Rama Mantra*, the *Krishna Mantra*, or any other *mantra*. So kill all the egoism and thoughts by the purifying power of your *mantra*. *Mantra*s are not ordinary letters—they are the subtle form of Mother Divine.

Sarva mantrātmike sarva yantrātmike sarva tantrātmike
Sarva yogātmike sarva jnānātmike sarva sarvātmike
Sarva rūpātmike sarva nāmātmike sarva śaktyātmike
Sarva mokṣātmike sarva svarūpe hé Jagan Maṭrke
Pāhi mām Devī namo tubhyām namo namaḥ

In the *Vedas,* Mother is said to be the *atma* of all the *mantra*s. The *atma,* you know—the soul. Without Mother, without soul, there is no existence at all—no body, no mind and no limited intellect. Soul alone works in our entire life. Mother is the only source of energy for every *mantra*, *tantra* and *yoga.* She alone is the source of energy for everything.

So pray to Mother. Fill your heart with cosmic love, not dry feelings. We are always talking about business and worldly matters. It is not good to listen to all these things. When our heart is filled with divine love for Mother, we have a tender heart and tender feelings. We never expect anything from anyone. We give everything without any expectation—not even for a word of thanks. That is great! That is a grand life, a very grand inner life.

So children, experience Mother in your heart. Dwell always in *atma jnana, Brahma jnana.* Pray to Mother, "Please grant me cosmic love and pure devotion for Your lotus feet. Give me liberation from all these six weeds, and bless me with wisdom!" Bother Mother for all these things. Bother Her again and again. You have that right! And go inside; enjoy Mother in your heart and everywhere in the universe. Feel that Mother is with you, within you, every second of your life—not only in your meditation room, not only in temples, not only in Amma's presence. That is beautiful!

If you feel love and devotion in front of Amma and afterwards you forget everything, that is not true devotion, that is not beautiful. You must feel divinity in each and every cell of the universe, in each and every cell of the cosmos! See Mother's divinity everywhere, all the time, in everything. That is real spirituality; that is true spirituality, children. Elevate to that level. Do not be in this lowest, worldly level. Elevate yourself, you *must* elevate to the highest level—that is beautiful. That is beautiful, beyond beautiful, beyond everything!

So utilize the boon of this life. This birth is a great boon, the greatest of boons. Utilize this great boon and offer your entire life to Mother Divine. Offer yourself to Her with the prayer: "O Mother, I worship You with all the fragrant inner flowers. The thousand-petalled lotus of the *sahasrara* blooms only by Your pure devotion. So Mother, grant me pure devotion. Open the *sahasrara* lotus and bless me with oneness with You!"

I get thousands of letters from suffering children and senior citizens in pain. Oh, I cannot bear that pain. So pray for all these people. Not only for them, pray for everyone suffering with illness and sadness. They are all alone in a very pathetic, very sad condition. Pray for the welfare of all mankind, for all the beings in the universe. That is our responsibility. This universe, this nature, gives you so much, but you never give anything in return—you are always taking. Give something, at least give your prayer. Pray for the welfare and peace of all. So children, pray with a pure heart.

Purify your inner life. Inner values are your *dharma,* they are very important. *Dharma* is wisdom; *dharma* is Truth; *dharma* is forgiveness; *dharma* is contentment. If you lead a *dharmic* life you have contentment inside. In spiritual life only can we experience that contentment—not in anything else in this world. So cultivate contentment with pure devotion and mental detachment. That is the only path to peace. Mental detachment, discriminative knowledge, compassion, detachment, inner beauty, purification, truth, cultivation of all the divine attributes—all these are *dharma*. The word *"dharma"* does not mean "righteousness" only. So many hundreds and hundreds of divine attributes are contained in *dharma*. Divine Mother is beyond *dharma:*

Dharmādharma vivarjitāyai namaḥ

She is beyond *dharma*. The rules of *dharma* are only for you. Rules in the home, rules on the road, rules in the hospital, in court, in our life—we need rules in every aspect of our lives. Without rules our life cannot be disciplined. Without discipline there is no spirituality at all. Discipline is extremely important in spiritual life. *Dharma* is discipline. *Dharma* rules the entire cosmos. *Dharma* is very, very powerful. *Dharma* burns all the impurities and immoral tendencies in our heart. We attain spiritual elevation and inner richness when we cultivate *dharma. Dharma* alone can stand without any worldly support. So children, be always in *dharma.* Cultivate *dharma*, meditate and live only for *dharma.* Your breath must be *dharma*—each and every cell of your body, blood and bones must always be saturated with *dharma* only. That is beautiful!

And pray for eternal peace in the entire universe. At the end of your meditation or prayer, you must pray for everyone:

Lokāḥ samastāḥ sukhino bhavantu

In *Sanatana Dharma*, there are innumerable beautiful prayers for world peace. One of these is:

Om taccham yorāvṛṇī mahe
Ghātum yajnāya ghātum yajnapataye
Daivī svastir astu nah
Svastir mānusẹbhyaḥ
Ūrdhvam jigātu bheṣajam
Śam no astu dvipade śam catuṣpade

Om namaste astu Bhagavan Viśveśwarāya
Mahādevāya Trayambakāya Tripurāntakāya
Trikāgni Kālāya Kālāgni Rudrāya
Nilakanthāya Mṛtyunjayāya Sarveśwarāya
Sadāśivāya Śriman Mahādevāya namaḥ

Om namaḥ Śambhave ca Mayobhave ca
Namaḥ Śankarāya ca Mayaskarāya ca
Namaḥ Śivāya ca Śivatarāya ca

In these universal prayer *shlokas*, *"Rudra"* means "the angry and fierce one." But here *"Rudra"* means "One who open the third eye." He opens our third eye, the eye of knowledge and wisdom. So the meaning of the *shloka* is: "O God, give awareness to everyone in the universe. Open everyone's third eye and bless them with *brahmic* awareness. Let only noble thoughts always come from every side into our life."

So these are the beautiful prayers in *Sanatana Dharma*. Not five thousand years before, not ten thousands years before, ages and ages and ages before, the sages prayed for the entire universe, because India is very rich in spirituality. India belongs to everyone in the universe. In the prayers from India, ages and ages before, the *rishis* prayed for the welfare of all mankind. India is a beautiful *karma bhumi*. *"Karma bhumi"* means "the land of selfless service"—the land of dedication, the land of *Veda,* the land of purity, the land of bliss! I cannot express the spiritual beauty of India in words, children. India belongs to everyone. This sacred land is full of so much spirituality—like nectar, beyond nectar.

So children, be always in *dharma*. Without *dharma,* we lead a blind life, maddened by worldly intoxication. Even with our eyes open we are blind. We are always seeking for money, name and fame—spending our life in meaningless things like eating, walking and talking. All these activities are a million times meaningless! So when we attain purity inside, when we attain divinity inside, realization inside, that is beautiful. Our life has meaning. So be a real *yogi* inside; be a real swan inside. That is Amma's expectation for her children.

Hari Om Tat Sat!

Children, come in two lines for blessings and be in silence. Meditate on your own *mantra* as you come to Amma in line. When you chant your *mantra* mentally, all the inner flowers begin to bloom. So when Amma touches your forehead, here, at the third eye, it will be more beautiful. So come to Amma in silence, chanting your own *mantra* mentally. It is beautiful when we maintain silence in the presence of holy ones and in spiritual places. You must learn to maintain silence, because silence is the language of Mother Divine! Thank you, children.

Philadelphia *20 May 1997*

ॐ

THE BEAUTIFUL DIVINE LAW OF COSMIC LOVE

Sri Vidyām jagatām dhātrīm
Sṛṣti sthiti layeśwarīm
Namāmi Lalitām nityām
Mahā Tripura sundarīm

Om praṇatānām prasīdasya
Devī viśvārti hāriṇī
Trailokya vāsinām iti
lokānām varadā bhavām

Embodiments of Divine Souls, Amma's Most Beloved Children,

There is a beautiful law in divinity. What is that law, children? It is the beautiful law of divine cosmic love. Cosmic love means equal and unconditional love for all beings. A mother very naturally loves her infant baby. We see the same love in birds and animals also. It is a beautiful, gentle, and common natural law. But the harmony in the universe now lacks balance because of lack of love. However, meditation remodels us completely. It awakens divine cosmic love in our heart and elevates us to the highest level. Where there is love, there only is purity. Where there is purity, you find *dharma* and peace. And where there is *dharma,* there only is wisdom. So children, this is the eternal spiritual law.

Honesty is the foundation of spiritual life—it is the gate to wisdom. We need honesty in our inner life as well as in our daily life—in the office, in our home, on the road, in court—everywhere. Imagine what we would be like without honesty. We would be neither sweet nor pure. We need honesty. If we have purity inside, that purity itself is the greatest honesty. Honesty is the greatest virtue—it is a dynamic virtue! Honesty is the greatest wisdom. Without honesty life is impure and unbalanced.

Why does this imbalance of the natural law occur in our universe again and again? It is because of lack of honesty, noble thoughts, inner purity, and inner beauty, etc. These divine attributes bloom in our inner life when we meditate. The black curtains of selfishness, egoism, limited negative feelings, etc. are burned by the fire of purity. We attain real purity only in *bhakti,* devotion. If we do not have inner purity it means our *bhakti* is on the surface level. So my dear babies, ask Divine Mother again and again for pure one hundred percent devotion. Bother Mother for pure devotion. Ask Her again and again, "Mother, grant me pure *bhakti,* only the purest devotion." If you have pure *bhakti* in your heart, you have everything. In devotion and spirituality alone can we find contentment.

There is no contentment in worldly life. Even if you are a billionaire, you cannot find real peace in the intoxication of material pleasures. Only in spirituality will you find contentment. Contentment is the greatest natural treasure. Do not lose this treasure, children! In Sanskrit, contentment is called *"tripti."* There is no greater treasure than *tripti.* It is so beautiful! All over the world, we see that some people are full of contentment because of their devotion, honesty and nobility. My dear children, you *do* have devotion. But ask Mother Divine for more and more and more devotion.

Just now one of Amma's beloved daughters sang a beautiful song, "Kanya Kumari." Imagine the map of India in front of your third eye, with Kanya Kumari at the bottom as the root *chakra*, the *muladhara chakra*. "Kanya Kumari" means "a young maiden." Devi is worshipped as a pure, lovely young girl named Kanya Kumari in a beautiful temple located at the southernmost tip of peninsular India.

A little further north is the *svadhishthana chakra.* This is Jambukeshwara, where there is a beautiful temple of *Akhilandeshwari Devi.* Her name means that the whole universe is within Her—it is Her Self only. Even today many divine miracles occur in Jambukeshwara!

At the third *chakra*, the *manipura chakra,* is the temple of *Madurai Meenaskshi*, or *Madhura Meenakshi Devi. "Madhura"* means "sweet as nectar." Mother is beyond nectar, beyond motherly love. When you pray to Mother Divine, She takes you to Her eternal home.

And still further up, at the *anahata chakra,* the heart *chakra, Bhamarambika Devi* rules in Sri Sailam. Our heart becomes a pure white lotus when we attain pure devotion. Pure *bhakti* fills our heart with the nectar of all the divine attributes, such as contentment, inner beauty, nobility, equal vision, etc. Then Mother Divine, in the form of *Bhramarambika Devi*, comes and resides in the lotus of our heart. *"Bhramaramba"* means "Mother Bee." Sometimes we may pray, "I want to be a bee, always hovering around Divine Mother's lotus feet." But here, Mother Herself becomes a bee, and She wants to live eternally in the beautiful, fragrant lotus of the devotee's heart!

Just see the beauty of Mother, the beauty of the law of spirituality! The law of divinity is cosmic love. Children, cultivate cosmic love. Like *dharma,* cosmic love rules this entire universe. So children, when you pray to Mother Divine, She comes and resides in your heart. She fills you with all the divine attributes, such as nobility, purity, honesty, wisdom, inner beauty, equal vision and forgiveness. Each and every cell of your body is drenched with the purity and fragrance of Mother Divine. She is always inside you, in your heart.

So pray to Mother for liberation: "O Mother, never leave the temple of my heart. My life belongs to You. Please kill my egoism—send it permanently from my heart, and give me liberation from all limited, immoral tendencies" That should be your only prayer.

What is our eternal home, babies? *Om! Om* is our eternal home. This body is a hostel. You are living in a hostel just now. (Laughter) You are always unhappy. For a little happiness in this world, you work so hard and get so tired. You play so many games simply to earn money. Again and again you get entangled in *maya.* To attain a little happiness, you live in unhappiness. (Amma laughs.) This is very sad.

Children, when Mother blesses you with the greatest boon of contentment and pure devotion, you have everything. *"Madhura"* means "nectar." When Mother is in your heart, your entire life becomes nectar, and you feel Her divine presence in each and every cell of the entire universe. That is the beautiful love of Mother Divine!

So the *anahata chakra*, the heart center, is the sacred *pitha,* the holy altar, of *Bhamarambika Devi*. Her beautiful temple is located at Sri Shailam in Andhra Pradesh. There are *ashtadasha pithas*—eighteen important altars of worship—sacred temples of energy for Mother in India. Actually, there are one thousand *Devi pithas* all over the world. Of these, one hundred and eight are most important. As it may not be possible for people to visit one hundred and eight places, eighteen—*ashtadasha pithas*—are said to be the most holy and most powerful. The Bhramaramba Pitha is one of these. So if you get a chance to come to India, you must visit that sacred temple. It is also a very powerful *pitha* in the human body. Actually Mother is right here in your heart. When the purity in your heart has made it blossom like a beautiful white lotus, Mother can never leave you, babies. Mother will always be in your heart in the form of *Bhramarambika*, the Divine Bee. She loves to drink the nectar of your *bhakti!* It is so very sweet and beautiful!

And the *vishuddhi chakra* is at the throat center. This is Kashi, the beautiful *pitha* of *Vishalakshi Devi.*

The next holy center is the *ajna chakra,* between the eyebrows. This is Nepal. Do you know the state of Nepal? But this isn't about Nepal. There is another meaning hidden here. The "pal" in Nepal stands for *"phala."* The Sanskrit word *"phala"* means "the forehead." Here Devi resides as *Guhyeshwari Devi. "Guhyeshwari"* means "the secret Mother." The secret is not in books but in our lives. We have brochures of parks or gardens. In these brochures, we find pictures of animals and birds, flowers and plants that may be seen in those gardens. But simply by looking at pictures of the birds, animals and flowers, can you get the satisfaction of actually being there and seeing them? Never! Seeing things for yourself is a totally different experience. Similarly, if you are always reading books, you will never experience *samadhi.* It is only when you put all those books aside and sit in meditation that you will experience divine love and peace inside. And after some time you will experience *samadhi.* So children, do not lose yourselves in books. God is beyond all books. Go beyond everything. Meditate on Mother Divine with a longing heart, with tears in your eyes. If you have pure devotion and intense desire for Mother, you will attain everything.

And finally there is the *sahasrara chakra.* This is Mt. Kailasa. Kailasa is a beautiful, beautiful Sanskrit word. This is where all the souls are assembled in one place—the countless billions and billions of souls. Even the souls of ants, the sun, moon and all the galaxies, including the soul of Brahma, the Creator Himself, are assembled in Kailasa. That is Mother's eternal home, sweet home. So children, come back to your home, the thousand-petalled universal lotus in the crown of the head!

Mother does not stay at any one *chakra*—as *kundalini* She travels through all the six *chakras.* When Mother is in the heart *chakra,* the *anahata chakra,* how are we? We have humility, devotion—pure devotion without any desire—truthfulness, honesty, wisdom and great contentment and detachment. We feel that God is one. Every belief in the entire universe, all religions, all paths, agree that everything belongs to God, who is only one. We have no turbulent emotions at all. Strong emotions are not good—they are not conducive to meditation. Uncontrolled emotions are the enemies of meditation. Anger is the foremost enemy of meditation. So give up all your emotions and anger to Amma. Yes, give all the emotions and angers to Amma and become a real *yogi.* When our lives are filled with divine cosmic love, we have all the divine attributes of wisdom, nobility, honesty, purity, inner beauty, detachment, dispassion and discrimination.

When Mother comes to the *vishuddhi chakra* in the throat center, we are pure like the beautiful white swan on a pond. A pond without a swan or without a lotus has no beauty. If our words and thoughts are pure, the pond of our heart is greatly beautified by the tender lotuses of our words and thoughts. At the *vishuddhi chakra,* we have *para vak, pashyanti, madhyama* and *vaikhari,* the four levels of speech. At the *para* level we are always in pure Consciousness. We understand divinity and constantly experience the nectar of divinity. We are immersed in thoughts of purity and divinity only. When *para* is always in our hearts, we never speak ill of anyone. Our lives become sweeter than nectar. *Devatas,* the Gods, experience death even though they have drunk *amrita,* ambrosia. But to the blessed soul who drinks the nectar of *samadhi,* there is no death at all. He merges in Mother's divine personality.

Such is *samadhi.* So children, when Mother as *kundalini* comes to the *vishuddhi chakra* we are like divine swans, and whatever we say becomes *Veda vakya,* the truth. We are in bliss. We can see the entire cosmos with our third eye. The vision of our physical eyes is very limited. But when the third eye opens, the entire cosmos lies before us!

What happens when *kundalini* reaches the *ajna chakra* between the eyebrows? The lotus of the *ajna chakra* has two petals—one is Siva, the other Shakti. One petal is *Narayana*, the other Lakshmi. One petal is Sri Rama, the other Sita Devi. One petal is Brahma, the other Saraswati.

When we meditate on *Omkara*—the *Om nada*, the sound of *Om*—all the six *chakras* open and begin to bloom.

Śaḍkārāgana dīpikām Śiva satīm śad yoginī sevitām

"When Mother as *kundalini* enters the gates of the six *chakras,* She fills them with radiance. She is the eternally loyal consort of Lord Siva, served by a hundred divine energies."

The word *"angana"* means "entrance." The farther *kundalini* enters into the lotus of the *ajna chakra,* the more the sweet fragrance of peace pervades the entire body. When Mother wants to enter the other *chakras*, the doors of their entrance gates open automatically. So invite Mother: "O Mother! Please come and sit in the lotus of my heart." Every lotus waits for Mother. We must have pure devotion and purity in our heart, with no lust, greed, jealousy or desire for worldly intoxication. So purify yourself with just a tiny atom of *dharma* in your life—that is enough for Mother Divine. When She sees even a little bit of *dharma*—not a mountain of *dharma*, only a tiny atom of *dharma* in your heart—Mother will never leave you, children! If we leave *dharma*, *adharma* will destroy our lives completely.

Dharmo rakṣati rakṣatiḥ

If we live in *dharma*, *dharma* will protect us. If we do not live in *dharma*, our *adharma* or unrighteousness will burn us. This is the law—the law of the *Vedas*. That is why the people in India are afraid to tell lies. They are afraid to be in *adharma*. They live for *dharma* and die for *dharma*. I see so many people all over the world who would die for *dharma*. *Dharma* alone can stand in this world without any support. That is the beauty of divine *dharma*. Children, cultivate *dharma;* cultivate purity; cultivate humility; cultivate pure devotion, and ask Amma again and again: "Mother, please grant me a grand inner life as my heart is so full of poverty. I have poverty in devotion, wisdom and knowledge. So please bless me and grant me a rich and grand inner life."

Dharma is righteousness. When you practice *dharma* you have everything. When you are in unrighteousness, you are on the wrong path. That is why Amma says again and again, "O children, Divine Mother has already blessed you with intellectual power, so be careful and do not miss your exits. If you miss your road, you miss everything." There are only two paths in life, *dharma* and *adharma*. So let me emphasize again and again: "Be very careful." One of our legs is *dharma*, the other is truth. If both legs are strong and function correctly, we can keep moving forward on the right path. But if one leg is weak or injured—either the leg of *dharma* or the leg of truth—we cannot walk on the correct path.

You know all these things more than Amma, my babies! You know all these things. You read so many books; so many great *gurus* and sages have given you so much knowledge out of love for you. However, you cannot repay them in any way for all the love and knowledge they have given you. You need to practice *dharma,* not just speak about it. You *must* practice *dharma* in your life. That is beautiful!

Lord Krishna says in the *Bhagavad Gita:*

Svalpamapyasya dharmasya trāyate mahato bhayāt

"O Arjuna, the practice of even a little of this *dharma* saves one from great fear. So cultivate *dharma.*" Bhagavan Krishna tells Arjuna to cultivate *dharma.* But one may say, "My life is nearly over. How much *dharma* can I cultivate now?" How much *dharma* can you cultivate? *"Swalpamasya dharmasya,"* just a little. Take a pin and put it on a piece of paper. The point of the pin is so small that it is almost invisible, you can hardly see it. Likewise, a pin-point of *dharma,* just an atom of *dharma,* is enough. A tiny spark of fire is enough to burn everything here on Earth. *"Agni"* means "fire." Children, *dharma* is a great fire! There are many fires—the fire of purity; *jnanagni,* the fire of knowledge; *yogagni,* the fire of *yoga;* the fire of divinity and *Sivagni,* the fire of Siva. Anger is fire, lust is fire, desires are fire, worldly intoxications are fire—all worldly things are fire.

In spiritual life also there are many fires: *Dhyana,* meditation, is a beautiful fire that burns all our inner impurities. *Jnana,* knowledge, is the greatest and most beautiful fire of all. When this fire enters into all the *chakras,* they glow with the light of self-illumination, *dharma* and purity. When we have self-illumination and purity inside, we feel "I am the Self, I am perfect and complete. I am beyond the three cages of body, mind and intellect. I am eternal. The entire cosmos belongs to me only!" Here "I" and "me" do not mean the limited, egoistic "I," but the "I" that is the Self—eternal, unlimited and boundless, indestructible, pure, divine and full of benediction.

So children, when we pray to God, all the *chakras* bloom in our inner cosmic garden. And when Mother comes to the *ajna chakra*, the two beautiful petals of this divine lotus come together and Siva and *Shakti* mingle with each other, filling the *chakra* with radiance.

That is why when the program is over, children, do not talk. Do not make this holy place into a market place. Be in silence, silence, silence. Maintain continued silence. Come in silence and go in silence. Chant your *mantra* mentally. When you chant the *mantra* even once with a pure heart, all the inner flowers truly bloom immediately. So chant your *mantra* as you come in line. When you come to Amma, she will touch your *ajna chakra*, the divine lotus of the third eye, which is full of nectar. The *sahasrara chakra* is the universal lotus—Mother's eternal home. Come back to your home, children! Your home is blissful. Your home is indestructible divine and pure. Your home is the very source of energy. Your home is *Omkara.* Your home is *Ayimkara.* Your home is *Srimkara.* Your home is *Hrimkara.* The seed letters in the *Saraswati Mantra—Ayim, Srim, Hrim* and *Om*—are our home. They are our subtle form. The *bijaksharas* of all *mantras* are the subtle forms of our soul. The *sahasrara* is our real home. When will you come back to your true home, children?

Do not mistake the sleep state for *samadhi.* When we are tired, sleep is very natural to the body, very natural. Even the great sages experience deep sleep when their bodies become tired. But you must not confuse sleep with *samadhi*. *Samadhi* is completely different—it is boundless. It cannot be described in words, it can only be experienced. So do not mistake sleep for *samadhi*.

When you meditate, and the *kundalini* gets established at the *ajna chakra,* even the sound of *Om* gradually ceases. Then you are in complete silence and the entire cosmos is yours! Your soul belongs to everything and everything belongs to your soul. When you attain *samadhi*, you yourself are God. You yourself are wisdom. You yourself are *dharma*. You yourself are *Veda*. You yourself are everything! You are Saraswati, Lakshmi, *Maha Kali*, *Chamundeshwari*, *Raja Rajeshwari*, *Lalita Parameshwari*, Rama, Jesus, Buddha—you yourself are every divinity!

The *sahasrara* is your eternal home. Come back to your Mother's sweet home, children! When I say this, my children think, "Oh, Amma is calling us to Bangalore or Penusila." Penusila is not my only home. I am not limited only to Bangalore or to India. Nor am I limited to this little Earth. Compared to the cosmos, Mother Earth is like a tiny atom. Only when you go beyond body consciousness does your soul touch the entire cosmos. That is the beauty of the soul.

When you meditate, you experience so much bliss inside. You play with Mother Divine, you sing with Mother Divine, and gradually your soul merges in Mother Divine just as the Ganga merges into the ocean. How beautiful it is! From its source at Gangotri, the Ganga touches so many cities—Allahabad, Kanpur, Benares and Calcutta. And at the Sundarvana Forest the Ganga merges into the ocean. Passing through more than two hundred cities on its course to the ocean, the sacred river gives us a mighty message. It teaches us to purify ourselves like the Ganga and merge in the ocean of divine Consciousness. Beautiful!

So children, meditate, meditate! There are twenty-four hours in a day. Amma never asks her babies to sit always in meditation. But start the day with meditation—half an hour, one hour or two hours. If that is not possible for you, at least spend fifteen minutes a day in meditation. When you meditate, all of the negative, unruly emotions are suppressed very quickly, and there is no lust, anger or jealousy in you at all. All these limited natures are burned completely in meditation because *dhyana* is *yogagni,* the fire of *yoga;* it is *jnanagni,* the fire of knowledge, and *Sivagni,* the fire of Siva. When this fire rises from the root *chakra* during meditation, tremendous heat develops in the body and great energy is produced. But if we sit in meditation for only a few minutes, no heat will be generated in the body. However, if we meditate for longer periods, even our touch will have the energy of a very powerful magnet.

The pure Consciousness of the divine lotus blooms at the *Brahma kupa* or *Brahma randhra,* the tenth gate of our body. So when the *sahasrara* lotus opens, you automatically attain *samadhi*. Then you become a *Brahma jnani.* Many great sages such as Vishvamitra and Durvasa meditated—not for one hundred or two hundred years, but for thousands of years! They encountered many failures but, like Buddha, they continued to sit in meditation until they attained the ultimate goal of Self-Realization.

Just imagine Buddha. One dark night, He left everything. He never cared for His kingdom or anything else. He even left his wife, his beautiful son, his father, mother, and all his wealth. He only wanted to realize the Self.

Buddha's life is beautiful, but it is not possible for most householders to renounce everything. At least try to sit in meditation for one hour in the morning, and one hour before going to bed. And be honest in your life—that much is possible for us. And always have positive thoughts and speak positively. Do not speak negatively under any circumstances. Do not soil the hearts of others with your negative thoughts. Honesty is the greatest, most dynamic virtue; it is the very greatest wisdom. Be always in honesty. And pray to Mother for the boon of bliss. If Mother wishes, everything is possible. If Mother fills your heart with pure cosmic love, you will be full of contentment and nobility. Your heart will always be inward. External things will have no attraction for you. They will be like meaningless dust with no taste at all.

When there is sweet sugarcane juice in one glass, and dry sugarcane pulp in another, any intelligent person will prefer the sugarcane juice to the pulp. An ignorant person, not knowing the difference, will take the squeezed-out pulp. Similarly, because of ignorance, illusion and *maya,* we are eating only the tasteless pulp of worldly pleasures. We are always running after money, name and fame and worldly happiness, not after the bliss of experiencing Mother Divine. So babies, drink the sugarcane juice, do not touch the pulp.

Children, pray to Mother, "You know everything Amma. So do not let me walk on the wrong path. Show me the right path in time. If I learn about You in my ninetieth or ninety-fifth year, it will be of no use at all, because I will not be able to meditate on You. I will not have the strength and energy to sit in meditation; I will be unable to do any spiritual practices. If you show me the path at the beginning of my life, I can try my best to climb higher and attain Self-Realization one day."

Spirituality is like a huge mountain and our *karma* load is heavy. But when we pray to God with deep sincerity, the entire *karma* load is burned by our purity in a fraction of a second. One *Rama nama* is enough; one *Siva nama* is enough; one *Vishnu nama* is enough; one *Devi nama* is enough to burn the mountain of billions of *karmas*—only the prayer must come from the bottom of our hearts. One name of Jesus, one name of Buddha, just one name of God in whatever faith you have is enough. Without faith, prayer is powerless, a million times powerless. Prayer without faith is meaningless. If the prayer does not come from the heart, it is just lip-service. Children, avoid lip-*Vedanta,* lip-devotion and lip-service.

When you call "Ma," with your whole heart, Mother immediately receives your prayers. There should be no desire behind your prayer. Even if there are desires, Mother will fulfill them all, no doubt. Whatever your wish, She must fulfill it. If you wish for money, She will give it to you. But if you wish for Her, She will test you again and again, "How much true devotion does my child have? If she really wants me, she will never like money." A seeker with a real longing for Mother will not like anything in this world. If he still has a desire for worldly things, his devotion is superficial—it is really worthless. All the monies, gold and diamonds in the entire universe are equal to an insignificant, tiny dust particle under Divine Mother's lotus feet. What appears to be valuable and great to you is a mere atom of dust to Mother.

So children, ask Mother for liberation only. Ask for liberation from bad temper. Anger is our first enemy. Where there is anger, there is no God at all. Ask for liberation from lust—where there is lust, there is no purity. Ask for liberation from dishonesty—where there is no honesty, there is no wisdom whatsoever. We do not want to experience all these negative qualities again and again in our lives.

When we attain pure devotion we have *dharma*, purity, humility, and all the divine virtues. We attain wisdom. So start your morning early with prayer. Prayer purifies our physical body, mental body and spiritual body. It gives us a connection to divine cosmic love. So pray! Pray with tears. Pray with your *mantra.* The meanings of all the *mantras* are beautiful.

Anyathā śaraṇam nāsti tvameka śaraṇam mama

"There is nobody else in this world for me but You."

Just now a devotee sang a song expressing the same feeling. "How many births must I take, Amma? Why am I always caught in the play of *maya?* When will You give me liberation from this *maya?*" There is a beautiful feeling in this song. "All this is only *maya, maya, maya!* I am always in the intoxication of *maya*. O Mother, I understand that You are the cause of this *maya*. If you continue to let me be deluded by Your *maya*, how can I attain realization in this life? You alone can liberate me from *maya*. Lead me to the goal of Self-Realization, O Mother! I want to attain bliss at least in this birth."

If Mother grants you the boon in your lifetime, it is beautiful. But even if it is on your deathbed, it is okay. If we keep praying to Mother, at least we will have hope for our next birth. In some faiths, there is no belief in rebirth—there is no hope at all. If there is rebirth, at least we can cultivate *dharma* and *bhakti* in our next life. But if there is no other birth, we can do nothing.

So pray! Do not wait for one more birth—make this birth your last! If even one desire remains in our hearts, we will be born again. So burn all desires and impurities in the fire of pure devotion, children. Devotion is a great fire, a dynamic fire—it is a dynamic virtue. Cultivate pure, pure, pure devotion. Without devotion, though we may talk about many things such as *chakras* and *jnana,* our feelings will remain dry. There will be no sweetness or fragrance in our words. So pray to Mother for *bhakti:* "Amma, bless us with the purest divine cosmic love that rules this entire cosmos! Please grant us the boon of Your love. Only love can conquer this entire universe—only love! Divine love is nectar; divine love is beautiful beyond words; divine love is sweeter than anything in this world!"

With Mother's blessing you will be able to understand the inner Reality. If there is no inner vision, you will never hear the inner voice. The inner eye of knowledge will never open. But when you open the third eye, the eye of knowledge, you will have everything. Everything belongs to your Self only. That is beautiful!

So my dear embodiments of divine souls, pray to Mother early in the morning. Start the day, the beautiful day, with prayer. When we pray to Mother Divine, we are filled with love and our hearts become tender, for Mother is the very embodiment of tenderness.

Pray and meditate regularly. If there are any immoral tendencies in your heart, get rid of them slowly and permanently. Tell yourself, "This is not good! I am not living in honesty. It is very bad. I have been meditating for so many years, so why do I still have negativity in my heart? This is not good at all!" Try to understand yourself—watch yourself. Watch your words; watch your thoughts; watch your deeds—that is enough. Do not find faults in others; find only your own faults. Such an attitude is beautiful for a *sadhaka.* A *"sadhaka"* is a "seeker," a "spiritual aspirant." If you want to find faults, the world is full of faults. But we cannot change the world, we can only change ourselves. When we understand this truth, it is beautiful.

So children, ask Mother: "Grant me the purest and best devotion. Now I have devotion, Mother, but it is so little. Bless me with more and more devotion. I want to see You in all the *chakras* in the form of self-illumination—not in a limited physical form. I want to see You inside." Children, pray daily to Mother, and cultivate beautiful devotion—true devotion—in your lives.

Pray to Divine Mother for *bhakti* only, not for anything else. If you have *bhakti,* you have everything. So ask Mother for devotion only. If we keep asking Her continuously for useless, worldly things, She will stop talking to us. She gives everything. But when you ask Mother for Herself, She does not give Herself to you easily. She puts you through many tests to see the true condition of your heart—how much longing you have for Her, and how true your love is.

Babies, if you pray to Divine Mother sincerely, She *must* give you salvation. She *must* give it—there is no doubt about this at all!

See you all again next year! Thank you, children.

Hari Om Tat Sat!

Philadelphia *21 May 1997*

APPENDICES

Stotra, Shloka and Kirtana

The following are listed alphabetically by the first word. Unless indicated otherwise, all verses are in Sanskrit. The International Standard of Sanskrit Transliteration has been used. Please refer to the key on page x.

Ājnā cakrāntarālasthā
Rudra granthi vibhedinī
Sahasrārāmbuja ārūḍhā
Sudhāsārābhivarṣiṇī

-Śrī Lalitā Sahasranāma: shl. 39

Establishing herself in the subtle center of the ajna chakra, the kundalini pierces the Rudra granthi in that lotus. She then climbs to the sahasrara chakra at the crown of the head and showers the seeker's whole subtle system with purest nectar.

Ānati niyyave Devī sannuti cheyyagā
Sannidi cheragā ānati niyyaveDevī
Ni āna lenide jagāna sāguṇā
Vedāla vāṇito Virinci viśva nāṭakam

O Divine Mother! Please give us permission to pray to You, to praise You, and to reach Your divine presence. Without Your permission, nothing can happen in this world. Even Lord Brahma and Saraswati Devi cannot create this world-play without Your command.

Antara mukha jana ānanda
phaladāyinyai namo namaḥ

Salutations to Devi who, when She is worshipped within, blesses the devotee with the choicest boon of supreme bliss.

Antar mukha samārādhyā
bahir mukha sudurlabhā

-Śrī Lalitā Sahasranāma: shl. 162

Worship Mother Divine within for it is very difficult to attain Her outside.

Bhavānī tvam dāse mayi *Vitara dṛṣtim sakaruṇām* *Iti stotum vāncan kathayati* *Bhavānī tvam iti yaḥ* *Tadaiva tvam tasmai* *Diśasi nija sāyujya padavī* *Mukunda Brahmendra sphuṭamakuṭa nīrājita padām* *-Saundarya Laharī. v.22* *Ādi Śankarācārya*	Even before Your devotee can utter the word "Bhavani," when he wants to call out to You and begs You for one compassionate glance, You bestow on him the status of oneness with Your divine feet. Your sacred lotus feet are eternally adored by Lord Vishnu, Brahma and Indra, King of all the Gods, by placing their dazzling, jeweled diadems on them as they bow down before You.
Brahmānandā Maṇidvipa vāsinī *Brahma jnāna sukhkam dehī*	See: Brahma Vishnu Maheshwara janani….
Brahmā Viṣṇu Maheśwara jananī *Devī Bhavānī* *Brahmānandā Maṇidvipa vāsini* *Devī Bhavānī* *Brahma jnāna sukham dehī* *Brahmānanda sukham dehī* *Devī Bhavānī Lalitā Bhavānī*	O Devi Bhavani! You are the Mother of the three deities Brahma, Vishnu and the great Lord Siva. Ever blissful, You reside in the jeweled isle of Manidwipa. O most tender and loving Mother Lalita, bless me with the supreme knowledge of the Absolute and fill me with the bliss of Brahman!

Caitanya kusumārādhyā *Caitanya kusuma priyā* *-Śrī Lalitā Sahasranāma: shl.170*	Mother Divine should be worshipped with the flower of consciousness—the fully bloomed sahasrara lotus, fragrant with divine inner qualities—for this is the flower She loves best.
Darśanam divyāmṛtam *sparśanam divyāmṛtam* *sambhaṣaṇam divyāmṛitam*	Being in the presence of the holy ones—seeing their blessed form—is divine nectar; being touched by them is divine nectar and having a conversation with them is also the purest divine nectar.
Devī Bhavānī Ammā Karuṇāmayī Ammā *Dayā karo Ammā Kṛpā karo Ammā* *Jaya Mā jaya Mā Jaya Devī Bhavānī Ammā* *Jaya Penuśila vāsinī Ammā* *Vijayeśwarī Bhavānī Ammā* *Ammā Ammā Ammā*	O Mother Bhavani Devi, O Karunamayi Amma, have mercy on us, shower Your grace on us. Glory to You, victory to You, O Mother Divine! O Mother Devi Bhavani, Salutations to You, whose home is in Penusila. You are our Mother Vijayeswari Devi Bhavani!
Devī caraṇam praṇamāmyaham *-Line from Devī bhajan.*	I offer salutations at the divine lotus feet of Devi.
Devī pūjā madhuram *Hṛidaya nivāsam madhuram* *Devī pādam madhuram* *Sarvam Devī madhuram* *-Devī bhajan*	It is supremely blissful to worship Devi. Her constant presence in the heart showers the devotee with ambrosia. There is nothing more blissful than meditation on Her divine lotus feet, which are the very source of nectar. Everything about Devi is indescribably sweet.

Dharatī jala aura agni pavana ākāśa *Nāśavanta ye carācara mein tū hī hai avināśa* *-Hindi bhajan*	All the five elements—earth, water, fire, air and ether—will be destroyed one day. Of all sentient and non-sentient things, You alone are indestructible and eternal!
Dharmādharma vivarjitāyai namaḥ *-Śrī Lalitā Nāmāvalī: Name 255*	Salutations to Divine Mother who is beyond all concepts of right and wrong action.
Dharmo rakṣati rakṣatiḥ	Dharma protects; it verily protects one who lives in dharma.
Dhyāyet padmāsanasthām.... *Sarvālankāra yuktam....* *-Śrī Lalitā Sahasranāma dhyāna shls.*	See: Sinduraruna vigraham….
Duradhigama nissīma mahimā Mahā Māyā *Viśvam bhramayasi Para Brahma Mahiṣī* *-Saundarya Lahari. v 97* *Ādi Śankarācārya*	O Mother Durga Devi! You are difficult to attain; Your glory is boundless and indescribable. You are Maha Maya, the feminine aspect of Para Brahma, the Absolute. You cast the veil of illusion on all living beings and it is Your energy that endlessly revolves all the planets in the universe!
Ekamevadvitīyam Brahma *nānyad asti akincanaḥ*	Brahman is the only One, without a second. Nothing else exists.

Hari Om Tat Sat	Hari: Vishnu, the Lord in His manifest protective, all-pervading form + Om: Shabda Brahman, primordial sound vibration—symbol of the Absolute—that arose at the beginning of creation + Tat: the Absolute, the one self-existent supreme Spirit, without beginning or end, without name or form, without vibration, eternal, all-pervading, and all-powerful + Sat: the manifested universe, apparently so real, yet transitory and illusory in nature—all these are one—Brahman alone!
Hrīmkārāsana garbhitānala śikhām *Sauḥ Klīm kalām bibhṛtīm* *Sauvarṇāmbara dhāriṇīm vara sudhām* *Dhautām trinetrojjvalām* *Vande pustaka pāśānkuśa dharām* *Sragbhūṣitām ujjvalām* *Tvām Gaurīm Tripurām Parātpara kalām* *Śrī Cakra sancāriṇīm* *-Dhyāna śloka for Sri Devi Khaḍga Mālā*	Salutations O Gauri Devi, You are divine nectar. Seated in the heart of the sacred and powerful seed letter Hrim, You shine like a dazzling flame of fire. The sacred seed letters Sauh and Klim add to Your brilliance. O lovely Goddess of three divine eyes, You are arrayed in golden raiment, decorated with jewelled ornaments, and hold a noose, a goad, and a book (the *Vedas),* in Your hands. Salutations to You, O luminous Tripura Devi, sovereign ruler of all the triads, the light beyond all lights. O Mother, You are supreme Consciousness, eternally pervading the Sri Chakra.
Jāgrat svapna suṣuptinām *sākṣi bhūtyai namo namaḥ*	Salutations to Devi who is the sole witness of the three states of waking, dreaming and deep sleep.
Jai Karuṇāmayī	Victory and salutations to Sri Karunamayi, the compassionate Mother Sri Sri Sri Vijayeswari Devi!

Lokāḥ samastāḥ sukhino bhavantu *-Peace invocation*	May all beings in all the realms of this beautiful cosmos be happy and free from all suffering.
Madhura madhura Meenākṣī *Madhurāpurī nilaye* *Ambā Ambā Jagadambā (2x)* *Madhura madhura Meenākṣī* *Vāgvilāsinī madhura madhura Meenākṣī* *Mātangī marakatāngī* *Madhura madhura Meenākshī* *-Devī bhajan*	Meenakshi Devi, with lovely, large, fish-shaped eyes, is the sweetest of the sweet! She resides in the sweet city of Madhurapuri. She is my mother—She is the mother of the whole universe! She revels in poetic words. Her limbs glow like precious emeralds. Born as Matangi, the daughter of Matanga Muni, Meenakshi Devi is the sweetest of the sweet!
Mānasa bhajare Guru caraṇam *Devī caraṇam praṇamāmyaham* *-Śrī Guru bhajan*	O my mind, always meditate on and adore Sri Guru's divine lotus feet! I offer loving and humble salutations at the *divine* lotus feet of Devi.
Manda hāsa vadanī manoharī *Vijayeśwarī Mātā Ambā Vijayeśwarī Mātā* *Jagat Jananī śubha kariṇī Vijayeswari Mātā* *Ambā Vijayeśwarī Mātā Īśwarī Ambā* *Maheśwarī Ambā* *-Śrī Karuṇāmayī bhajan*	Mother Sri Vijayeswari Devi's sweet and gentle smile steals the heart. She is the supreme sovereign who creates the universe, and rules over it. Mother is Maheshwari, consort of the great Lord Siva, who takes care of the welfare of all Her children.

Manuṣyatvam mumukṣatvam *Mahā puruṣa samṣrayaḥ*	One obtains a human birth by great good fortune. One is very blessed indeed if one also has an intense desire for liberation, and is further blessed with the company and protection of a Self-Realized soul.
Mokśa dvāra kavāṭa pāṭanakarī *Bhikṣām dehi kṛpāvalambanakarī* *Mātā Annapūrṇeśvarī* *-Śrī Annapūrṇā Stotram*	O Divine Mother, You alone can open for us the doors of the entrance-gate to liberation. Remember Your naturally compassionate nature and bless us with the alms of Your divine grace. O Mother Annapurna, You alone nourish and support all beings in the universe.
Nāma sahasra pāṭhaśca yathā carama janmani *Tathaiva viralo loke Śrī Vidyācāra vedinaḥ* *-Śrī Lalitā Sahasranāma Phala śruti: Shl.75*	Only a rare one, for whom this is the last birth, will be able to recite the thousand names of Sri Lalita Devi, and know how to worship the Divine Mother.
Namaḥ Śivābhyām navayauvanābhyām *Paraspara sliṣta vapudharābhyām* *Nagendra kanyām Vriṣa ketanābhyām* *Namo namaḥ Śankara Pārvatībhyām*	Salutations to the auspicious Lord Siva and His Shakti, the ever-young divine couple in eternal embrace. Salutations again and again to Parvati Devi, daughter of the Himalayas (Nagendra) and to Lord Siva, who have the bull (Vrishabha) on their banner.
Om bhūr bhuvaḥ suvaḥ tat savitur vareṇyam *Bhargo devasya dhīmahi dhiyo yonaḥ pracodayāt*	Om! We glorify and adore the supreme Divinity in the form of the effulgent sun, Creator of Earth, Ether and Heaven. May that

Āpo jyoti rasomṛtam Brahma bhūr bhuvassuvarom *-Srī Gāyatrī Mahā Mantra*	supreme Consciousness inspire and illumine our mind and understanding. Brahman is Om, the immortal, luminous essence of all waters; Brahman alone is the earth, the sky and the celestial realms.
Om Gurur Brahmā Gurur Viṣṇu *Gurur devo Mahesvaraḥ* *Guru sākṣāt Para Brahma* *Tasmai Śrī Gurave namaḥ* *-Śrī Guru Gītā: shl. 32*	Salutations to the glorious Guru who is Brahma, Vishnu and Maheshwara; to the Guru who is verily supreme Brahman.
Om namaḥ Śambhave ca Mayobhave ca *Namaḥ Śankarāya ca Mayaskarāya ca* *Namaḥ Śivāya ca Śivatarāya ca* *-Śrī Rudram: Namakam. 8th Anuvāk v.3*	Om! Salutations to the very source of auspiciousness and happiness. Salutations to the Lord who bestows both earthly welfare and divine bliss on all beings. Salutations to Siva, the very embodiment of auspiciousness, more auspicious than anything. Salutations to the luminous supreme Lord!
Om namaḥ Śivāya namaḥ Om (4x) *Om namaḥ Śivāya namaḥ Om Om Om (4x)* *Durgā Bhavānī namaḥ Om Om Om* *Durgati nāśinī namaḥ Om Om Om* *Kailaśa vāsinī namaḥ Om Om Om* *Ātma nivāsinī namaḥ Om* *-Śiva and Devī bhajan*	Om! Salutations to Lord Siva. Salutations to Durga Devi, creator of the universe who destroys all misfortune. Salutations to Divine Mother who lives in Kailasa, and dwells eternally in my heart!

Om namaste astu Bhagavan Viśveśvarāya *Mahādevāya Trayambakāya Tripurāntakāya* *Trikāgni Kālāya Kālāgni Rudrāya Nilakanthāya* *Mṛtyunjayāya Sarveśvarāya Sadāśivāya* *Śriman Mahādevāya namaḥ* *-Śrī Rudram: 1st Anuvāk. v.16*	Om! Salutations to You, O Lord of the Universe, the supreme Lord, the three-eyed one, destroyer of the demon Tripurasura and the three cities. You are the fire known as trikagni; You are the fierce and terrible Rudra, who consumes creation at the end of a kalpa (time cycle) as the blaze of the Kalagni fire. O blue-throated one who has conquered death, ruler of all, eternally auspicious and peaceful, O luminous and glorious supreme Lord, salutations once again!
Om praṇatānām prasīdasya *Devī viśvārti hāriṇī* *Trailokya vāsinām iti* *lokānām varadā bhavām* *-Devī Māhātmya: ch.11 v.35*	Om! O Devi, remover of the afflictions of all beings, be pleased with us, who bow at Your lotus feet. You pervade the three worlds, so please shower Your grace on us and bless us all.
Om śaraṇāgata dīnārta *paritrāṇa parāyaṇe* *Sarvasyārti hare Devī* *Nārāyaṇī namōstutē* *-Devī Māhātmya ch.11 v.11*	Om! O Mother, Your heart melts at the sight of suffering. It is Your nature to relieve the pain of those who take refuge in You. You are the remover of all afflictions. I surrender to You O great Goddess Narayani, Lakshmi Devi, consort of Lord Vishnu!

Om sarva mangala māngalye *Śive sarvārtha sādhake* *Śaraṇye Trayambike Devī* *Nārāyaṇī namostute* *-Devī Māhāmya: ch.11 v.9*	Om! O Consort of Lord Siva, O auspicious Mother with three divine eyes, You are the very essence of everything auspicious! You fulfill all desires, both material and spiritual. I take refuge at Your lotus feet Mother, for You are also Lakshmi Devi, known as Narayani consort of Lord Vishnu. Please accept my humble salutations.
Om Śrī Cakra vāsinyai namaḥ *Om Śrī Lalitāmbikāyai namah* *-Śrī Lalitā Devī Mantra*	Om! Salutations to the lovely and most tender Mother, Sri Lalita Devi, who resides in the Sri Chakra.
Om Śrī Vidyām jagatām dhātrīm *Sṛiṣṭī sthiti layesvarīm* *Namāmi Lalitām nityām* *Mahā Tripura Sundarīm* *-Sri Devi Khaḍga Mālā invocation mantra*	Om! You are Saraswati Devi, Goddess of Knowledge, the eternal supreme Divine Mother of all! I offer my humble and loving salutations at Your lotus feet, O Devi Tripurasundari, the most beautiful and magnificent Goddess in all the three worlds! You are the tender and playful Lalita Devi, who sports in the divine play of creating, sustaining and re-absorbing this universe into Yourself.
Om Śuklāmbara dharam Viṣṇum....	See: Śuklāmbara dharam Viṣṇum....
Om taccham yorāvṛṇī mahe *Ghātum yajnāya ghātum yajna pataye*	Om! We worship and pray to the supreme Lord for the welfare of all beings. May all miseries and shortcomings leave us

Daivī svastir astu naḥ svastir mānuṣebhyaḥ *Ūrdhvam jigātu bheṣajam* *Śam no astu dvipade śam catuṣpade* *-Peace invocation of Śrī Puruṣa Sūktam*	forever so that we may always sing for the Lord during the holy fire ceremonies. May the Gods rain peace on us. May all medicinal herbs grow in potency so that all diseases may be cured. May all men and animals be happy and at peace.
Om Tat puruṣāya vidmahe Mahādevāya dhīmahi *Tanno Rudraḥ pracodayāt* *-Śrī Śiva Gāyatrī*	Om! Let us meditate on the great Lord Rudra, the destructive aspect of Lord Siva, the Supreme Being. May that great God inspire and illumine our mind and understanding.
Om Vighneśvarāya namaḥ *-Śrī Gaṇeṣa Mantra*	Om! Salutations to Lord Ganesha who is the remover of all obstacles.
Prānadā Prāna rūpiṇyai namaḥ *-Śrī Lalitā Nāmāvalī: Names 783,784*	Salutations to Devi, Mother Divine, the embodiment of supreme energy, who gives life and vital energy to all beings.
Prātaḥ smarāmi Lalitā vadanāravindam *Bimbādharam prathula mauktika śobhi nāsam* *Ākarṇa dīrgha nayanam maṇikuṇḍalāḍhyam* *Manda smitam mṛgamad ojjvala phāla deśam* *-Śrī Lalitā Pancaratnam*	At dawn I meditate on the beautiful lotus face of Lalita Devi, whose lips are as red as a pomegranate flower. A pearl ornament enhances the beauty of Her nose; Her large eyes extend to the ears, which look charming with earrings set with precious gems. She smiles gently, and Her forehead glows with the deep red mark of kasturi.

Purṇa sarvajna Satcidānanda *Brahmānanda*	Brahman is complete and omniscient. It is of the form of supreme Truth, divine Consciousness and eternal bliss.
Rāvammā Ammā Rāvammā *Rāja Rājeśvarī Rāvammā* *Nirmala jīvana sudhālu tonakagā* *Śānti tīramuna mammu cherpagā* *Rāvammā Ammā Rāvamma* *-Telugu song*	O Mother Raja Rajeshwari! Please come to us. Make our life pure and sweet as nectar. Lead us to the shores of peace. Come, come O Mother!
Rogān aśeṣān apahamsi tuṣṭā *Ruṣṭā tu kāmān sakalān abhīṣṭān* *Tvām āśṛtānām na vipannarāṇām* *Tvām āśṛtā hyāśrayatām prayānti* *-Devī Māhātmya: v.29*	O Mother Divine! When You are pleased, You remove all ailments and sorrow, and fulfill every desire of Your devotee. Even when angry, no harm can befall those who take refuge at Your lotus feet. In fact, they themselves become a refuge for others.
Śaḍkārāgana dīpikām Śiva *satīm śad yoginī sevitām* *Śatkārāngana dipikām Śiva satīm* *Śaḍ vairi vargāpahām*	O pure and stainless eternal consort of Lord Siva! You illumine the courtyard of six entrances. You dwell in the six chakras of all beings, and are eternally served and adored by six pure and blemishless divine energies, who are Your constant attendants. You put to flight the six inner enemies from the hearts of Your devotees.

Śaraṇāgata dīnārtā....	See: *Om śaraṇāgata dīnārtā....*
Śrī Vidyām jagatām dhātrīm....	See: *Om Śrī Vidyām jagatām dhātrīm*
Śuklāmbara dharam Viṣṇum *śaśi varṇam catur bhujam* *Prasanna vadanam dhyāyet* *sarva vighnopa śāntaye* - *Śrī Gaṇeṣa Mantra*	We meditate on the ever-smiling, four-armed Lord Ganesha, arrayed in white garments. We pray to the all-pervading Lord, whose complexion glows like the moon, for the removal of all obstacles.
Sakunkum vilepanām alika cumbi kastūrikām *Samanda hasitekṣaṇām saśara cāpa pāśānkuśām* *Aśeṣa jana mohinīm aruṇa mālya bhūṣojjvalām* *Japā kusuma bhāsurām japa vidhau smared* *Ambikām* -*Śrī Lalitā Sahasranāma dhyana shl.*	I meditate on Devi, whose lovely form is decorated with kumkum designs; Her forehead is kissed by the fragrant mark of musk; She glows in red silk garments, and is adorned with crimson hibiscus garlands and ruby ornaments. Her hands hold the sugarcane bow, five flower arrows, the noose and the goad. With Her gentle smile and sweet glances, She captivates the hearts of all!
Samsāra panka nirmagna samuddharaṇa *panḍitāyai namaḥ* - *Śrī Lalitā Nāmavalī: Name 880*	Salutations to Divine Mother, the supreme expert who knows how to redeem those who are deeply sunk in the mire of worldly existence.
Sarva mantrātmike sarva yantrātmike	O Devi, You are the embodiment of all mantras, yantras and

Sarva tantrātmike Sarva yogātmike
Sarva jnānātmike sarva sarvātmike
Sarva rūpātmike sarva nāmātmike
Sarva śaktyātmike Sarva mokṣātmike
sarva svarūpe hé Jagan Matṛke
Pāhi mām Devī namo tubhyām namo namaḥ

tantras. You are the personification of yoga and jnana. You pervade the whole world. You manifest in all names and forms, You are divine energy. O Mother! You alone are moksha, liberation from the pain and bondage of this world. Protect me, O Mother of the Universe. I bow to You again and again!

Sindūrāruṇa vigrahām trinayanām
Māṇikya maulī sphurat
tārānāyaka śekharām smita mukhīm
Āpīna vakṣoruhām

O Mother with three divine eyes, I meditate upon Your radiant red form.. Sweetly smiling, You have adorned the crescent moon like a jewel in Your crown of rubies. I adore Your full-figured beauty

Pāṇibhyām alipūrṇa ratna caṣakam
Raktotpalam bibhratīm
Saumyām ratna ghaṭastha rakta caraṇām
Dhyāyet Parām Ambikām

In one divine hand You hold a crimson lotus, and in the other, a jewel-encrusted bowl thronged by bees. I meditate on Your peaceful, gently smiling face, and painted lotus feet, red upon a golden foot-rest inlaid with precious gems.

Aruṇā karuṇā tarangitākṣīm
Dhṛta pāśānkuśa puṣpa bāṇa cāpām
Aṇimādibhir āvritām mayūkhair
Ahamityeva vibhāvaye Bhavānīm

O Mother, Goddess of Dawn, Your eyes ever overflow with tender compassion. You hold a noose, a goad and five flower arrows in Your hands. I envision You surrounded by all the supernatural energies, which are Your own luminous rays.

Dhyāyet padmāsanasthām vikasita vadanām
Padma patrāyatākṣīm

O Bhavani, I meditate upon Your beautiful form seated in the lotus, a gentle smile on Your face, and lovely soft eyes large as

Hemābhām pīta vastrām karakalita
Lasad hema padmām varāngīm

Sarvālankāra yuktām satatam abhayadām
Bhakta namrām Bhavānīm
Śrī Vidyām śānta mūrtīm sakala suranutām
Sarva sampat pradātrīm

- Śrī Lalitā Sahasranāma dhyana shls.

lotus petals. Radiating golden effulgence, dressed in yellow silk, You hold a golden lotus in one hand.

O Mother, embodiment of peace, adorned with jeweled ornaments, Your heart is full of tender love and compassion for all Your devotees. You grant them prosperity and freedom from fear. You are Sri Vidya personified and adored by all the Gods.

Śivaḥ śaktyā yukto yadi bhavati śaktaḥ prabhavitum
Na ca Devam devo na khalu kuśulaḥ spanditumapi
Atas tvāmārādhyām Hari Hara Virincādibhir api
Praṇantu stotum vā kathamakṛta puṇyaḥ prabhavati

- Saundarya Laharī v.1

Siva, the Lord of Gods, has no expansion or power unless He is connected with Shakti. Without Her, He is incapable of any movement whatsoever. Therefore who except those with great merit accumulated in past births, can adore and sing Your praises, O Mother Divine? Even the great Gods Brahma, Vishnu and Siva worship You.

Srī Mātā Jai Mātā Srī Mātā
Tana mana prāṇa mé Srī Mātā
Pavana gagana mé Srī Mātā
Nayana nayana mé Srī Mātā
Aṇuva aṇuva mé Srī Mātā
Janana maraṇa mé Srī Mātā

- Devī bhajan

Glory to the luminous Mother! Victory to Her, salutations to Her! She is in the body, mind and vital breath. She pervades both ether and air. She dwells in every eye. Every atom vibrates with Her divine energy. She alone is birth as well as death.

Sŕīṣti sthiti laya kāriṇī	Devi alone creates, maintains and dissolves the entire cosmos.
Tat tvam asi *-Vedic mahā vākya*	That thou art: You and the supreme Reality, the Absolute, are one and the same. One of the four maha vakyas, great truths, of the Vedas.
Trividham narakasyedam *dvāram nāśanam ātmanaḥ* *Kāmaḥ krodhas tathā lobhas* *Tasmād etat trayam tyajet* *-Srīmad Bhagavad Gita: Ch.16 v.21*	There are three main entrances to hell: desire, anger and greed, which destroy the soul.
Vāsānsi jīrṇāni yathā vihāya *navāni gṛhṇāti naro parāṇī* *Tathā śarīraṇi vihāya jīrṇān* *anyāni sanyāti navāni dehī* *- Srīmad Bhagavad Gītā: Ch.2 v. 22*	Just as a person discards old, worn out garments and puts on new ones, the embodied soul discards the old, worn out body and takes a new one.
Viśveśvarāya narakārṇava tāraṇāya *- From Dāṛdrya Dahana Stotra*	Lord Siva is the supreme sovereign of the universe. He liberates souls from the ocean of worldly hell.
Yā kundendu tuṣāra hāra dhavalā	The luminous Goddess Saraswati Devi glows like the moon,

Yā śubhra vastrāvṛtā *Yā vīṇā vara daṇḍa maṇḍita karā* *Yā śveta padmāsanā* *Yā Brahmācyuta Śankara prabhṛtibhir* *Devaiḥ sadā pūjitā* *Sā mām pātu Sarasvatī Bhagavatī* *Niḥ śeṣa jādyāpahā*	wears a snow-white garland of fragrant jasmine blossoms, and is arrayed in pure white raiment. She is seated on a white lotus, holding a beautiful vina (a stringed musical instrument) in Her hands. She is eternally worshipped by Brahma, Achyuta (Sri Krishna, an incarnation of Lord Vishnu), Shankara and all the other Gods. May She ever protect me and completely remove my ignorance
Yatra nāryantu pūjyante tatra ramante Devatāḥ	The Gods are happy to dwell in the land where women are treated with respect.

GLOSSARY

Wherever possible the etymology of the Sanskrit words has been given in parenthesis. Words that have been explained in the text, and words that occur in the glossaries of Blessed Souls Vols. 1 and 2 are not included here.

A

Āditya Hridayam: A Sanskrit stotra or hymn extolling the Sun God as the giver of life.

Advaitic: (a: without + dvaita: duality) Adj. for advaita, non-duality, i.e., the knowledge that the same divine Consciousness pervades everything.

Āgama: A name for the *Vedas* derived from "agam," birth, origin. The original sacred shastras or scriptures of Indian spirituality

Akrita punyah prabhāvati: (akrita: uncreated, natural + punyah: merit of pure deeds + prabha: radiance + vati: one who has) Divine Mother, with the effulgence of natural, perfect purity.

Allāhābād: (Allah: Urdu word for God + abad: Urdu word for abode) The abode of God. Modern name for Prayaga, the holy town that stands on the banks of the sangam, the confluence, of the three sacred rivers, the Ganga, Yamuna and Saraswati—popularly known as the Triveni Sangam.

ardha padmāsana: (ardha:half + padma: lotus + asana: posture) Half padmasana, one of the yogic postures of hatha yoga. See: hatha yoga.

artha vishanna: (artha: money, wealth + vishanna: depressed and unhappy) A person who is unhappy due to lack of money.

ashta madas: (ashta: eight + mada: intoxication of pride) The eight kinds of pride are: pride of caste; 2. Pride of wealth; 3. pride of strength; 4. Pride of learning and scholarship; 5. pride of personal beauty; 6. pride of youth; 7. pride of aishvarya—accomplishments and power; 8. pride of tapas, austerities.

ashvattha vriksha: Sanskrit name for the sacred bodhi tree, Ficus religiosa, the sacred pipal tree. A tree of great longevity, it has heart-shaped leaves with long tips. Lord Buddha attained nirvana, the supreme bliss of liberation, after meditating for a long time under the pipal tree.

Aurobindo Āshram: The ashram founded in Pondicherry, South India, by the famous sage Aurobindo (1872-1950) He is well known for his great philosophical works: *Savitri, Life Divine* and *Integral Yoga.*

Ayim: (<Ayi: Mother) Bijakshara for Goddess Saraswati. The powerful second seed syllable in the Saraswati Mantra. It purifies the seeker at all levels, removes negativities and leads to liberation.

Ayimkāra: The sound of the seed syllable Ayim. See: Ayim.

B

Bālā Mantra: The mantra sacred to Bala Devi.

Bālā Tripura Sundari Mantra: The mantra sacred to Bala Devi as Tripura sundari—the most beautiful Divinity and supreme Empress of the three worlds—Heaven, Earth and the nether regions, or Hell.

Bhadra Kāli: (Bhadra: good, auspicious + Kali: the fierce and terrible form of Durga Devi) A name for Durga Devi in Her auspicious, benign form.

Bhaja Govindam: a Sanskrit stotra or hymn by Adi Shankaracharya extolling Govinda, Lord Krishna, as the all-pervading Reality, and exhorting us not to be entangled in the transitory world created by maya, illusion.

Bhayāpahā: (bhaya: fear + apaha: one who takes away or removes) Devi removes all the fears of Her devotees.

Bhopāla rāga: A raga is a mode in classical Indian music. The Bhopala raga is played or sung only in the morning.

Brahma granthi: (Brahma: Brahma the creator + granthi: knot) The knot of Brahma, a subtle energy center—the junction point of many nadis (subtle nerves)—located at the base of the spine in the muladhara chakra. See: chakra.

Brahma kūpa: (Brahma(n): the Absolute + kupa: well) The well of Brahma. See: Brahma randhra.

Brahma randhra: (Brahma(n): the Absolute + randhra: hole, aperture) The spot on top of the head (which is soft for many months after birth) is called "the hole of Brahman," and "the Brahma kupa." It is known as the tenth gate of the body, and is situated at the sahasrara chakra, the subtle energy center at the crown of the head. The soul of jnanis, Self-Realized ones, is said to leave through this aperture.

brāhmic: Adj. For Brahman, the Absolute, the One, Self-existent Spirit, without beginning or end, eternal, all-pervading, and all-powerful.

Brahmo Samaja: Raja Ram Mohan Rao, a scholar of Sanskrit and Arabic, was a highly intellectual man. He was a protagonist of social reform and women's education. He founded the Brahmo Samaja in Calcutta in 1828. The members of the samaja rejected the traditional beliefs and rituals of Hinduism, including idol worship and worship of multiple Gods and Goddesses.

C

chakra: A chakra is a center of the divine energy, kundalini, in the subtle body of human beings

Chāmundeshwari Temple: Chamundeshwari Devi is the Goddess Kali, who emanated from Durga Devi. She assumed this fierce form for the destruction of the demons Chanda and Munda, hence Her name. She is worshipped in a prominent hilltop temple in Mysore, Karnataka.

cosmic love: Equal and unconditional love for everything in the cosmos—living as well as non-living—for everything is divine Consciousness only.

D

dashāvatāras: (dasha: ten + avata-ras: incarnations) The ten incarnations of Lord Vishnu.

Devi: Divine Mother, Shakti, the primal energy that eternally creates, sustains and reabsorbs the universe into Herself.

dhoti: A long piece of white cloth worn gracefully round the waist—the traditional dress of Hindu men.

G

Ganesha prārthanā: (Ganesha + prarthana: prayer) A prayer to Lord Ganesha.

Gangotri: Name of the place in the high Himalayas where the sacred Ganga River has its source.

H

hatha yoga: (hatha: stubborn insistence + yoga) The form of yoga which emphasizes relentless practice—physical disciplines and exercises, including breath control—for the achievement of withdrawal of the mind from external objects.

Hrim: The fourth and most powerful bijakshara of the Saraswati Mantra, repetition of which bestows energy at the physical, mental, emotional and spiritual levels.

Hrimkāra: The sound of the seed syllable Hrim. See: Hrim.

J

jyotisha: The esoteric science of Indian astrology.

K

kartittva: The sense or feeling of doership.

Kāshi: A name of the holy city of Benares, which lies on the bank of the sacred Ganga River.

Ketu: The descending node in astronomy. The name of a demon said to devour the sun or moon at the time of an eclipse. See: Rahu.

khadga: A broad sword; a scimitar.

L

laya: (To merge with; to be absorbed into.) At the end of a kalpa, a time cycle, all creation is re-absorbed into Divine Mother.

M

mahā purusha samshrayah: (maha: great + purusha: man + samshrayah: grace and protection) The blessing of the grace and protection of the Sad Guru.

mokshatvam: The intense desire for moksha, salvation.

muhūrta: An auspicious time. A period of time, according to Indian calculations, equal to 48 minutes.

mūlādhāra kunda: (muladhara + kunda: hollow) The hollow of the muladhara chakra, the subtle energy center at the base of the spine. See: chakra.

Mysore: The capitol of the state of Karnataka in South India.

N

Nepāl: An independent Himalayan country to the north of India.

Nigama: 1. Passages or words quoted or derived from the *Vedas*. 2. Name given to the scriptures based on *vedic* thought, especially the *Tantras,* which propagate the worship of the Supreme as Shakti. See: Devi.

nirukta: Etymology. Etymological interpretation of words connected with *vedic* compositions.

P

Pancharatna shlokas: (pancha: five + ratna: precious gems + shlokas: verses) A hymn of five verses glorifying a deity. Here the reference is to *Sri Lalita Pancharatna,* a very beautiful Sanskrit stotra praising Lalita Devi.

pavitratā: Purity.

Prānadā: (prana: life-giving energy + da: one who gives) Divine Mother alone bestows life and consciousness on all living beings.

pranāms: Reverential salutation; bowing with respect.

R

Rahasya Sahasranāma: (rahasya: secret + sahasra: thousand + nama: names) The secret thousand names of Devi.

Rāhu: The ascending node in astronomy. In mythology, a demon who, together with Ketu, swallows the sun or moon at the time of an eclipse. See: Ketu.

Rāmakrishna Āshram: The ashram in Bengal, East India, of the famous nineteenth century saint, Sri Ramakrishna Paramahamsa, (1836-1860). He was the revered Guru of Swami Vivekananda, who brought the philosophy of Advaita Vedanta to the west.

Revati r̄aga: A beautiful mode in Indian classical music which is played or sung in the afternoon.

Rudra granthi: (Rudra: the fierce form of Lord Siva + granthi: knot) The knot of Rudra, the junction point of many nadis, subtle nerves, located at the ajna chakra between the eyebrows. See: chakra.

S

sālokya: (sa: the same + loka: world) The blessing of living in the same realm as the Divine Mother.

sama drishti: (sama: equal + drishti: vision) Seeing everything as pervaded by the same supreme Atman or Soul.

sāmipya: (samipya: closeness, nearness) The blessing of always being close to Divine Mother.

Sampūrna Prajnā: (sampurna: complete + prajna: higher knowledge) The knowledge of oneness attained at the time of Self-Realization.

Sanātana Dharma: (sanatana: ancient or eternal + dharma: the laws of righteousness or moral living and virtue) The ancient laws of righteousness which lay the foundation for leading a truly moral, virtuous life. Their precepts are true for all time.

sārupya: (sa: the same + rupa: form) The blessing of having the same form as Divine Mother.

sāyujya: (sa: the same + yuj: united or joined with) To become one with Divine Mother.

Sharmadā: (sharma: happiness + da: giver) One who gives happiness. See: Sharma dayini.

Sharma dāyini: (sharma: happiness + dayini: one who gives) Divine Mother showers happiness on all.

Shodashākshari Mantra: The mantra of 16 syllables sacred to Devi.

shraddhā: Faith.

Siva keshavādi janani: (Siva + Keshava: a name of Lord Vishnu + adi: and others + janani: mother) Devi is the mother of Lord Siva, Vishnu and all the other Gods.

Soham Mantra: The supreme divine mantra that every living being repeats unknowingly with every breath throughout life—"So" with the incoming breath and "Ham" with the outgoing breath. The meaning of "Soham" is, "I am That," "I am the supreme Reality" When this sacred mantra is chanted mentally and consciously, it leads the seeker to liberation.

Srim: (<Sri: Lakshmi Devi, Goddess of Light and Wealth) Bijakshara for Lakshmi Devi, who is the embodiment of auspiciousness. The third seed syllable of the Saraswati Mantra. Devotional repetition of Srim blesses the seeker with divine light—physically, mentally and spiritually.

Srimkāra: The sound of the seed syllable Srim. See: Srim.
srishti: Creation.
sukha: Happiness
Sundarvana Forest: "The beautiful forest." Name of a wooded area on the delta of the river Ganga where it enters the Bay of Bengal.
svarūpa: (sva: of the Self; one's own + rupa: form) The atman, soul, is our true Self.
svasvarūpa: (sva: one's own + svarupa: form) Our true form, which is the eternal and all-pervading supreme Soul, not the body.

V

Vāmadeva: A *vedic rishi,* author of many hymns, who was reluctant to be born in the usual manner. He came forth from the womb by the power of yoga, as he was endowed with divine knowledge from conception.
Vashinyādi Vāg devatās: (Vashinyadi: Vashini and others + vag: speech + devatas: Gods) Vashini and the seven other Goddesses of Speech
Vedānta: (*Veda* + anta: end or conclusion) The ultimate wisdom of the *Vedas* contained in the *Upanishads.* These are attached to the end of the *Vedas* and were taught to the aspirants while seated near the feet of the master, hence the name (upa: near + nishad: sitting). They all declare with one voice that the individual soul and the supreme Soul are one.
Vishālākshi: (vishala: large + akshi: with eyes) The Goddess with large eyes. Name of Devi in the temple at Benares, Kashi.
Vivek Chudāmani: (viveka: discrimination between Reality and the transitory + chudāmani: crest jewel) The crest jewel of the priceless diamond of discrimination. Name of a famous Sanskrit book by Adi Shankaracharya revealing the basic principles of Vedanta.

Y

Yogini nyāsa: (Yogini: A woman who practices yoga, meditation: Mother Divine, the supreme yogini + nyasa: rules laid down) The names of Devi in the fifth section of *Sri Lalita Sahasranama* which indicate the rules regarding meditation.